BEHAVIOR MODIFICATION IN THE HUMAN SERVICES
a systematic introduction to concepts and applications

Martin Sundel, Ph. D.
River Region Mental Health-Mental Retardation Board

Sandra Stone Sundel, M. S. S. W.
University of Louisville
Louisville, Kentucky

John Wiley & Sons   New York London Toronto Sydney

Library of Congress Cataloging in Publication Data

Sundel, Martin, 1940-
    Behavior modification in the human services.

    Includes bibliographies and index.
    1. Behavior modification. I. Sundel, Sandra Stone, 1948-   joint author. II. Title. [DNLM: 1. Behavior therapy. 2. Concept formation. WM420 S957b]

BF637.B4S9   361'.06'019   74-23342
ISBN 0-471-83566-8
ISBN 0-471-83567-6 pbk.

Printed in the United States of America

10 9 8 7 6 5 4 3 2 1

To our parents, to our students, and to each other

preface

The purpose of this book is to provide a systematic introduction to behavioral concepts and techniques for students in the fields of social work, psychology, psychiatry, nursing, special education, and other relevant social and behavioral sciences. The book is also appropriate for practitioners in these fields who have had little or no formal exposure to behavioral concepts. Case examples are used to illustrate representative applications of behavior modification practice.

The behavioral concepts are presented in order of increasing complexity; each chapter, therefore, builds on the knowledge and skills covered in the preceding chapters. As the student progresses through the book, course materials are arranged so that he can demonstrate his ability to utilize and integrate course content. A course post-test is provided in which the student must apply the concepts covered in the course to specific case material.

A variety of case vignettes are included as a basis for critical analysis and discussion of problematic client behaviors and controlling conditions, treatment goals, and implementation of behavioral intervention strategies. These vignettes represent composites drawn from actual cases in human service settings. All names referring to clients in the course materials are fictitious. Sufficient information is presented in the vignettes so that the student can learn to apply the methods of behavioral analysis to these cases. Throughout the book, the student is asked specific questions related to these cases to determine (1) his or her comprehension of the subject matter and (2) his or her ability to apply behavioral concepts to practice situations. The content covered represents a variety of problems and situations relevant to social work, psychology, psychiatry, education, nursing, and other human service professions. These disciplines frequently serve clients with similar complaints, life circumstances, and aspirations.

The behavioral approach presented here attempts to provide a common framework for students of different disciplines and for practitioners performing a wide range of human services. Throughout the book, various professional caregivers are identified in terms of their professional titles to illustrate the applicability of the behavioral approach to specific professional groups. In most cases, however, the professional who is a competent behavioral practitioner could apply the behavioral approach regardless of his job title or professional affiliation. In addition, other caregivers such as parents, teachers, and clergymen can learn to apply behavioral principles under the direction of professional behavioral practitioners.

Since a number of introductory behavioral textbooks are currently available, the reader may wonder why we have written this one. We have attempted to develop a course that integrates behavioral concepts with practical applications. We have placed special emphasis on the knowledge and skills required in behavioral assessment and treatment planning. In this way, behavioral concepts and techniques are related to an overall strategy and rationale for behavioral intervention. The book is also designed to provide frequent and immediate feedback to the student regarding his or her mastery of course content. The chapters are purposefully brief and are primarily designed to include the essential knowledge required to achieve the objectives. The pretests and post-tests are instructional aids in that the answers were formulated to illustrate additional applications of the concepts tested.

Growing awareness and concern about social services, mental health, mental retardation, education, corrections, and health have created a burgeoning interest and demand for innovative methodologies and approaches that are effective with clients from all socio-economic groupings. The funding sources of social programs have placed greater emphasis on accountability, and the behavioral approach stands out as a model for determining the effectiveness and efficiency of service delivery. Behavior modification techniques are based on the experimental analysis of behavior. They have been used with a variety of clients in institutional and community settings, including mental patients, the mentally retarded, drug abusers, the physically handicapped, and alcoholics. They have also been extensively applied in educational settings. Behavior modification techniques have been applied to the entire spectrum of age groups, from infants to geriatric citizens. They have been applied to remedy dysfunction in inpatient and outpatient treatment settings and in preventive programs such as parent training and classroom management.

The course materials have been used with students and practitioners from a variety of educational backgrounds and human service settings. The questions and answers have been revised on the basis of their performances. The book has benefited from the challenging questions, comments, and suggestions offered by our students.

The major concepts presented in this book are based on the operant conditioning approach developed by B. F. Skinner and his followers, and the classical conditioning approach developed by Ivan Pavlov. We are indebted to our many colleagues, too numerous to mention here, who have provided conceptual, experimental, and clinical foundations for the body of knowledge incorporated in this text. Many of their names will be found in the references at the end of each chapter.

We would like to thank Dr. George L. Geis who served as both a discriminative stimulus and a positive reinforcer for our behavioral pursuits. We acknowledge the contribution of Dr. Reuben Chapman who provided valuable assistance in the development of the instructional design and format of the course. We thank Dr. William H. Butterfield for his critical review of the manuscript and for his help in clarifying several issues. The book also reflects the contribution of Dr. Harry Lawrence to a number of the clinical examples and assessment instruments. We extend our thanks to Ms. Carol Silvernagel for her diligent and efficient typing of the final manuscript. Finally, we wish to express our appreciation to our colleagues and friends who offered comments and suggestions on the manuscript. We take full responsibility, however, for the final product.

Martin Sundel
Sandra Stone Sundel

contents

BEHAVIOR MODIFICATION IN THE HUMAN SERVICES:
A Systematic Introduction to Concepts and Applications

introduction

The purpose of this book is to present a systematic approach to behavioral concepts and techniques. We have attempted to arrange the textual materials in a logical and sequential manner. The early chapters are brief and require mastery of a few basic concepts so that you can become familiar with the format of the book as well as with technical terms used in behavior modification. The chapters become increasingly complex and require integration and application of concepts presented in earlier chapters.

Each chapter begins with a set of objectives and ends with a post-test. The objectives specify what you should be able to do after completing the chapter. The teaching unit is directed primarily toward meeting the objectives and contains a minimum of extraneous material. The post-test questions were formulated in accordance with the objectives and require you to demonstrate achievement of the objectives.

HOW TO USE THIS BOOK

Textual Materials

The book contains the following materials:

1. Eight vignettes demonstrating the application of concepts taught in this course to representative practice problems. These vignettes are located in Appendix 1 and should be referred to wherever indicated throughout the text.
2. Twelve questions and answers, constituting a pretest for the course. The questions are representative of the course post-test. The course pretest is found in Appendix 2. Answers to the course pretest are found in Appendix 3.
3. Sixteen chapters presenting behavioral concepts and applications. Each chapter contains a list of objectives, a pretest, a teaching unit, a post-test, and

answers to the pretest and post-test. All chapter pretests are found in Appendix 4, pretest answers in Appendix 5, and answers to the post-tests in Appendix 6. Because subsequent chapters build on concepts and test items from previous chapters, we recommend that you work through the teaching units in the order in which they are presented.

4. Thirty-five questions and answers, constituting a post-test for the course.

Vignettes

The eight case vignettes are referred to throughout the text to illustrate the application of various behavioral concepts. Questions on the course pretest and course post-test require answers based on the information found in these vignettes. Chapter pretests and post-tests also frequently require answers based on the information from the vignettes. In addition, reference to specific vignettes is made at various points in the teaching units.

Scoring

Many of the questions require examples that demonstrate mastery of course concepts; therefore, a number of different correct answers may be possible for a particular question. In these cases, criteria for correct answers are delineated. If your answer includes the criteria stated, you receive the maximum number of points. If your answer includes two out of three correct parts, for example, you receive 2 points for the question. If your answer does not include any of the stated criteria, you receive 0 points for that question. The tests make frequent use of open-ended questions, rather than true-false or multiple-choice questions. In this way, you can demonstrate your ability to generate applications of concepts, rather than merely identifying which of two or more answers is correct. Although determining whether or not criteria for a certain answer have been met may be difficult initially, we have found that students quickly improve their ability to make the discriminations required for accurate scoring. Sample answers are given for each open-ended question that meet the criteria specified for a correct answer.

We offer the following guidelines for scoring certain types of questions that are asked frequently throughout the tests.

1. When a question asks for a description of a procedure, the answer should list the operations or steps required to carry out that procedure in a manner that could be replicated.
2. When a question asks for an example that describes a procedure or technique, the answer must include a specific example, listing the steps involved in implementing that procedure or technique.
3. When the question asks for a paradigm of a procedure, the correct symbols and their explanations must be included. If the question asks for a paradigm showing an example, the symbols of the paradigm must be drawn

correctly, and the explanation of the symbols must be stated in relation to the specific example.

4. When a question asks for a description of the effects of a certain procedure, the answer must describe the typical results of using that procedure.

5. When a question asks for an example that describes the effects of a certain procedure, the results of using that procedure must be stated in relation to information based on that example. When a case example is given, the answer must be stated in relation to information obtained from that example.

6. When a question asks for an evaluation of the effectiveness of a certain procedure or technique, the answer must state a specific criterion for dertermining whether or not the procedure or technique accomplished its intended goal.

Following are several examples of completely correct, partially correct, and completely incorrect answers to the same question to illustrate some of the points discussed above.

Question: Describe the positive reinforcement procedure and its effect on the strength of a response.

Correct answer: The presentation of an object or event following a response (procedure) that increases the strength of that response (effect).

Partially correct answer: Present a positive reinforcer to someone immediately after he performs the target behavior (procedure). Its effect is to modify that behavior.

Incorrect answer: 1. Indicate reinforcer before desired behavior to entice person to act in desired way. 2. Give positive reinforcer immediately after behavior as a reward.

The acceptable score for each test was established as 90% of the questions answered correctly. This is indicated as the *criterion score* shown at the bottom of each test. The value of each question reflects the number of components required for a complete answer. In the above example, the total number of points possible for a completely correct answer is 2; 1 point for the correctly stated procedure, 1 point for the correctly stated effect. The first answer above received 2 points. The second answer was only half correct; therefore, it received 1 point. The third answer was incorrect and received 0 points. Point values are specified beside each question.

The Course Pretest

After working through the *course pretest*, you will have obtained an overview or sampling of the course content. The purposes of the course pretest are (1) to orient you to the type of questions that you will be required to answer correctly upon completion of the course and (2) to help you assess your entering knowledge of the course content. In addition, the course pretest provides you with a measure of your current level of behavioral knowledge in relation to a set of performance criteria. After completing the text, your performance on the course pretest can be compared with your score on the course post-test. We recommend that you take the course pretest (Appendix 2) before reading any of the teaching material. When you have answered all the questions, score the test by comparing your answers to those given in Appendix 3. You are not expected to achieve criterion score on the course pretest unless you have had prior exposure to behavioral concepts. If you do achieve criterion score (that is, 90%) on the course pretest, you may take the course post-test (p. 163). If you also achieve criterion score on the course post-test, you have demonstrated sufficient mastery of the material and have passed the course.

The Chapters

Objectives are stated at the beginning of each chapter to describe the results to be achieved after completing the chapter materials. Each chapter has a *pretest* (Appendix 4) that will orient you to the content presented in the teaching materials. The pretest also determines your familiarity with the material to be presented. Score the pretest before reading the teaching unit by comparing your answers to those given in Appendix 5. Again, as an introductory student, you are not expected to achieve criterion score on the chapter pretests. Taking the chapter pretests, however, will expose you to the types of questions and answers that will appear on the post-tests. If you achieve criterion score on the chapter pretest, you may wish to take the chapter post-test without reading the teaching unit. If you also achieve criterion score on the chapter post-test, you should/go on to the next chapter pretest, as you already have met the objectives for that particular chapter. If you achieve less than criterion score on the chapter pretest, you should read the teaching unit. Each *teaching unit* covers the content necessary to meet the objectives. The *chapter post-test* is typically taken after you have studied the teaching unit. You should try to answer the questions without looking back at the teaching unit. Score the chapter post-test by comparing your answers to those given in Appendix 6. If criterion score is not achieved, refer back to the teaching unit or previous chapters for review and retake the test until you achieve criterion score. Successful performance on each chapter post-test constitutes an intermediate step to achieving criterion performance on the course post-test.

    References are included at the end of each chapter. The references cited were selected according to their relevance for specific principles or applications and constitute a small sample of available literature. They provide theoretical foundations, case studies, and empirical research that can be consulted to further clarify and elaborate the concepts and applications covered in that chapter.

The Course Post-Test

The *course post-test* is taken after you have completed the sixteen chapters. Answers to the course post-test are found in Appendix 7. If you do not achieve criterion score, you should review the chapters related to the incorrect answers. Chapters covering the content required for a correct answer on the course post-test are indicated. When you achieve criterion score on the course post-test, you have mastered the content of this course.

A *summary of notational symbols and paradigms* used throughout the text is found in Appendix 8.

The *glossary* contains definitions of technical terms which are italicized in the text. Terms that appear to have technical meaning or are italicized for emphasis but are not found in the glossary retain their common usage meaning.

RECOMMENDATIONS FOR INSTRUCTOR USE OF THIS BOOK

A variety of instructional formats can be utilized with this book. The instructor can use the book by itself or with supplementary readings. Chapters should be assigned in sequential order to be completed by the student prior to class sessions. The instructor can use class time to clarify, elaborate, and discuss the chapters and readings. Class time can also be used for demonstrations of relevant concepts and practice skill sessions in which the students participate in role-plays involving applications of principles and techniques. The students can be assigned to report their pretest and post-test scores each week and chart them over the period of the course. The instructor could also require that the students retake each deficient post-test until 90% criterion or better is achieved, so that students have the opportunity to restudy chapters to improve both their knowledge and scores.

An alternative for the instructor also requires that the students complete the chapter pretests and teaching units outside of class. The students take the chapter post-tests in class, however, either scoring their own papers, exchanging papers for grading, or handing them in for scoring by the instructor.

The course pretest can be administered during the first class session, or it can be assigned for the students to complete outside of class. The course post-test can be used as a final exam for the course, either to be taken in class or completed at home.

The instructor can use additional readings in both basic and applied research to supplement this book and can draw from the recommended references included at the end of each chapter. Other sources include:

Annual Review of Behavior Therapy
Behaviour Research and Therapy
Behavior Therapy
Journal of Applied Behavior Analysis
Journal of Behavior Therapy and Experimental Psychiatry
Journal of the Experimental Analysis of Behavior

chapter 1
specifying behavior

OBJECTIVES

After completing this first chapter, you should be able to:

1. describe events according to observable behaviors or responses,
2. discriminate between vague and behaviorally specific statements,
3. rewrite the vague statements into behaviorally specific ones, and
4. rewrite a statement so that it includes a frequency measure of response strength.

The behavioral practitioner strives for specificity in his descriptions of actions performed by individuals. These actions are called *behaviors* or *responses*; these terms will be used interchangeably throughout the text. A human response is defined as any observable, measurable movement or activity of an individual. Responses include verbal behaviors such as lecturing to an audience, screaming, or talking on the telephone, and nonverbal behaviors such as smiling, throwing a baseball, perspiring, or raising an eyebrow.

Human service practitioners frequently encounter problems that are presented in nonspecific language. The behavioral practitioner attempts to delineate an individual's problem in words that clearly specify his verbal and motor responses. The individual's situation should be described in *positive, observable* terms. Negatively stated descriptions such as "Harold *does not* turn in his class assignments" are insufficient in that they fail to describe what Harold *is* doing in the problematic situation. In the example above, an appropriate description of Harold's problematic behavior might be, "Harold looks at comic books instead of writing his assignment." A description of an individual's behavior in observable terms specifies what he *says* or *does*. Reference to unobservable constructs such as "ego impairment" or "striving for masculinity" are insufficient to measurably describe a person's behavior. These terms lack descriptive clarity and do not contribute essential information about his behavior. For example, in Vignette 7, if the teacher complained that Harold was "inattentive and poorly motivated" in class, there would be some doubt as to how he was "inattentive and poorly motivated." Did he sit under his desk? Did he walk around the room? Did he throw papers out the window? A more acceptable description might be, "Harold stared out the window in class and completed only one out of ten math problems." Thus, a stranger reading this description would be provided with a concrete, observable instance of Harold's "inattentive and poorly motivated" classroom behavior. Similarly, a statement such as, "He refused to do his chores" or "She denied spilling the milk" fails to describe what these individuals said or did in those situations. Refusing to do chores could mean the individual said, "I refuse to do the chores," or that he rode his bicycle all morning while his mother did his chores for him.

In specifying behavior, the *topography* or form of the response should be described. For example, in the statement "Tim struck his brother on the arm," the topography or form of Tim's response could be further delineated by the statement, "Tim struck his brother with a closed fist about two inches below the shoulder." A still more precise description of *response topography* would be, "Tim raised his right arm straight up and swung down with a closed fist landing about two inches below his brother's shoulder." How precisely one should specify response topography depends on the description required for analyzing or modifying the behavior. An adequate description provides enough detail so that other individuals could accurately identify the responses. Some English words are defined so that topographical aspects are included; for example, slug (strike with closed fist) or slap (strike with open hand).

Response strength is a major concept used in describing behavior. In this book, response *rate* or *frequency* (per interval) will be considered as the primary measure of response strength. Response rate or frequency indicates how often or how many times a response occurs during a given period; for example, Mrs. Jones washed her hands eight times in the past hour. Other important measures of response strength include *latency* (the interval between presentation of a stimulus and occurrence of the response), *intensity*, and *duration*. For example, Mother rang the dinner bell and Bert came to the table immediately (latency); the students' talking in the classroom registered 70 decibels (intensity). Sometimes two or more of these measures are used to describe a particular response; for example, Mrs. Jones screamed at her neighbor's cat for over ten minutes (duration) three times this week (rate). Measures of response strength will be discussed in more detail later.

POST-TEST QUESTIONS

(10)　1-A.　Indicate with a (+) which of the following statements are written in behaviorally specific terms, and with a (−) statements that are vague and require further specification.

1-B.　After completing 1-A above, rewrite in specific terms only those statements in which the responses are not described behaviorally.

　a.　Eddy took two cans of beer from the refrigerator.

　b.　Johnny expressed his feelings of inadequacy at the ball game.

　c.　Norman showed hostile feelings toward his probation officer this week.

　d.　Mr. Smith asserted his authority over use of the car.

　e.　He thinks of his girlfriend often.

    f. Susan placed dirty dishes in the sink.

(1) 2. In Vignette 7, Harold is described as having a "negative attitude toward learning." Specify a behavior that might have led the counselor to describe him in that way.

(1) 3. Rewrite the following statement so that it includes a frequency per interval measure of response strength: Emily read the story to her brother.

chapter 2
positive
reinforcement

OBJECTIVES

After completing this chapter, you should be able to:
1. specify a target behavior and its appropriate baseline measure,
2. give an example illustrating the positive reinforcement procedure and its effect on the strength of a response,
3. describe how baseline data are used in evaluating the effectiveness of a positive reinforcer,
4. indicate the temporal condition that maximizes the effectiveness of a positive reinforcer, and
5. draw a paradigm showing how positive reinforcement can be used to increase the frequency of a response.

A *stimulus* (plural, stimuli) can be any object or event. It can include physical features of the environment (e.g., a telephone) as well as an individual's own behavior or the behavior of others (e.g., a smile). Stimuli can precede or follow a specific response. In this chapter, we are concerned with stimuli that follow a specific response and thereby increase its strength.

Positive reinforcement is a procedure for *increasing* the response strength or probability of occurrence of a specific behavior. A *positive reinforcer* is a stimulus whose presentation following a response increases the strength of that response or its probability of occurrence. The presentation of any event or object that increases the likelihood that the behavior it follows will recur under similar conditions is called a positive reinforcer. Thus, the principle of positive reinforcement states that the strength of a behavior can be increased

- by certain consequences, that is, presentation of a specific reinforcer that follows the behavior.

A behavioral *paradigm* (a stimulus-response model indicated by a set of notational symbols) depicts relationships between stimuli and responses. Paradigms are used throughout this book to provide schematic representations of behavioral concepts and procedures. A paradigm can be used to represent the positive reinforcement procedure in which a response is conditioned:

R	$\longrightarrow$	S^+
a response (or behavior) is emitted or occurs	and is followed by	a positively reinforcing stimulus

The S^+ in the above paradigm indicates a stimulus (S) whose presentation increases (+) the strength of the response it follows. The effect of the positive reinforcement procedure is that the response (R) is conditioned; that is, it increases in strength over its previous rate. Behaviors that are conditioned in this manner are referred to as *operant* behaviors, that is, behaviors that are controlled by their consequences. (This is in contrast with *respondent* behavior, which is elicited by specific antecedents or events occurring prior to the response; respondent behavior will be discussed in Chapter 14.)

You may have observed from your own experience that if someone performs a certain behavior and it is followed by a particular event, he will tend to perform that behavior on other similar occasions. For example, Fred tells jokes when among a group of his friends. His friends laugh at his jokes. If Fred tells jokes again under similar circumstances, the friends' laughter serves as a positive reinforcer for Fred's joke-telling. In paradigm form, the above example would look like this:

R	$\longrightarrow$	S^+
Fred tells jokes	is followed by	friends laugh

The effect of the positive reinforcement procedure is that Fred's joke-telling increases in strength; that is, the likelihood that it will recur under similar conditions is increased.

Another example of positive reinforcement involves getting Donna to wash the dishes. For the past three months, Donna has only washed the dishes once each week. A plan is arranged whereby each time Donna washes the dishes, she receives a quarter. The quarter will serve as a positive reinforcer for dishwashing if the rate of Donna's dishwashing increases. The *target response* in this example is Donna's *washing the dishes*. As long as the money serves as a positive reinforcer, Donna will continue to wash the dishes. In subsequent chapters we will examine some of the factors involved in maintaining response strength without having to present the reinforcer each time the response occurs.

The *target response* is the behavior to be observed or counted; it is the focus of modification. Depending on the desired behavioral change, there are five treatment outcomes or directions in which a target behavior can be modified. Modification techniques can be applied so that a behavior is (1) acquired or developed, (2) increased in strength, (3) maintained at a particular rate or pattern of occurrence, (4) decreased in strength, or (5) completely suppressed.

Some common positive reinforcers include food, water, sex, attention, praise, and money. Although stimuli may differ in their ability to serve as positive reinforcers for different individuals, almost any object or event can act as a positive reinforcer for specific responses under certain conditions. The term reward is sometimes inappropriately used synonymously with the term positive reinforcer. A reward is an object or event that is identified as pleasant, satisfying, desirable, and that the individual will seek out or approach. Rewards can, and frequently do, serve as positive reinforcers. A stimulus is only called a positive reinforcer, however, if its presentation increases the strength of the response or likelihood that the behavior it follows will recur under similar circumstances.

The effectiveness of a reinforcer may be related to the size, amount, type, or quality of the reinforcer. Bubble gum may increase the frequency of 10-year-old Tom's going to the store on an errand, but probably will not increase the strength of Mr. Jones' doing the same errand. The relativity of reinforcer effectiveness becomes evident when we observe that Tom runs an errand for a piece of bubble gum, but that one piece of bubble gum will not serve as a positive reinforcer for other responses such as mowing the lawn or shoveling snow from the driveway. For $5.00, however, the likelihood is greatly increased that Tom will mow the lawn or shovel the snow. An individual's estimate of the effort required to perform a response can influence the effectiveness of the reinforcer. For example, an average person would probably not walk from downtown Los Angeles to Santa Monica for $25.00, although this same individual might eagerly attempt to do so for $25,000.00. On the other hand, a cross-country runner might accept $25.00 for the same walk.

Behavioral assessment is a method used to evaluate a client's problem or circumstances so that an appropriate intervention plan can be formulated. The first step in behavioral assessment is to specify the problem in observable terms. In the last chapter you learned how to specify behaviors that were stated in vague terms. A second step in behavioral assessment, carried out after specification of the target behavior, involves the collection of *baseline data*. Baseline data indicate significant measures of response strength used in formulating an intervention strategy. They also provide a basis for evaluating the client's progress. Baseline data involve measures of *response rate, latency, intensity,* and/or *duration. Response rate* is obtained by counting the frequency or number of times a behavior has occurred within a given interval. Response rate (frequency of the response per unit of time) is typically obtained as the baseline measure and will serve here as the focus of our discussion. For example, "Harold completed two out of three school assignments this week"; "Jane cried at the dinner table once on Monday, twice on Tuesday, and once on Thursday." These data are obtained during assessment and indicate the *baseline rate* of Harold's completing his assignments and of Jane's crying; that is, the frequency with which these behaviors occur prior to implementation of treatment or modification techniques. The effectiveness of treatment techniques can be evaluated by comparing the frequency of the target behavior after treatment with the baseline rate.

The effectiveness of any reinforcer for a particular behavior can be evaluated by comparing the baseline rate of the behavior with its rate after delivery of the reinforcer. For example, if you did not know the baseline rate of Gary's making his bed without being paid for doing so, you could not evaluate the extent to which subsequent payment for making his bed increased his bed-making. A baseline rate might indicate that Gary only made his bed once a week over a four-week period prior to payment. After payment for bed-making, Gary made his bed six times a week over six months. These data provide measures of the effectiveness of the money as a positive reinforcer for Gary's bed-making.

The temporal relationship between a response and its reinforcer influences the effectiveness of the reinforcer. A stimulus identified as a positive reinforcer is most effective when delivered or made available *immediately after* the response to be strengthened. If you give Nathan an ice cream cone *before* he mows the lawn, it is less likely that he will mow the lawn than if you give him an ice cream cone *after* he mows the lawn. If you wait too long to give Nathan his ice cream cone for mowing the lawn, however, you might find him less willing to mow the lawn again. A delay in reinforcement could also result in unintentionally conditioning a behavior occurring at the time of reinforcement rather than conditioning the desired behavior. Therefore, in order to maximize the effectiveness of a positive reinforcer, the reinforcer should be presented not only *after* the response has occurred, but *immediately* after.

Deprivation and *satiation* are other factors that influence the effectiveness of a reinforcer. *Deprivation* refers to a condition in which the individual has not been exposed to a reinforcer for a specified period; for example, eight hours, or four days. *Satiation* refers to a condition in which a reinforcer has been continuously available to an individual until it loses its reinforcing effect. For example, if you offer Nathan an ice cream cone for mowing the lawn and he has just eaten a triple scoop ice cream cone, the probability of his mowing the lawn will be low. He is satiated on ice cream. If, however, he has not been allowed to have ice cream for several days, the probability of his mowing the lawn for an ice cream cone will be higher. He has been deprived of ice cream. In general, a reinforcer is most effective in increasing response strength when a high level of deprivation exists. A reinforcer is less effective in increasing response strength during a low level of deprivation and ineffective when the individual is satiated with regard to that reinforcer.

REFERENCES

Bachrach, A.J., Erwin, W.J., and Mohr, J.P., "The Control of Eating Behavior in an Anorexic by Operant Conditioning Techniques," in Ullmann, L.P. and Krasner, L. (Eds.), *Case Studies in Behavior Modification,* Holt, Rinehart and Winston, Inc., New York, 1965, pp. 153–163.

Haughton, E. and Ayllon, T., "Production and Elimination of Symptomatic Behavior," in Ullmann, L.P. and Krasner, L. (Eds.), *Case Studies in Behavior Modification,* Holt, Rinehart and Winston, Inc., New York, 1965, pp. 94–98.

Keller, F.S. and Schoenfeld, W.N., *Principles of Psychology,* Appleton-Century-Crofts, Inc., New York, 1950, Chapter 3, pp. 36–66.

Madsen, C.H., Jr., "Positive Reinforcement in the Toilet Training of a Normal Child: A Case Report," in Ullmann, L.P. and Krasner, L. (Eds.), *Case Studies in Behavior Modification,* Holt, Rinehart and Winston, Inc., New York, 1965, pp. 305–307.

Skinner, B.F., *Science and Human Behavior,* The Free Press, New York, 1953, Chapter 5, pp. 59–90.

POST-TEST QUESTIONS

(2) 1. Describe the positive reinforcement procedure and its effect on the strength of a response.

(2) 2. Give one example of an object or event that you think acts as a positive reinforcer for yourself. State your proof.

(3) 3. From Vignette 7, draw a paradigm showing how positive reinforcement could be used to increase the frequency of Harold's completing his class assignments, labeling the appropriate components. What evidence could be used to evaluate the effectiveness of this procedure?

(4) 4. Rewrite the following statements, specifying the target behavior and indicating a baseline measure.
    a. Hank is always annoying his brother.

    b. Mary was often depressed.

(2) 5. Correct these statements so that the effectiveness of the candy bar and the movies as positive reinforcers can be maximized.
    a. Mrs. Jones gave Edward a candy bar and told him to take the dog for a walk.

b. Harvey washed his father's car and his father took him to the movies three weeks later.

(1) 6. Describe how baseline data can be used in determining if going shopping immediately after doing housework served as a positive reinforcer for Lillian's doing housework.

chapter 3
extinction

OBJECTIVES

After completing this chapter, you should be able to:
1. give an example of a behavior that is decreased in strength through application of the extinction procedure,
2. determine empirically whether or not a given stimulus serves as a positive reinforcer for a specific response,
3. describe the role of positive reinforcement in the extinction process, and
4. describe how spontaneous recovery is considered in a treatment plan.

In the previous chapter, we described positive reinforcement as a procedure for increasing response strength. This chapter is concerned with decreasing the strength of a behavior by applying a procedure called *extinction*. Like positive reinforcement, the extinction procedure deals with the consequences of behavior. By systematically withholding the reinforcing consequences for a behavior, the response strength is decreased. The extinction procedure consists of withholding the positive reinforcer continuously, that is, each time the target response occurs, until the response strength decreases to a prespecified level. The extinction procedure can be represented in paradigm form:

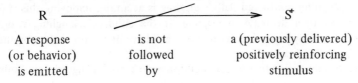

R		S⁺
A response (or behavior) is emitted	is not followed by	a (previously delivered) positively reinforcing stimulus

19

The $\not> S^+$ in the above paradigm indicates that a positively reinforcing stimulus (S^+) is no longer presented (withheld continuously) until the strength of the preceding response decreases to a designated level.

The effect of the extinction procedure is that the target response (R) decreases in strength to (1) a prespecified level or to (2) its own *operant level*, that is, the response strength prior to conditioning. For example, in the previous chapter we found that the baseline rate (or operant level) of Gary's making his bed was once a week. When he was paid every time he made his bed, the frequency increased to six times per week. When he was not paid for making his bed, the rate of his bed-making decreased to its baseline rate of once a week. Aside from demonstrating the effect of extinction in decreasing response strength, this example also demonstrates the effectiveness of money as a positive reinforcer for Gary's bed-making. If the money were not the positive reinforcer, taking it away would have no effect on decreasing Gary's bed-making. In paradigm form, the above example can be represented as follows:

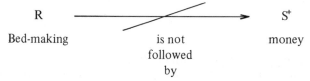

R		S^+
Bed-making	is not followed by	money

Gary's bed-making was extinguished. In this example, we can probably reinstate Gary's bed-making behavior by paying him again (see Figure 1).

In real life, however, behavioral practitioners do not always have the opportunity to condition a behavior, extinguish it, and recondition it. Often we are asked simply to eliminate or decrease an undesired behavior, for example, Sally's giggling in class. In this type of situation, we must determine what the reinforcing consequences are for Sally's giggling in class. The first step is to observe what happens when Sally giggles in class and try to identify a potential reinforcer. We observe that other students laugh when Sally giggles. Second, we measure the number of times Sally's giggling occurs during a given interval to determine the rate of occurrence of giggling. We decide to count each occurrence of giggling as a separate giggling response if it is separated by at least 10 seconds from a preceding giggle. We find that Sally giggles an average of six times an hour. Third, we remove the social consequences of her giggling in class. We instruct the other students to continue working, turn their faces away from Sally, and remain silent when she giggles. If our initial observation that the students' laughing reinforced Sally's giggling is accurate, removing this stimulus should result in a decrease in giggling. If the children's laughing is not the reinforcer for Sally's giggling, its removal will have little or no effect on the rate of Sally's giggling in class.

In withholding positive social reinforcement to extinguish an undesired

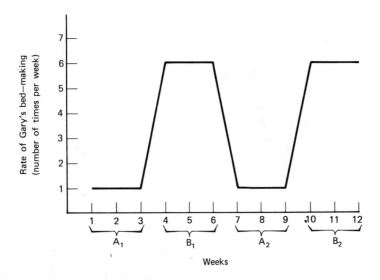

FIGURE 1. Graph of Gary's bed-making. A_1, baseline; B_1, Gary is paid every time he makes his bed; A_2, extinction: bed-making is no longer followed by money; B_2, reinstatement of payment for bed-making.

behavior, the behavior modifier should ignore the individual by turning away from him, avoiding eye contact, and refraining from conversation. He should not scowl, grimace, or exhibit other facial or verbal behaviors that could possibly reinforce the response to be extinguished.

Besides decreasing the frequency of Sally's giggling, we have also determined the positive reinforcer that conditioned or maintained Sally's giggling in class : laughter of the other students. We could reinstate Sally's giggling by telling the children to laugh at Sally when she giggles in class, and we could again decrease Sally's giggling by telling the children to turn their faces away and remain silent when she giggles in class (see Figure 2).

It must be noted here that the target response usually does not immediately disappear. The initial effect of extinction is often a sharp increase in strength of the target behavior. For example, the first hour the students ignore Sally's giggling, she might giggle eight or ten times. Disruptive or "emotional" responses such as kicking, hitting, or screaming might also be part of the initial effects of extinction. For example, the first day Gary is not paid for making his bed, he may kick the bed, scream at his mother, or mumble under his breath. But if reinforcement is continuously withheld, the target behavior will gradually decrease until it reaches the baseline or operant level. In Sally's example,

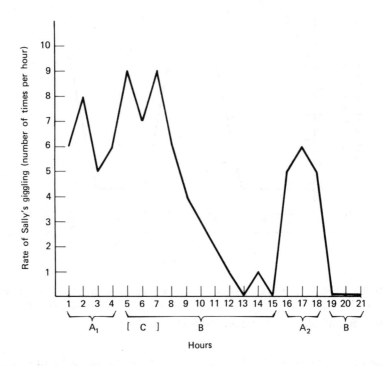

FIGURE 2. Graph of Sally's giggling in class. A_1, baseline; c, initial burst of responding; B, extinction; A_2, reinstatement of student laughter after Sally giggles.

however, having been called in on the case after the behavior was already conditioned, we could not determine the operant level (unconditioned rate) of giggling. In this case, our criterion measure for effective reduction of Sally's giggling could be the teacher's estimate of a reasonable and normative frequency for that behavior under appropriate circumstances. Extinction, then, is judged to be effective when the target behavior decreases to its operant level, if it can be determined, or to a prespecified criterion.

Two practical difficulties might be encountered in implementing an extinction procedure. The first is *consistency*; that is, positive reinforcement should be withheld each time the behavior occurs. There is often a tendency to "give in" by reinstating the reinforcer, especially during the burst of increased responding or disruptive behavior that may occur during the initial period of extinction. "Giving in" reinforces exactly that response which is to be decreased. If a response is reinforced *intermittently,* that is, not every time it occurs but on some occasions and not others, it will be more difficult to extinguish. The second major difficulty is in controlling the *dispensing of reinforcers.* When we are not in control of the individual's reinforcing environment, someone else might be reinforcing the exact behavior that we are attempting to extinguish. This has the same effect as inconsistency; that is, the response is reinforced intermittently and becomes more difficult to extinguish.

As we have seen, the extinction procedure can be applied to decrease the strength of a response. For example, Gary's bed-making was conditioned by a positive reinforcer—money; Sally's giggling was shown to be conditioned or maintained by the class laughing. In each of these cases the target response decreased when the positive reinforcer was withheld. In practice, however, when we extinguish an undesired behavior, we should also positively reinforce desirable behavior in the problematic situation. When we extinguish Sally's giggling in class, we should also positively reinforce appropriate classroom behaviors that are *incompatible* with giggling; for example, speaking appropriately to other students and to the teacher, reading aloud for the class, and answering questions asked of her by the teacher.

One additional feature of extinction important to the behavior modifier is the concept of *spontaneous recovery.* Frequently, after a behavior has been extinguished, it will *recur* at a future time when similar stimulus conditions are present. This spontaneous recurrence of the target behavior appears when the individual finds himself in the same or a similar situation that previously set the occasion for reinforcement of the extinguished response. For example, at bedtime, five-year-old Jerry screamed and his father allowed him to watch more television. In order to extinguish Jerry's screaming, the father was instructed to turn off the television at Jerry's bedtime. At first, Jerry's screaming increased in duration and he kicked the couch. After Jerry's father turned off the television at Jerry's bedtime each night, however, Jerry's screaming gradually decreased in duration. By the fourth night, he no longer screamed at bedtime. Jerry's father continued this procedure successfully for two weeks. One evening the following week, Jerry's mother turned off the television at his bedtime. Jerry screamed, but the television remained off. The mother's turning off the television and leaving it off when Jerry screamed constituted another extinction trial in which reinforcement was withheld for Jerry's screaming. In implementing the extinction procedure, therefore, it is essential to identify those individuals who have control over the delivery of reinforcement in the client's environment. These individuals must consistently follow the designated treatment plan. In Jerry's situation, both the mother and father, as well as babysitters or relatives, must turn off the television and leave it off at the designated time.

In anticipation of the possible spontaneous recovery of Jerry's screaming, the therapist instructed Jerry's parents to hold firm in leaving the television off if he screamed on future occasions when the television was turned off. The therapist also instructed them to inform anyone else who would be responsible for turning the television off at Jerry's bedtime to ignore his screaming, should it occur, under the designated circumstances.

A systematic follow-up plan should be incorporated into a treatment program. Prior to termination, arrangements should be made with the client, where indicated, for one month, six months, one year, and/or other designated follow-up contact. If maladaptive behavior has recurred, further intervention should be arranged to ensure maintenance of the individual's treatment gains.

REFERENCES

Ayllon, T. and Michael, J., "The Psychiatric Nurse as a Behavioral Engineer," *Journal of the Experimental Analysis of Behavior,* 2 (1959), pp. 323–334.

Pinston, E.M., Reese, N.M., LeBlanc, J.M. and Baer, D.M., "Independent Control of a Pre-School Child's Aggression and Peer Interaction by Contingent Teacher Attention," *Journal of Applied Behavior Analysis,* 6, 1 (1973), pp. 115–124.

Williams, C.D., "The Elimination of Tantrum Behavior by Extinction Procedures," *Journal of Abnormal and Social Psychology,* 59 (1959), p. 269.

Wolf, M., Birnbrauer, J., Lawler, J. and Williams, T., "The Operant Extinction, Reinstatement, and Re-Extinction of Vomiting Behavior in a Retarded Child," in Ulrich, R., Stachnik, T., and Mabry, J. (Eds.), *Control of Human Behavior, Volume Two,* Scott, Foresman and Co., Glenview, Illinois, 1970, pp. 146–153.

POST-TEST QUESTIONS

(3) 1. Describe the procedure for extinguishing a response by giving an example in which you specify a response and its reinforcer.

(4) 2. After observing a mother's response to her son's crying, what would you do to determine whether or not the child's crying was conditioned by his mother?

(1) 3. Describe the effects of extinction on the rate of a target response.

(2) 4. Using the information from Vignette 3, indicate how positive reinforcement played a part in the following:
a. in conditioning an undesired behavior

b. in conditioning desired behavior

(1) 5. In what way is spontaneous recovery considered in a treatment plan?

chapter 4
positive reinforcement contingencies

OBJECTIVES

After completing this chapter, you should be able to:
1. give an example of a positive reinforcement contingency,
2. compare self-contingency management with accidental contingencies,
3. define and give an example of the Premack Principle,
4. indicate when it is appropriate to use a continuous schedule of reinforcement,
5. state two advantages of using an intermittent reinforcement schedule rather than a continuous reinforcement schedule, and
6. compare response strength on a continuous versus an intermittent schedule of reinforcement.

In the chapter on positive reinforcement, we saw how positive reinforcers were arranged to follow a response. The effect of this arrangement or *contingency of reinforcement* was to increase the likelihood of the target behavior recurring. The conditions under which a specific behavior must occur in order for a positive reinforcer to become available is called a *positive reinforcement contingency*. A positive reinforcement contingency dictates an "if . . . then" functional relationship involving the behavior that must be emitted in order for a positive reinforcer to become available. It must be stated in positive terms with clear specification of the behavior, the reinforcer, and the circumstances under which reinforcement will occur. For example, "if you trim the hedges, Leroy, we'll go fishing"; "after you finish your piano lesson, Diane, you may go shopping with Sherry." As stated previously, the positive reinforcer is more effective when it immediately follows the desired behavior than when it is delayed.

A behavioral contingency, then, is a statement that specifies the conditions under which certain consequences will follow a response. Contingency management is a term that describes the use of such arrangements within a program of behavioral change. A positive reinforcement contingency is one type of behavioral contingency. Self-control contingencies, accidental contingencies, punishment contingencies, and negative reinforcement contingencies are other types of behavioral contingency statements.

Positive reinforcement contingencies can be stated explicitly, as above, or they can serve as rules that control an individual's behavior without his awareness or ability to describe them. In a marital relationship, for example, one partner may be unaware of the positive reinforcement contingency that exists between the behavior he or she emits and the affection received from the spouse.

Sometimes an individual's behavior has been conditioned by a positive reinforcer that has been accidentally related to that behavior. We call that "superstitious" behavior, and it is the result of the accidental relationship between a response and a reinforcer. For example, a gambler twirls his "lucky" ring while playing blackjack and attributes his win to the twirling of the ring. Some event other than his twirling the ring produced the reinforcer of the win, and the response accidentally became associated with its delivery. The gambler may continue to twirl his ring while playing blackjack, although this behavior is not responsible for producing the reinforcer. Winning is not contingent upon ring-twirling; that is, ring-twirling is not a behavior that produces winning. The gambler would have drawn the winning cards on the reinforcing occasion whether or not he twirled his ring.

Individuals can employ self-control techniques using reinforcement contingencies. In this way, the individual becomes a self-contingency manager who can increase the strength of desired behaviors. For example, a student is in danger of flunking math because he fails to complete his assignments. By arranging to play basketball only after completing his math work, the student can increase the frequency of completing his math assignments. Another example is the person who arranges to complete the housework before visiting a neighbor. In these situations, the individual arranges conditions so that the desired response is predictably followed by reinforcement.

The *Premack Principle* is a special kind of contingency management. The Premack Principle states that any behavior occurring more frequently than another behavior can serve as a reinforcer for the behavior that occurs less frequently. In other words, a high-frequency behavior can increase the response strength of a low-frequency behavior. For example, Jane frequently talks to her friends on the phone, but rarely does her chores. The Premack Principle would indicate that talking on the phone can serve as a reinforcer for doing chores if talking on the phone is made contingent on completing the chores.

In the previous chapters on positive reinforcement and extinction, the contingencies described for conditioning or extinguishing a behavior specified that reinforcement be given or withheld continuously, that is, each time the response occurred. We can say that those behaviors were conditioned on a continuous reinforcement *schedule* and extinguished on a schedule of continuous nonreinforcement. A *schedule of reinforcement* indicates the frequency with which reinforcement is given for a response.

We have demonstrated the use of a continuous reinforcement schedule in conditioning Donna to wash the dishes every night. Once a response becomes established, however, it is not necessary to provide positive reinforcement each time the response occurs. The response can be maintained on a less-than-continuous or *intermittent schedule of reinforcement*. In general, intermittent schedules of reinforcement specify that we selectively reinforce the response on some occasions and withhold reinforcement on other occasions when it is emitted. Chapter 5 describes various kinds of intermittent schedules of reinforcement.

An intermittent reinforcement schedule has two advantages over a continuous schedule of reinforcement. First, fewer reinforcements are required to maintain a behavior. Second, a response maintained on an intermittent reinforcement schedule is more resistant to extinction. In other words, an individual will emit a greater number of responses during extinction of a response if it had been maintained on an intermittent rather than a continuous schedule of reinforcement, as shown in Figure 1. Thus, another measure of response strength involves the number of responses an individual will emit during extinction.

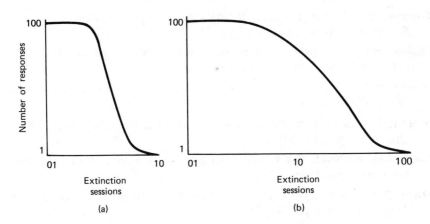

FIGURE 1. Comparison of resistance to extinction under continuous and intermittent reinforcement. (*a*) Response previously maintained on a continuous reinforcement schedule. (*b*) Response previously maintained on an intermittent reinforcement schedule.

It is appropriate to use a continuous reinforcement schedule to condition a response or to strengthen a response that occurs with low frequency. Attempting to condition a response on an intermittent reinforcement schedule may lead to extinction of the response before the functional relationship between the response and the reinforcer is established. After the response has been established at a desired strength, it is appropriate to introduce an intermittent schedule of reinforcement. Not only will this procedure require fewer reinforcements and make the response more resistant to extinction, but it also more closely simulates reinforcement schedules in the natural environment.

REFERENCES

Cohen, H. L. and Filipczak, J., *A New Learning Environment*, Jossey-Bass, Inc., San Francisco, 1971.

Homme, L., "Contiguity Theory and Contingency Management," *Psychological Record*, 16 (1966), pp. 233–241.

Homme, L., *How To Use Contingency Contracting In The Classroom*, Research Press, Champaign, Illinois, 1969.

Mahoney, M.J., "Self-Reward and Self-Monitoring Techniques for Weight Control," *Behavior Therapy*, 5 (1974), pp. 48–57.

Marston, A., "Self-Reinforcement: The Relevance of A Concept In Analog Research in Psychotherapy," *Psychotherapy: Theory, Research and Practice*, 2 (1965), pp. 1–5.

Premack, D., "Toward Empirical Behavior Laws: I. Positive Reinforcement," *Psychological Review*, 66 (1959), pp. 219–233.

Skinner, B.F., "Contingencies of Reinforcement in the Design of a Culture," *Behavioral Science*, 2 (1966), pp. 159–166.

Skinner, B.F., " 'Superstition' in the Pigeon," *Journal of Experimental Psychology*, 38 (1948), pp. 168–172.

Skinner, B.F., *Science and Human Behavior*, The Free Press, New York, 1953, Chapter 15, pp. 227–241.

Smith, J.M. and Smith, D.E.P., *Child Management*, Ann Arbor Publishers, Ann Arbor, Michigan, 1966.

Stuart, R.B., "Behavioral Control of Overeating," *Behaviour Research and Therapy*, 5 (1967), pp. 357–365.

POST-TEST QUESTIONS

(2) 1. State a positive reinforcement contingency related to Vignette 7 that

you might use with Harold in relation to completing his class assignments.

(2) 2. As described in this chapter, self-control of contingencies is more desirable than accidental contingencies. What is the difference between an accidental contingency and self-controlled reinforcement?

(1) 3. When is it more appropriate to use a continuous reinforcement schedule than an intermittent reinforcement schedule?

(1) 4. What evidence indicates that intermittent reinforcement makes a response more resistant to extinction than continuous reinforcement?

(2) 5. State two advantages of using an intermittent reinforcement schedule rather than a continuous reinforcement schedule?

(3) 6. Define the Premack Principle and give an example of its use and effect.

chapter 5
schedules of reinforcement

OBJECTIVES

After completing this chapter, you should be able to:
1. match four schedules of reinforcement with their characteristic effects on response pattern and rate,
2. give an example of "straining the ratio," and
3. describe how to schedule reinforcement to maintain a response after it has been conditioned, given a case example.

The purpose of this chapter is to present the major intermittent schedules of reinforcement and their effects on response rates and patterns of responding. Four types of intermittent schedules are described: *fixed-ratio* (FR), *variable-ratio* (VR), *fixed-interval* (FI), and *variable-interval* (VI).

An intermittent schedule of reinforcement is typically applied after a response has been established at a desired strength. A response maintained on an intermittent reinforcement schedule requires fewer reinforcements and is more resistant to extinction than a response maintained on a continuous reinforcement schedule (abbreviated CRF). After a response has been conditioned, reinforcement can be gradually shifted from a continuous to an intermittent schedule. If intermittent reinforcement is used before a response occurs regularly, the response may extinguish.

A cumulative recorder is a recording instrument used to plot the number of responses emitted as a function of time. A cylinder of paper with a pen attached turns continuously while the pen marks horizontally on the graph paper. When a response is emitted, the pen moves vertically, leaving a mark on the paper to indicate the response. Therefore, the faster the rate of responding, the steeper the vertical line or slope. The cumulative recorder provides a graph of all the responses made by an individual within a given period of time, or a cumulative record of responses. Figure 1 is a schematic representation of three different response rates plotted cumulatively. Figure 1 (*a*) represents a zero response rate; no responses were made during that time. Figure 1 (*b*) shows a slow response rate; the slope shows a steady but slow rate. Figure 1 (*c*) shows a moderate rate of responding; the slope is steeper than that in Figure 1 (*b*).

Intermittent reinforcement procedures can be applied to strengthen low frequency behaviors. For example, Harry rarely speaks in class, and his second-grade teacher is concerned about his silence and lack of participation in class discussion. After consultation with the school social worker, she has decided to call on him more frequently and praise him for responding. During the first week she calls on Harry and praises him each time he responds. Soon Harry raises his hand with approximately the same frequency as other children during class discussions.

Now that Harry speaks appropriately in class, his teacher would like to maintain this behavior without having to call on him and praise him each time he raises his hand. In the real world people are not reinforced every time they emit an appropriate response. We do not get an answer every time we ring a doorbell, nor are we positively reinforced every time we see a play or read a book. Nevertheless, we continue to call on our friends, go to the theatre, and read. Harry's teacher, after consulting with the social worker, decided to shift gradually from a continuous reinforcement schedule to *fixed-ratio* (abbreviated FR) and *variable-ratio* (abbreviated VR) schedules of reinforcement. On Monday and Tuesday of the second week the teacher continued to call on Harry and

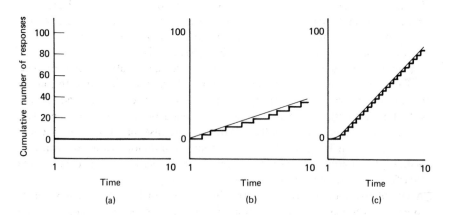

FIGURE 1. Schematic representation of cumulative response rates (*a*) No responses emitted; (*b*) slow rate of responding; (*c*) moderate rate of responding.

praised him every time he raised his hand. On Wednesday and Thursday, she called on Harry every second time he raised his hand and praised him every second time (FR 2). On Friday, she called on him and praised him every fourth time he responded (FR 4).

In an *FR schedule*, a prescribed number of responses must be emitted in order for reinforcement to be delivered. An *FR 2* schedule indicates that two responses must be emitted before reinforcement will occur. In the above example, the teacher began with a continuous reinforcement schedule (CRF or FR 1). She shifted to an FR 2 schedule after the response was well established at the desired frequency. Then she shifted reinforcement again to an FR 4 schedule.

Under laboratory conditions, the FR schedule typically generates high rates of responding with minimal hesitation between responses until the ratio is completed. A post-reinforcement pause is also associated with the FR schedule. This means that after every reinforcement, the organism "takes a short break" from responding. This type of schedule does not exist very often with humans under normal circumstances. Even in the above classroom example, the FR schedules were used only temporarily in order to maintain the response at a high strength with fewer reinforcements, approximating everyday, variable reinforcement schedules. A typical FR schedule would be a worker on a piecework wage, who is paid for every three pieces completed, for example. A worker on this schedule generally works at a high, consistent rate, taking little time off until he completes the three pieces. After reinforcement is obtained, the worker rests a little while (post-reinforcement pause), then begins the ratio again. Figure 2 shows a cumulative record of an FR 3 schedule.

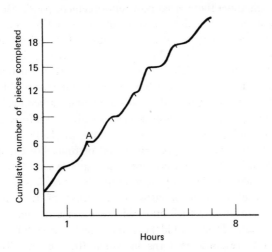

FIGURE 2. Cumulative record of an FR 3 schedule. The slash (\) marks indicate delivery of reinforcement. A: post-reinforcement pause.

When applying FR schedules, each ratio should be increased gradually. For example, if the teacher had shifted from CRF immediately to FR 15, Harry would probably not have emitted fifteen responses for reinforcement, so that no reinforcement would have been delivered, and his responding in class probably would have extinguished. This rapid shift from CRF to an FR that is too large to support the response is called *straining the ratio*. The same effect could have occurred had the teacher shifted from FR 2 to FR 15. The fifteen responses required for reinforcement would probably have been too many, and the response would have extinguished.

Going back to our classroom example, by the third week of the program, the teacher was calling on Harry with the same approximate frequency that she called on the other children, and praised him only when he gave the correct answer. A second type of schedule is the *variable- ratio schedule* (VR). In VR schedules, reinforcement is delivered after an *average* number of responses is emitted. Thus on a VR 10 schedule, reinforcement would occur after an average of ten responses has been emitted. This means that reinforcement could occur after one response, after ten responses, or after twenty responses, as long as the average number of responses producing reinforcement is ten. Our classroom example does not involve a strict VR schedule, but an approximation of one. According to the teacher's judgment of variable ratio, Harry could be reinforced after one response, two responses, or ten responses. This schedule might more accurately be called a random ratio, since reinforcement is not delivered according to a prespecified number of responses. VR schedules, like FR schedules, generate extremely high rates of responding with minimal hesitation between responses. In fact, VR schedules generate the highest rates because, unlike the FR schedule, there is no post-reinforcement pause. Slot machines are typically programmed to deliver reinforcement on a VR schedule. Since the gambler never knows exactly what ratio is required for reinforcement, he inserts coins and pulls the handle at a high rate, with minimal hesitation between responses, to maximize the delivery of reinforcement. Unfortunately the slot machine is programmed on a high VR schedule to take more of his money than it pays out. Figure 3 shows a hypothetical slot machine schedule, VR 75.

The next type of schedule we will discuss is called *fixed-interval* (abbreviated FI). In FI schedules, reinforcement becomes available when a response is made after the passage of a specified period of time. For example, FI 2 min means that two minutes must pass before a response can be reinforced. It is important to remember that not only must the time interval pass, but the response must also be emitted after that period of time has elapsed. If reinforcement were given based only on the passage of time, some behavior other than the desired one could be conditioned accidentally. Fixed-interval schedules generate response patterns in which there is an initial low rate of responding and a terminal high rate of responding. Thus, the response pattern is

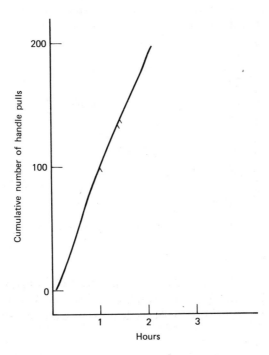

FIGURE 3. Hypothetical slot machine schedule, VR 75. The slash marks (\)
indicate delivery of reinforcement.

shaped like a scallop. Once again, FI schedules are rarely programmed as such in
real life. The closest example of an FI schedule would be any situation involving
a deadline. For example, if examinations are scheduled at the end of the month,
a student might exert little effort in studying during the first few days of that
month, somewhat more, perhaps, around the middle of the month, but by the
last few days before the exam, his study behaviors would increase until the day
of the exam. A reinforcer for his studying could be the passing grade he receives.
A cumulative record of this student's study behaviors is shown in Figure 4.

The next schedule we will describe is the *variable-interval schedule* (abbreviated VI). Variable-interval schedules pay off after an average amount of
time has passed. The interval is varied around a given time value with a
designated range, e.g., one minute to seven minutes. With this range, VI 4 min
would indicate that reinforcement is made available after an average of four
minutes has passed; the individual might be reinforced after one minute has
passed or after seven minutes have passed. Once again, not only does the
designated time period have to elapse, but the response must also be emitted in

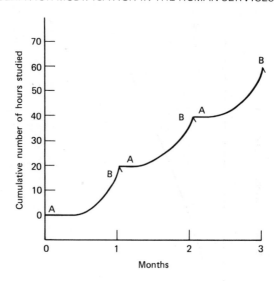

FIGURE 4. Cumulative record of three months study behavior with exams at the end of each month. A, initial low rate of responding; B, terminal high rate of responding. The slash marks (\) indicate delivery of reinforcement.

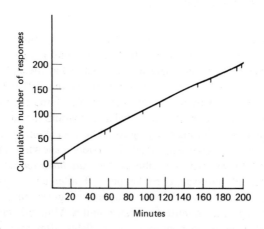

FIGURE 5. Cumulative record of a VI 20 min schedule. The slash marks (\) indicate delivery of reinforcement.

Fixed-Ratio (FR)	Variable-Ratio (VR)	Fixed-Interval (FI)	Variable-Interval (VI)
High response rate with minimal hesitation between responses	High response rate with minimal hesitation between responses	Initial low rate of responding; terminal high rate of responding	Consistent, moderate rate of responding
Scallop			
Post-rein-forcement pause			

FIGURE 6 Characteristics of four schedules of reinforcement.

order for reinforcement to occur. Variable-interval schedules typically generate consistent and moderate response rates with no post-reinforcement pause. A cumulative record of a VI 20 min schedule is shown in Figure 5. Real-life approximations to variable-interval schedules are standing on the corner waiting for a taxicab or looking out the window waiting for the mail to arrive.

Figure 6 compares characteristics of the four schedules of reinforcement discussed in this chapter. Response rates under these schedules is a function of the size and range of the ratio or interval employed.

REFERENCES

Bijou, S. W. and **Orlando, R.**, "Rapid Development of Multiple-Schedule Performances with Retarded Children," *Journal of the Experimental Analysis of Behavior* 4 (1961), pp. 7-16.

Ferster, C. B. and **Skinner, B. F.**, *Schedules of Reinforcement*, Appleton-Century-Crofts, New York, 1957.

Morse, W. H., "Intermittent Reinforcement," in Honig, W. K. (Ed.), *Operant Behavior: Areas of Research and Application*, Appleton-Century-Crofts, New York, 1966, pp. 52-108.

Skinner, B. F., *Cumulative Record*, Appleton-Century-Crofts, Inc., New York, 1961, pp. 178-182.

Skinner, B. F., *Science and Human Behavior*, The Free Press, New York, 1953, Chapter 6, pp. 91-106.

POST-TEST QUESTIONS

(1) 1. Give an example of "straining the ratio."

(3) 2. Using the information from Vignette 4, how could you schedule reinforcement to maintain Mr. C.'s increased vocalizations after session ten?

(7) 3. Match the schedules in Column A with their characteristics from Column B. (Items from Column B can be used O, 1, or more times in Column A and each schedule in Column A can have 1 or more characteristics from Column B.)

   Column A

   Fixed-Interval _____

   Variable-Interval _____

Fixed-Ratio   ──────────

Variable-Ratio   ──────────

Column B

1. Initial low rate of responding, terminal high rate of responding.
2. Post-reinforcement pause.
3. Consistent, moderate rate of responding; no post-reinforcement pause.
4. Characteristic slot machine schedule.
5. Very high response rate with minimal hesitation between responses.
6. Scallop.
7. Initial burst of responding, tapering off to low rate of responding.

chapter 6
shaping
and response
differentiation

OBJECTIVES

After completing this chapter, you should be able to:
1. define and give an example of an operant,
2. give an example of response differentiation,
3. describe how a DRO schedule can be used to decrease the frequency of an undesired response,
4. describe the use of a DRO schedule as a control, and
5. describe the·steps involved in shaping a behavior.

In this chapter we will discuss *differential reinforcement*, a method for refining an already established behavior. We will also discuss *shaping via successive approximation*, a method by which we can establish behavior that an individual currently does not emit, may never have emitted, or has a low probability of emitting. Before we proceed, there are several concepts that require explication.

Variability is an essential characteristic of operant behavior because a behavior is rarely repeated in exactly the same form. When a response occurs and is followed by a reinforcer, the probability of that response recurring has increased. The reinforcer also serves to increase the future probability of other responses that have the same or similar effect on the environment as the reinforced response. Thus, not only is the individual response reinforced, but a class or group of behaviors is also reinforced. This class of behaviors, each member of which produces the same or similar effect on its environment, is called an *operant* or a *response class*. For example, there are many different ways of opening a door: you could shove it with your shoulder, you could kick it with your foot, or you could push the door knob with your right hand or left hand. All these responses have the same effect, that is, they open the door. The operant, therefore, would be defined as "those responses that open the dour," and members of that operant include, among others, the operant responses stated above. We can define an operant as broadly or narrowly as we choose. For example, we could require that the door be pushed open two inches, two feet, or wide enough so that an individual can enter through it. The main point is that the definition of an operant is determined by the behavioral outcome that is established.

Differential reinforcement is a procedure in which some responses are reinforced while reinforcement is withheld from other responses, according to prespecified criteria such as form or intensity of the response. When the reinforced response occurs frequently, to the exclusion of responses from which reinforcement is withheld, we say that the response has become *differentiated*. For example, most of us have been consistently reinforced for *walking* through the doorway of a room when we want to leave it. Therefore, given the operant, "leaving the room," for most adults the response of walking through the doorway has become differentiated from crawling or running through. There are a number of ways to walk through the doorway, however. In this example, all the responses one can make to walk through the doorway are strengthened. This differentiated response—walking through the doorway—can also be defined as an operant, including all the different responses one can make in walking through the doorway, for example, walking through forwards or walking through backwards. The words "response" and "behavior", therefore, refer not to a discrete response, but rather to a defined operant or class of responses. Similarly, one member of an operant is not one discrete response, but rather a subset of responses that meet certain criteria or specifications.

As another example, if we wanted to teach a child to pull the lever on a candy machine with enough force to deliver the candy, we could define the operant as "responses causing the candy to fall into the tray" or "responses of 25 grams of force or more" (if that were the determined amount of force necessary). The only responses that are reinforced by the candy appearing in the tray are responses of 25 grams of force or more; these responses are strenghtened or increase in frequency. Responses that are not reinforced are those under 25 grams of force; since these responses are not reinforced, they decrease in frequency. Thus, responses of lever pulling with 25 grams of force or more have become differentiated, that is, they occur with greater frequency than any other responses.

We could also set the machine's mechanism so that only responses between 25 and 30 grams of force would be reinforced by candy falling into the tray. By selectively reinforcing responses between 25 and 30 grams of force, these responses would become differentiated, that is, they would occur with greater frequency than other responses in the operant "responses of 25 grams or more." Similar processes of differential reinforcement are involved in the highly differentiated responses we observe in expert craftsmen, public speakers, and professional athletes.

Differential reinforcement involves both reinforcement and extinction. Some responses are positively reinforced, while reinforcement is withheld continuously from other responses, that is, they are extinguished. Differential reinforcement can also be used to *weaken* an undesired behavior by reinforcing behaviors *other than* the undesired response. The undesired response is thereby weakened or extinguished and desired behaviors are strengthened. For example, in Vignette 3, in addition to reinforcing Carla when she put her toys away, the worker could have instructed the mother to reinforce any appropriate behavior Carla did *other than* screaming, such as helping her mother put groceries on the shelf or fold the laundry, or playing quietly by herself. In this way, not only is reinforcement withheld from undesired behavior, but appropriate responses currently in the client's repertoire are strengthened and maintained. This procedure is called a *differential reinforcement of other*, or *DRO*, schedule.

There is another way differential reinforcement can be utilized. The DRO schedule can be used as a control device to test the effectiveness of reinforcers. We can use the DRO schedule to determine that the reinforcer and not some other aspect of the situation is, in fact, functionally related to occurrence of the behavior. For example, a retarded child receives a token after he brushes his teeth. The tokens can be exchanged for candy or toys. In order to test the effectiveness of the tokens as reinforcers for brushing his teeth, we could give him a token for any behavior *other* than brushing his teeth. If the frequency of tooth-brushing decreases while the frequency of other behaviors increase, we conclude that the tokens served as reinforcers for tooth-brushing. Further proof of the tokens' effectiveness would involve reconditioning the tooth-brushing with tokens.

In developing a new behavior, we can use the methods of *differential reinforcement* and *successive approximation*. Since a client can seldom perform the desired terminal behavior at the beginning of treatment, we establish a series of intermediate behaviors or succesive approximations to the terminal behavior. Shaping via succesive approximation is a procedure that can be used to develop a new behavior or one that rarely occurs.

The following steps can be implemented to shape a behavior:

(1) Specify the terminal response(s) or behavioral goal.

(2) Specify positive reinforcers to be delivered.

(3) Specify initial and intermediate responses. The initial response to be reinforced must bear some resemblance to the terminal behavior.

(4) Differentially reinforce the initial response until it occurs consistently.

When the desired response occurs, it should be reinforced immediately to ensure that reinforcement is delivered only for appropriate behavior.

(5) Shift the criterion for reinforcement to an intermediate response.

(6) Reinforce the intermediate response until it occurs consistently. Intermediate responses must successively approximate the terminal behavior; that is, the criterion for reinforcement is shifted to responses that are more and more similar to the terminal behavior.

(7) Shift criterion for reinforcement to the next intermediate response.

(8) Reinforce that response until it occurs consistently. Steps 7 and 8 of this procedure are repeated until the terminal behavior is achieved.

For example, shaping via successive approximation was used to reinstate speech in Mr. C. (Vignette 4). The terminal behavior was that Mr. C. speak in full sentences about slides he was shown. The positive reinforcers given Mr. C. were M & M candy, points, and verbal praise ("good") from the psychologist. The initial response included any vocalizations. Intermediate responses included monosyllabic responses, speaking in phrases, and answering questions about the slides. Initially, any vocalization made by Mr. C. was reinforced. When vocalizations occurred consistently, the criterion for reinforcement was shifted to monosyllabic responses. This meant that vocalization would no longer be followed by reinforcement. Mr. C. would be required to speak in monosyllables before receiving the M & M's, points, and praise. When Mr. C. was speaking consistently in monosyllables, the criterion for reinforcement was shifted to the next intermediate response, speaking in phrases, which more closely approximated the terminal behavior. This process of reinforcing a response until it occurs consistently, then shifting the criterion for reinforcement to the next intermediate response is continued until the terminal behavior is performed.

Shaping can also be used to condition a physically handicapped girl to use crutches to walk instead of using a wheelchair. The terminal response would be walking 50 steps on crutches. Positive reinforcers are candy and praise ("very good"). The initial response is movement toward the crutches, which are placed within her reach. Intermediate responses include touching the crutches with her hands, holding the crutches in her hands, using the crutches to raise herself from the wheelchair, standing up with the crutches properly positioned, and taking one step on crutches. Initially, when the girl made any movement toward the crutches, she was reinforced. When she consistently reached out toward the crutches, the criterion for reinforcement was shifted to the next intermediate response, touching the crutches. This procedure of reinforcing one response until it occurs consistently, then shifting the criterion for reinforcement to the next intermediate response continues until the terminal behavior is performed.

Shaping via successive approximations involves a gradual process in which a response must be appropriately developed at one level before reinforcement is shifted to the next level of approximation. If the criterion for reinforcement is shifted to the next level too quickly, or if insufficient reinforcement is given, the response will extinguish. On the other hand, if one response receives too much reinforcement, it becomes difficult to alter the individual's responding in the direction of the next approximation.

REFERENCES

Allen, K.E. and Harris, F.R., "Elimination of a Child's Excessive Scratching by Training the Mother in Reinforcement Procedures," *Behaviour Research and Therapy*, 4 (1966), pp.79-84.

Ayllon, T. and Azrin, N.H., "The Measurement and Reinforcement of Behavior of Psychotics," *Journal of Experimental Analysis of Behavior*, 8 (1965), pp. 357-383.

Ferster, C.B., "The Use of the Free Operant in the Analysis of Behavior," *Psychological Bulletin*, 50 (1953), pp. 263-274.

Hingtgen, J.N. and Trost, F.C., Jr., "Shaping Cooperative Responses in Early Childhood Schizophrenics: II. Reinforcement of Mutual Physical Contact and Vocal Responses," in Ulrich, R., Stachnik, T., and Mabry, J. (Eds.), *Control of Human Behavior*, Scott, Foresman and Co., Glenview, Illinois, 1966, pp. 110-113.

Isaacs, W., Thomas, J. and Goldiamond, I., "Application of Operant Conditioning to Reinstate Verbal Behavior in Psychotics," *Journal of Speech and Hearing Disorders*, 25 (1960), pp. 8-12.

Kerr, N., Meyerson, L. and Michael, J., "A Procedure for Shaping Vocalizations in A Mute Child," in Ullmann, L. P. and Krasner, L. (Eds.), *Case Studies In Behavior Modification*, Holt, Rinehart, and Winston, Inc., New York, 1966, pp. 366-370.

Schwitzgebel, R. and Kolb, D. A., "Inducing Behavior Change In Adolescent Delinquents," *Behaviour Research and Therapy*, 1 (1964), pp. 297-304.

Sidman, M., "Operant Techniques," in Bachrach, A. J. (Ed.), *Experimental Foundations of Clinical Psychology*, Basic Books, Inc., New York, 1962, pp. 170-210.

Sidman, M., *Tactics of Scientific Research*, Basic Books, Inc., New York, 1960.

Skinner, B.F., *The Behavior of Organisms*, Appleton-Century-Crofts, New York, 1938, Chapter 8, pp. 308-340.

Skinner, B. F., *Science and Human Behavior*, The Free Press, New York, 1953, Chapter 6, pp. 91-106.

Sundel, M., "Modification of Two Operants (Verbal and Non-Verbal) in

Near-Mute Schizophrenics Using Reinforcement and Modeling Procedures," in van Teslaar, A.P. (Ed.), *Studies in Language and Language Behavior*, VII, Center for Research on Language and Language Behavior, Ann Arbor, Michigan, 1968, pp. 506-620.

Wolf, M. M., Risley, T., and **Mees, H.,** "Application of Operant Conditioning Procedures To The Behaviour Problems Of An Autistic Child," *Behaviour Research and Therapy,* 1 (1964), pp. 305–312.

POST-TEST QUESTIONS

(3) 1. Define an operant and give an example of one, describing two of its members.

(6) 2. The steps involved in shaping a behavior are indicated below. Fill in the specific responses and/or reinforcers related to each step, using your own example of shaping a motor (nonverbal) behavior.

Fill in with examples

a. Specify terminal response.   a.
b. Specify reinforcer(s).   b.
c. Specify initial and intermediate   c.
    responses directed toward
    achieving terminal response.
d. Differentially reinforce initial   d.
    response until it occurs consis-
    tently.
e. Shift criteria for reinforcement   e.
    to next intermediate response.

f. Continue this procedure of dif-   f.
    ferential reinforcement and
    shifting criteria for reinforce-
    ment until the terminal beha-
    vior is achieved.

(2) 3. Describe how a DRO schedule can be used to decrease the frequency of a client's bragging about his sexual prowess.

(3) 4. Give an example of response differentiation, specifying an operant, the differentiated response, and the reinforcer.

(2) 5. Using the information from Vignette 4, describe how the psychologist could use a DRO schedule to determine if the M & M's and points served as reinforcers for Mr. C.'s increased vocalizations, rather than the reinforcers being primarily the attention he received in the experimental situation.

chapter 7
stimulus discrimination and stimulus generalization

OBJECTIVES

After completing this chapter, you should be able to:
1. describe the role of reinforcement and extinction in discrimination training,
2. give an example of an errorless discrimination training procedure,
3. describe a nonerrorless procedure for establishing a discrimination,
4. specify criteria for achievement of stimulus control, and
5. give an example of a stimulus generalization gradient.

The previous chapters focused on relationships between operants and their consequences. Because of the *functional relationship* between a response and its reinforcer, the presentation of the reinforcer increases the future likelihood of occurrence of the operant. Similarly, because in extinction there is a functional relationship between the operant and the withholding of the reinforcer, the probability or future likelihood of occurrence of the operant is decreased. We have shown that by changing the schedule of reinforcement, we can influence the rate and pattern of a response. We have also described a procedure for refining behavior by differential reinforcement and for shaping low-probability responses by a series of successive approximations. In summary, we have shown how consequences can be manipulated to *establish* or develop a low-probability behavior (by shaping via successive approximations); to *increase* the strength or frequency of a behavior (by positive reinforcement); to *decrease* the strength of a behavior (by extinction); and to *maintain* a behavior at a certain frequency or pattern (by employing a particular reinforcement schedule).

This chapter focuses on functional relationships that exist between behavior, its consequences, and its *antecedents*. Antecedents refer to those events that precede and are closely associated with the occurrence of a behavior. By considering both the antecedents and consequences of behavior in our analyses, we increase the range of behavior modification procedures that can be applied.

A *discriminative stimulus* (S^D, pronounced "ess-dee") is an antecedent stimulus in whose presence a response is followed by reinforcement. The S^D *sets the occasion for* or signifies the availability of reinforcement for a response made in its presence. Another antecedent stimulus, an $S^\triangle$ (pronounced "ess-delta"), indicates that responses made in its presence will *not* be followed by reinforcement. In paradigm form, the discrimination training procedure looks like this:

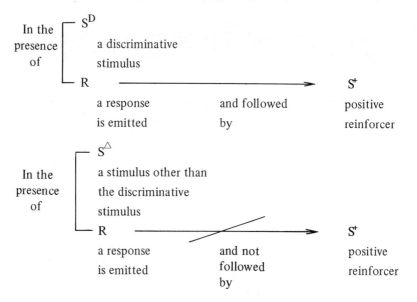

If the response is emitted in the presence of S^D, reinforcement will follow and increase the strength of that response. A response emitted in the presence of $S^\triangle$ is not followed by reinforcement and decreases in strength. For example, the telephone ringing serves as a discriminative stimulus for the response of answering (for example, picking up the receiver and saying "hello"), which is followed by the reinforcer of a reply. If the telephone does not ring ($S^\triangle$) and you lift the receiver, no reinforcer will be delivered; that is, no one will reply. Answering the telephone after it rings occurs with high frequency, whereas answering the telephone when it does not ring occurs with low frequency. In Vignette 4, the red light on served as the S^D for speaking about the slides. If Mr. C. spoke when the red light was on, he received M & M's, points, and praise. The red light off was the $S^\triangle$ for speaking about the slides. If Mr. C. spoke when the red light was off, he did not receive positive reinforcement. In paradigm form, this example of discrimination training would look like this:

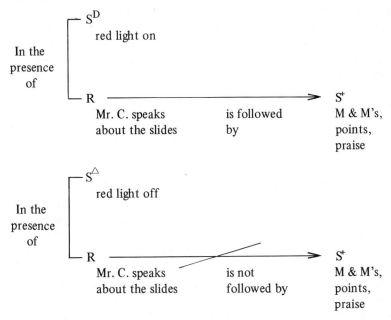

In the presence of

S^D
red light on

R ————————————————⟶ S^+
Mr. C. speaks   is followed   M & M's,
about the slides   by   points,
                                             praise

In the presence of

$S^\triangle$
red light off

R ————————————————⟶ S^+
Mr. C. speaks   is not   M & M's,
about the slides   followed by   points,
                                             praise

The red light on was the discriminative stimulus for Mr. C.'s speaking and subsequent reinforcement. In other words, it served as a cue indicating that speaking would be reinforced. As you can see, both positive reinforcement and extinction are involved in this *discrimination training procedure*. Correct responses occurring when the red light is on (S^D) are differentially reinforced and, therefore, increase in strength. Responses made when the red light is off ($S^\triangle$) are not followed by positive reinforcement and, therefore, are weakened. In teaching this discrimination, the correct response is reinforced only when it occurs under the S^D condition. Reinforcement is withheld when the response occurs in the presence of S^D. The response, however, must initially occur under both the reinforced S^D condition and the unreinforced $S^\triangle$ condition, so that discrimination between responding in S^D and $S^\triangle$ can be acquired. After differential reinforcement has been applied over a number of trials, the individual responds less frequently under the unreinforced $S^\triangle$ condition and more frequently during the reinforced S^D condition.

When the response occurs only during the condition of S^D and never under the condition of $S^\triangle$, we say that the response is under *stimulus control*. When stimulus control has been achieved, the response occurs only during S^D, and it occurs with short latency after the presentation of the discriminative stimulus. In Vignette 4, stimulus control is achieved when Mr. C. speaks only in the presence of the S^D (when the red light is on) and when he begins speaking immediately or soon after the red light goes on (short latency).

Errorless discrimination training is a stimulus fading technique used to establish difficult discriminations. This stimulus fading procedure makes use of discriminations that the individual has previously acquired. For example, a child has been reinforced for choosing black cards so that when shown black and white cards, he consistently chooses black over white. The child could not discriminate circles from squares, however. An errorless discrimination training procedure could be employed to teach the child to discriminate round from square. An S^D and $S^\triangle$ differing along two dimensions are specified; for example, the S^D could be black and round, the $S^\triangle$ white and square. The child chooses the S^D, the black circle, and is reinforced with praise, "That's good." The S^D is then gradually varied over a series of trials along one dimension, the color, until it is the same as the $S^\triangle$ along that dimension; the S^D is not varied along the second dimension, shape. The black circle (S^D) is gradually varied in color from black to gray, off-white, and white until it differs from the $S^\triangle$ only in shape. Now the child chooses the white circle over the white square. Initially, the child chose the black circle, having been reinforced for responding to black stimuli. The child continues to choose the circle, having now achieved the discrimination between round and square. This technique is called *errorless* discrimination training because the individual makes the correct response throughout the procedure, never or rarely responding in the presence of $S^\triangle$. Disruptive extinction effects due to an incorrect, unreinforced response are, therefore, avoided.

Stimulus fading techniques have been applied in situations where complex verbal or mechanical skills are taught through verbal instructions or cues. Initially, the individual performs appropriately only in the presence of these cues. The cues are gradually faded or removed until the individual responds appropriately to the existing stimulus dimensions of the situation. For example, an actor learning his lines on stage may rely on prompts or cues from the stage director. These cues are gradually faded until the actor responds to the S^Ds provided by the spoken lines of other actors on stage. Similar applications of fading techniques have been used in linear programmed instruction such as:

"A reinforcer is a stimulus that increases the probability of a response."
"A reinforcer is a stimulus that increases the probability of a _____."
"A reinforcer is a stimulus that _____ the probability of a _____."
"A reinforcer is a stimulus that _____ the _____ of a _____."
"A reinforcer is a _____ that _____ the _____ of a _____."

Fading and shaping procedures are both used to establish behaviors that initially have a low probability of occurrence. In shaping, the form of the response is gradually changed by manipulation of reinforcing *consequences*. The fading procedure, in contrast, involves gradual alteration of the *antecedent* stimulus conditions, or S^Ds, that set the occasion for the response to occur. The fading procedure, therefore, does not involve modification of the initial response; the response remains the same throughout the procedure but is emitted in the presence of gradually varied stimulus conditions.

Stimulus discrimination and stimulus generalization are important processes involved in behavioral adaptation. Just as we must discriminate appropriate occasions for performing a given behavior, so must we be able to apply what we have learned in one specific situation to other, similar situations. The principle of *stimulus generalization* states that a response conditioned in the presence of one stimulus, S^D (this S^D is called the original or training stimulus), will also occur in the presence of other similar, or functionally equivalent, stimuli. Stimulus generalization takes place when a response conditioned in the presence of one S^D is also emitted in the presence of similar or functionally equivalent stimuli. *Functional equivalence* in this case refers to the ability of particular stimuli, different from the training S^D, to set the occasion for the response to occur. In order to say that a response has generalized it must occur in the presence of a stimulus different from the training stimulus, without reinforcement.

In Figure 1, S^{D_1} is the training stimulus that sets the occasion for the response, R_1, to be reinforced. S^{D_2}, S^{D_3}, and S^{D_4} are three stimuli similar along some dimension(s) to S^{D_1}. Stimulus generalization takes place when R_1 is

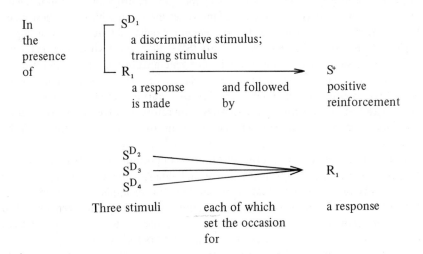

FIGURE 1. Stimulus generalization paradigm.

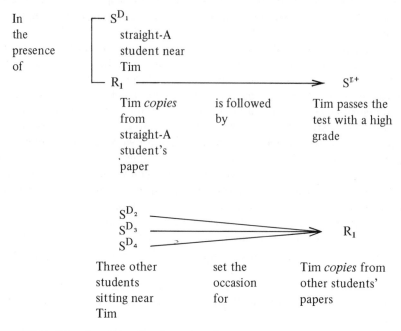

FIGURE 2. Stimulus generalization example.

emitted in the presence of S^{D_2}, S^{D_3}, or S^{D_4}. For example, Tim copies answers (R_1) from a nearby straight-A student's paper (S^{D_1}) during an exam in his math class, as a last resort to pass one test. Tim passes the exam with the highest grade he ever received in math (S^+). On subsequent exams in that class, Tim copies answers (R_1) from other nearby students $(S^{D_2}, S^{D_3}$, etc.) whose papers he can see. Figure 2 shows this example of stimulus generalization in paradigm form.

Stimuli, as well as responses, involve classes of events rather than discrete events. The word stimulus refers to a class or group of stimuli, each member of which can produce a similar effect. An S^D, therefore, involves a class of stimuli, each member of which can set the occasion for a response that will be reinforced.

The concept of stimulus generalization is important in human adaptation because of the many instances where individuals are required to transfer behaviors acquired in one situation to another. For example, most people learn to read from textbooks in school. Reading thereafter is frequently generalized to (1) other reading materials such as newspapers, magazines, and novels, and (2) other places such as home, the library, and the doctor's office. A person who learns to drive one standard shift automobile can usually drive other standard shift automobiles with little or no difficulty. This phenomenon is called stimulus generalization because the responses relevant to reading and driving learned in the original classroom and automobile have transferred to other rooms and automobiles.

From time to time, the therapist may encounter a client who is similar in some respect to a significant individual(s) in the therapist's life, such as a parent, colleague, spouse, or child. The therapist may respond to the client in the same way that he has behaved toward the significant individual. Stimulus generalization in such cases could be detrimental to the client, if the therapist fails to consider this factor in establishing and carrying out a treatment plan in the best interests of the client.

A *stimulus generalization gradient* demonstrates that as some property shared by a group of stimuli becomes more and more different from the training stimulus, the likelihood of the response occurring in their presence decreases.

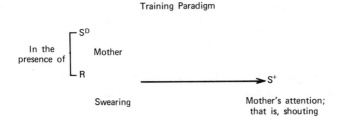

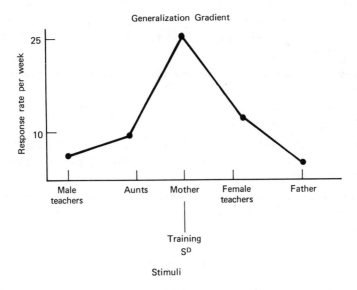

FIGURE 3.   Example of a stimulus generalization gradient.

The frequency of responding, therefore, is greatest in the presence of the training stimulus and decreases as the stimulus becomes less similar to the training stimulus. Stimulus properties include size, color, and form.

Johnny has been positively reinforced by his mother for swearing. The mother serves as the S^D for the response of swearing and the reinforcer is the attention she pays him by shouting at him when he swears. The mother's shouting is observed to increase rather than decrease Johnny's swearing. Johnny sometimes uses swear words with his aunts, female teachers, and other women, but rarely with his male teachers or his father. Johnny's swearing is observed to occur most frequently in his mother's presence and with decreasing frequency as the stimuli become less similar to his mother (training stimulus); this characteristic identifies the *gradient*. Figure 3 depicts this situation. A stimulus generalization gradient exists, therefore, when the response rate decreases as similarity to the training stimulus decreases. Accordingly, the response rate increases as similarity to the training stimulus increases.

REFERENCES

Barlow, **D.H.** and **Agras, W.S.**, "Fading to Increase Heterosexual Responsiveness in Homosexuals," *Journal of Applied Behavior Analysis,* **6,** No. 3 (1973), pp. 355—366.

Goldiamond, I., "Self-Control Procedures In Personal Behavior Problems," *Psychological Reports,* **17** (1965), pp. 851—868.

Lindsley, O.R., "Geriatric Behavioral Prosthetics," in Kastenbaum, R. (Ed.), *New Thoughts on Old Age,* Springer Publishing Co., Inc., New York, 1964, pp. 41—60.

Millenson, J.R., *Principles of Behavioral Analysis,* The MacMillan Company, New York, 1967, Chapter 9, pp. 187—207.

Skinner, B.F., *Science and Human Behavior,* The Free Press, New York, 1953, Chapters 7 and 8, pp. 107—140.

Sundel, M., Butterfield, W., and Geis, G., "Modification of Verbal Behavior in Chronic Schizophrenics," *Michigan Mental Health Research Bulletin,* **3,** No. **2** (1969), pp. 37—40.

Terrace, H.S., "Stimulus Control," in Honig, W.K. (Ed.), *Operant Behavior: Areas of Research and Application,* Appleton-Century-Crofts, New York, 1966, pp. 271—344.

POST-TEST QUESTIONS

(3) 1. Using the information from Vignette 5: (1) Describe the discrimination training procedure that was employed. (2) How were reinforcement and

extinction involved in this discrimination training? (3) Describe the effects of this procedure.

(3) 2. Jim, a retarded teenager, does not discriminate the Men's restroom sign from the Ladies' sign; that is, he sometimes walks into the Ladies' restroom, sometimes into the Men's. Give an example of an errorless discrimination training procedure you could use to teach Jim the appropriate discrimination.

(5) 3. Describe a procedure for establishing a discrimination (nonerrorless). In your example, include one S^D, one S^Δ, and one response. How would you know when stimulus control had been achieved?

(3) 4. Give an example of a stimulus generalization gradient that can be observed in an individual's behavior. What identifies this as a generalization gradient?

chapter 8
behavioral
assessment I

OBJECTIVES

After completing this chapter, you should be able to:
1. describe a problematic behavior in measurable terms,
2. give examples of deficit and excess problematic behaviors,
3. identify antecedents of problematic behavior and aversive or negative consequences of that behavior, given a sample case, and
4. identify problematic behavior, its antecedent and reinforcing consequences, given a sample case.

The purpose of this chapter is to summarize major concepts and procedures of behavioral assessment. We have thus far presented behavioral principles and techniques used in analyzing specific incidents or situations. Some of these concepts will now be considered within the framework of a behavioral assessment strategy. The behavioral assessment approach presented is applicable to a wide variety of individual and group practice settings.

Psychotherapists frequently encounter situations in which clients lack effective problem-solving skills or are unable to manage anxiety. In contrast to behavioral assessment, traditional psychodynamic approaches usually require lengthy diagnostic workups based on early developmental experiences of the client. These diagnostic procedures typically lead to classification of the client according to standardized categories of mental disorder. It is customary in psychodynamic approaches to attach diagnostic labels to a client, such as "paranoid-schizophrenic," "obsessive-compulsive neurosis", or "antisocial personality."

These labels frequently fail to indicate an explicit treatment strategy designed to ameliorate the condition specified by the label. In addition, clients given the same label often exhibit a wide range of maladaptive behaviors. Diagnostic labels can establish or reinforce the client's belief or fear that he has some permanent pathological condition that cannot be altered. Such labels may have further detrimental consequences for the client even after his maladaptive behaviors are no longer present; for example, he may experience difficulty in being hired for certain jobs.

Behavioral assessment involves systematic and continuous data gathering that focuses on current target behaviors and their controlling environmental conditions. In contrast to standardized diagnostic labels, behavioral assessment leads to specification of the client's problematic behavior(s), its controlling antecedents and consequences, and formulation of behavioral change goals. The behavioral change goals indicate the direction in which the target behaviors are to be modified. The treatment plan is based on these goals and involves selection of intervention techniques directed toward their achievement. The focus on *behavior* provides the client with the expectation that his situation can be improved. Cautela and Upper (1973) have proposed a behavioral coding system based on behaviorally specific categories, rather than diagnostic labels. It provides a uniform classification system that allows the therapist to focus on observable maladaptive behaviors rather than formulating abstract interpretations of behavior.

The client's *informed consent* should be obtained prior to carrying out a behavioral assessment. This can be formalized in a service or treatment contract in which the practitioner and client agree to perform certain activities that can lead to attainment of the client's treatment goals.

The practitioner initiates the behavioral assessment procedure by obtaining from the client a listing of major problem areas. The problem checklist, described later in this chapter, can be used along with interviewing to help identify major areas of difficulty. Sometimes a client agrees that all problem areas have been identified, but he later indicates the existence of other problems. These newly presented problems may indicate the necessity for reordering treatment priorities. Some clients, however, are "problem-switchers" who attempt to avoid dealing with any problem by presenting a new problem or crisis at each interview, insisting that the new problem take immediate priority.

A thorough behavioral assessment should be carried out prior to implementing a behavioral change program, so that intervention techniques are appropriately applied to the client's situation. This assessment provides baseline measures for evaluating effectiveness of treatment. In crisis situations, however, the practitioner may have to intervene prior to carrying out a systematic behavioral assessment, in order to provide the client with necessary resources, referrals, or direct assistance. Such emergencies include situations where the client is suicidal, requires immediate hospitalization, or where immediate action is required to provide food, housing, or medical care.

Behavioral assessment involves consideration of the following components: (1) problem area, (2) problem selection, (3) target behavior, (4) response strength, (5) antecedent and consequent conditions.

1. A *problem area* is often manifested in the role or position in which the individual experiences difficulty; for example, as a father, teacher, employee, or spouse. Thus, problem areas might include discipline of children, classroom management, social skills, or marital relations. The isolation of the problem area enables the practitioner to "zero in" or focus rapidly on the behavioral patterns related to maladaptive performance in role functioning. The Sundel-Lawrence Problem Checklist (Figure 1) for example, can be used to help a client specify problem areas. Fourteen areas are shown from which the client can check off problematic roles. Following this initial identification, the client is provided with sample problem descriptions that he can use as a guide in writing his own problem statements in behaviorally specific terms.

FIGURE 1. Sundel-Lawrence Problem Checklist*

Check ($\sqrt{}$) which of the following relationships are unsatisfactory to you or present problems for you.

Use a *double-check* ($\sqrt{}\sqrt{}$) for those that most concern you.

_____ Parents	_____ Teacher
_____ Brothers and sisters	_____ Co-workers
_____ Husband or wife	_____ Subordinates at work
_____ Children	_____ Persons of the same sex
_____ Other relatives	_____ Persons of the opposite sex
_____ Work supervisor or employer	_____ Myself
_____ Classmates	_____ Neighbors

For each of the relationships you *double-checked*, what are the one or two problems you are having with that person or persons that *most* concern you? Look at the examples below before you write your own. They should serve to guide your descriptions.

Examples:

Person(s)	Problems
1. Wife	We are constantly quarreling. She usually sleeps in the children's room instead of with me.

Sundel-Lawrence Problem Checklist Continued

2. Oldest son	When I ask him to do his chores, he doesn't obey me. He often fights with and beats his younger sister.
3. Girls at work	I do not participate in the conversations with the girls during lunch or coffee breaks.

Problems of major concern to me

Person(s)	Problems

*Reprinted with permission of Macmillan Publishing Co., Inc. from "Behavioral Group Treatment with Adults in a Family Service Agency," by Martin Sundel and Harry Lawrence in *Individual Change Through Small Groups* by P. Glasser, R. Sarri, and R. Vinter (Eds.) Copyright © 1974 by The Free Press, a Division of Macmillan Publishing Co., Inc.

2. If the client presents several problem areas for treatment, the practitioner can consider the following four criteria in determining *problem priorities* for treatment:

a. The problem that is the most immediate expressed concern of the client or significant others (e.g., family, friends, teachers).

Examples: A homosexual man wants to develop heterosexual relationships. A mother wants her son to stop screaming at bedtime.

b. The problem that has extensive aversive or negative consequences for the client, significant others, or society if not handled immediately.

Examples: Herman will be fired from his job unless he can start working cooperatively with co-workers. Sally will be expelled from school unless she attends more frequently.

c. The problem that can be corrected most quickly, considering resources and obstacles.

Example: Bob and Jean Jones decide to work on resolving their arguments over financial matters before dealing with their sexual problems.

d. The problem that requires handling before other problems can be treated.

Example: Mr. and Mrs. Smith decide to work on resolving child-rearing disagreements between them before working on their children's behavior problems.

In considering these criteria, the client should actively participate in ordering priorities.

3. The *target behavior* or problematic behavior of the client is stated in terms that clearly specify his response. The behavior is described in observable terms, without attaching labels or judgments such as "inadequate" or "passive-aggressive." Autonomic or covert responses such as anxiety or fear are described in terms of the client's overt behaviors, although measurements of physiological changes such as heart rate and galvanic skin response can be obtained.

Problematic behavior indicates either a *behavioral excess* or a *behavioral deficit. Behavioral excess* refers to high-frequency inappropriate behaviors emitted by the client; *behavioral deficit* refers to the absence or low frequency of appropriate behaviors. Examples of maladaptive excessive behaviors include lying, stealing, fighting, and crying; examples of deficient appropriate responses include smiling, talking, dressing, attending work regularly, and turning in class assignments. Behavioral deficits also occur when the client fails to discriminate the appropriate occasion for emitting a certain behavior. For example, talking in a loud voice might be appropriate on the playground, but inappropriate at the dinner table. Other words that are frequently used to signify problematic behavior include "maladaptive," "deviant," "inappropriate," and "undesirable."

4. The *strength of the target response* is determined by measures of frequency, duration, latency, and/or intensity. Frequency is the most typical measure of response strength. The number of times the target behavior occurs within a given time period is counted and recorded as baseline data. Time sampling is another method used to record frequency data. Time sampling involves observing and recording the occurrence of target behaviors at designated times. For example, the individual(s) may be observed at the end of every fifteen-second interval for a twenty-minute period twice a day. The observer would record the behavior emitted by the individual at the end of every fifteen seconds. When collected over a period of time, these data provide accurate accounts of baseline frequency. This method is particularly useful for recording behaviors that occur at very high rates, such as facial tics or head-banging. It can also be used when continuous observation of target behaviors is impractical, such as recording out-of-seat behaviors of several children in a classroom.

Where applicable the *duration* of a problematic behavior is also recorded; for example, "John slapped his brother in the face for five minutes"; "Sally shouted at the dinner table for ten minutes last Thursday and for fifteen minutes on

Friday." Another measure of response strength is *latency*. The latency of a response is measured by the interval between presentation of an antecedent stimulus and occurrence of the response. For example, Father called Sam to the dinner table, and he came immediately. The *intensity* or severity of behaviors such as punching, screaming, kicking, or crying are often difficult or impractical to measure as they occur in the client's environment, although instrumentation that can measure these behaviors in physical units such as decibels or grams is available in a laboratory setting. The problematic feature of these behaviors, however, involves the aversive consequences or effects that they have for the client or significant others. Because individuals differ in their tolerance for the behavior of others as well as in their own reactions to physical and social stimulation, examining the aversive or negative consequences of the problematic behavior for the client and significant others provides a useful method of judging the intensity of the behavior. For example, the degree of "noisiness" of Dick's playing in his room is determined by his father who reprimands him; the intensity of Sam's "tapping" a classmate on the arm is indicated by the victim's bruises or complaints to a teacher.

In assessing problems that occur infrequently, such as violent arguments between marital partners, the therapist should attempt to discover specific episodes that might not have been reported by the clients but that precede major problematic situations. The frequency of these lesser problematic interchanges should be obtained and the physical and verbal responses of both partners in these situations further delineated.

5. In behavioral assessment, the practitioner attempts to specify the *antecedent and consequent conditions* maintaining the target behavior. Antecedents refer to events that precede or trigger a specific behavior. In the previous chapter we discussed the cueing function of S^Ds. For example, an antecedent condition or S^D for Bob's striking Joe with his fist is Joe calling him "stupid." A second antecedent condition might have included two of Bob's friends urging him to strike Joe. It is sometimes difficult to specify antecedents that set the occasion for target behaviors. The controlling stimulus may be different to determine for a specific behavior. The therapist should describe in specific terms where the behavior occurs, when, who is present, and what is said or done by whom prior to the occurrence of the behavior. As a rule, the therapist focuses on contemporaneous factors that are closely associated with the target behavior. In some instances, however, the therapist may assess the influence of earlier antecedent events on the client's current behavior.

Reinforcing consequences refer to events that follow a problem behavior and strengthen or maintain it. For example, when Jim breaks into line ahead of the other children, he is positively reinforced by receiving his ice cream before the others. Aversive or negative consequences refer to events that follow a problem behavior that are undesirable or unpleasant to the individual or significant others. For example, when Bob hits Joe, the teacher cancels Bob's recess and reprimands him. Sometimes there can be both reinforcing and aversive consequences for the same behavior. In the above example, Jim is positively reinforced for breaking into line ahead of other children. Breaking into line also has aversive consequences for Jim, however, if his mother scolds him and sends him home after he receives his ice cream cone. The aversive consequences for the client and/or significant others frequently provide an incentive for modifying the problematic behavior.

Accurate, systematic data collection and recording are essential features of a behavioral assessment and modification program. Data indicating strength of the target response are recorded, along with relevant antecedent and consequent conditions. These measures constitute baseline data and should be obtained prior to implementation of an intervention plan. These data are also recorded throughout treatment and at follow-up, thus providing an ongoing basis for evaluating the effectiveness of treatment. The therapist can determine if target behaviors have increased or decreased in strength and if problematic antecedents and/or consequences have been altered.

Whenever feasible, graphs and charts depicting changes in the client's situation should be constructed. A graphic representation provides the client and practitioner with a summary of the recorded data and a visual indication of the direction of behavioral change. This feedback can serve as a positive reinforcer for the client and practitioner when desired change is readily apparent.

In addition to direct observations of the client's behavior and client reports, behavioral questionnaires or checklists may be used to obtain assessment information. The Fear Survey Schedule (Wolpe and Lang, 1969), for example, can be used in determining the extent to which certain events are anxiety-producing for an individual. The Fear Survey Schedule provides the therapist with information that otherwise would require extensive interviewing or be difficult to obtain. Other behavioral questionnaires and diagnostic instruments are listed in the references at the end of this chapter and include the Willoughby Personality Schedule, the Bernreuter Self-Sufficiency Scale, a Reinforcement Survey Schedule, and the Life History Questionnaire.

The therapist may also validate his observations by interviewing individuals associated with the client's problem. Sources of problem validation can include parents, relatives, neighbors, teachers, and peers as well as the client himself. A description of the problem as perceived by these individuals should be obtained, so that their roles in relation to the client's problem are made clear. Significant individuals can be instructed to observe and record the target behavior and the conditions under which it occurs. Frequently, this monitoring procedure is also effective in pointing out the monitor's role in generating or maintaining the target behavior; that is, how the significant other provides problematic antecedents or consequences related to performance of the undesired behavior.

Knowledge gained from such observation might be sufficient in some instances to suggest to the observer an immediate solution that would involve alteration of the observer's behavior in the problematic situation.

REFERENCES

Bernreuter, R.G., "Bernreuter S-S Scale and Scoring Key," in Wolpe, J., *The Practice of Behavior Therapy,* Pergamon Press, New York, 1969, Appendix 4, pp. 287-290.

Cautela, J.R. and Kastenbaum, R., "A Reinforcement Survey Schedule for Use in Therapy, Training, and Research," *Psychological Reports,* **20** (1967), pp. 115-130.

Cautela, J.R. and Upper, D., "A Behavioral Coding System," 1973.

Ferster, C. B., "Classification of Behavioral Pathology," in Krasner, L. and Ullmann, L. P. (Eds.), *Research in Behavior Modification*, Holt, Rinehart, and Winston, New York, 1965, pp. 6-26.

Mager, R. F., *Preparing Instructional Objectives*, Fearon Publishers, Palo Alto, California, 1962.

Sarbin, T., "On the Futility of the Proposition That Some People Be Labeled Mentally. Ill," *Journal of Consulting Psychology,* **31**, No. 5 (1967), pp. 447-453.

Sundel, M. and Lawrence, H., "Behavioral Group Treatment with Adults in a Family Service Agency," in Glasser, P., Sarri, R. and Vinter, R. (Eds.), *Individual Change Through Small Groups,* The Free Press, New York, 1974, pp. 325-347.

Ullmann, L.P. and *Krasner, L., A Psychological Approach to Abnormal Behavior,* Prentice-Hall, Inc., Englewood Cliffs, New Jersey, 1969.

Willoughby, J.R., "The Willoughby Personality Schedule (adapted from the Clark-Thurston Inventory)," in Wolpe, J., *The Practice of Behavior Therapy,* Pergamon Press, New York, 1969, Appendices 1 and 2, pp. 279-282.

Wolpe, J., *The Practice of Behavior Therapy,* Pergamon Press, New York, 1969, Chapter 3, pp. 22-54.

Wolpe, J. and Lang, P.J., "A Fear Survey Schedule for Use in Behavior Therapy," *Behaviour Research and Therapy,* **2**, No. 27 (1964).

Wolpe, J. and Lazarus, A.A., "Life History Questionnaire," in Wolpe, J. and Lazarus, A.A., *Behavior Therapy Techniques,* Pergamon Press, New York, 1968, Appendix 1, pp. 165-169.

POST-TEST QUESTIONS

(4) 1. Give two examples of individuals with behavioral deficits and two examples of individuals with behavioral excesses.

(4) 2. If a client tells you that her boyfriend is always late for their dates,
   a. Which of the two following questions would you ask her in order to obtain baseline measures of her complaint? (Circle the correct answers.)
      1. Why do you think he's always late?
      2. How many minutes late is he?
      3. How many times has he been late this month?
      4. What do you think his lateness means?
   b. Give two hypothetical answers to the questions you chose above that would provide assessment data indicating a baseline measure of the undesired behavior.

(3) 3. From the information given in the following paragraph, identify Shirley's problematic response, its antecedent, and its negative consequences.

   Shirley's boss frequently asks her to work late. Last week, he made four such requests. When her boss makes these requests, Shirley holds her head down and says, "O.K." She had unpleasant arguments with her husband twice over her working late, and on another night they arrived late to a play.

(3) 4. From the information given in the paragraph below, identify the problematic response, its antecedent, and the probable positive reinforcers.

Children are playing ball in a group; Howard is sitting by himself. When Howard tells jokes about himself, the other children gather around and laugh at him. The social worker observes that the other children rarely speak to Howard unless he is making fun of himself.

chapter 9
behavioral
assessment II

OBJECTIVES

Given a case example, you should be able to:
1. specify two antecedent conditions related to the problematic response,
2. state a negative consequence related to the problematic response,
3. state a probable reinforcer maintaining the problematic response, and
4. formulate a behavioral change goal based on the above information, including a desired client response, a relevant antecedent, and a probable positive reinforcer.

In this chapter, we will continue to focus on the major components of behavioral assessment. RAC-S is an acronym for *Response, Antecedent, Consequence*, and *Strength*, four major components of behavioral assessment. In gathering data for behavioral assessment, the therapist employs the following procedure, involving the client as much as possible at each step:

1. List the client's problems.
2. Select one problem for immediate attention.
3. Obtain a concrete example of the problem that includes a description of the following areas: (a) the target *response(s)*, (b) the controlling *antecedent(s)*, (c) the *negative consequences* for the client and/or significant others, (d) possible *positive reinforcer(s)*, and (e) response *strength* including measures of frequency per time unit (rate), latency, intensity, and/or duration.
4. Formulate terminal, intermediate, and immediate behavioral change goals, specifying (a) the desired *response(s)*, (b) the *antecedent(s)*, (c) the *positive reinforcer(s)* and (d) the desired response *strength*.

FIGURE 1. RAC-S schema.

———————————————————————————————————————

┌——————A
│   Antecedents
│
│   1. When does the target
│   behavior occur?
│   2. Who is present?
In the │ 3. Where is the client?
presence│ 4. What happens before
of   │   the target response?
│   a. What is said?
│   b. Who says it?
│   c. What nonverbal behavior is
│   emitted?
│   d. Who emits it?
│
└— R ——————————————————————————————————→ C

Target Response(s) or Behavior(s)	(S) Response Strength	Positive (C$^+$) or Negative (C$^-$) Consequences; (possible reinforcers or punishers)
1. What does the client say? 2. What nonverbal behavior does client emit?	1. How long has the behavior been a problem? 2. How long does an occurrence of the behavior persist (duration)? 3. How many times did the response occur during the past minute? Hour? Day? Week? Month? 4. How can the intensity of the behavior be described? 5. How quickly does the response occur after presentation of an antecedent stimulus?	C$^+$ and/or C$^-$ 1. What happens after the problematic response? 2. Who responds to the client? 3. When does this consequence occur? 4. Who judges the client's behavior to be problematic? 5. What behaviors do others emit that relate to the client's behavior? C$^+$ 1. What seems to maintain or support the response?

RAC-S schema (continued)

2. What attention does the client receive?
3. What benefit does the client receive?
4. What happens that could influence the client to perform the behavior again?

C^-

1. What losses are sustained by the client?
2. What physical or verbal assault is incurred by the client?
3. What losses are sustained by other individuals or society?

---

5. Specify response data to be observed and design a measurement plan.

The RAC-S assessment components are schematized in Figure 1. Sample questions relevant to each component are given.

The client and therapist select a problem for immediate consideration from among the various problem areas the client, significant others, and/or the therapist have identified. In order to delineate the client's problem, the therapist obtains an example of its occurrence either by direct observation or by asking the client and/or significant others to describe the problem the last time it occurred. The client is asked to give an explicit account of this event. *Behavioral re-enactment* is a role-play technique used to obtain specific data regarding the client's behavior in the problematic situation. This technique is particularly useful in validating a client's verbal report of a target behavior and its controlling conditions. In behavioral re-enactment, the client usually role-plays himself in the problematic situation and the therapist (and/or group members, if the assessment is occurring in group treatment) role-plays the parts of significant others according to the client's description. The therapist observes the client's verbal and nonverbal behaviors during the role-play and compares his observations with the client's earlier report. For example, Mrs. R., a high school teacher, complained that the principal singled her out for criticism; she insisted that nothing she did or said was responsible for it. Mrs. R. re-enacted a recent incident involving the principal's criticism, role-playing herself, while a group member role-played the principal. After the re-enactment, the therapist and group members pointed out discrepancies between Mrs. R.'s previous description of her behavior and the actual responses observed in the re-enactment. During the role-play, Mrs. R. spoke in short, clipped phrases, sneered, and stood with her hands on her hips. This feedback provided Mrs. R. and the therapist with a concrete example of her behavior in a simulation of the problematic situation. Behavioral re-enactment not only provides a concrete example of the client's problematic responses, but also helps to identify controlling antecedents and consequences.

Measures of the *response strength* (frequency, latency, intensity, and/or duration) of target behaviors should be obtained throughout treatment. The therapist gives the client various assignments that involve recording specific events and reporting RAC-S data at each interview. The client and therapist can record these data on prepared forms such as the RAC-S Data Form (Figure 2) and the RAC-S Data Chart (Figure 3). The client can also carry a 3 × 5-in. card in his pocket for conveniently recording target behaviors. Initially, the client may be assigned to record only the target behavior(s) and its frequency. When the client demonstrates his ability to observe and record these data, the therapist requests that he also record antecedents and/or consequences related to the target behavior(s). These RAC-S data are used in formulating goals.

FIGURE 2.   RAC-S Data Form.

---

1. State the problem and give an example of its occurrence.

2. Describe in specific terms the negative consequences of this problem for the client and/or significant others.

    1.
    2.
    3.

3. Specify the target response(s) to be observed in precise terms. Be sure that a stranger reading your description would know exactly what the client is *saying* or *doing*.

    Behavioral excesses:

    Behavioral deficits:

4. Describe below the antecedents and possible reinforcers related to the target response.

Antecedents:
1.
2.
3.
Possible reinforcers
1.
2.
3.

FIGURE 3. RAC-S Data Chart.*

Days	Antecedents	Possible Reinforcers	Description of Response	Response [a] Strength
Sunday[b]				
M				
A				
E				
				Total:
Monday				
M				
A				
E				
				Total:
Tuesday				
M				
A				
E				
				Total:
Wednesday				
M				
A				
E				
				Total:

*Reprinted with permission of Macmillan Publishing Co., Inc., from "Behavioral Group Treatment with Adults in a Family Service Agency," by Martin Sundel and Harry Lawrence in *Individual Change Through Small Groups* by P. Glasser, R. Sarri, and R. Vinter (Eds.) Copyright © 1974 by The Free Press, a Division of Macmillan Publishing Co., Inc.

RAC-S Data Chart (continued)

Days	Antecedents	Possible Reinforcers	Description of Response	Response[a] Strength
Thursday				
M				
A				
E				
				Total:
Friday				
M				
A				
E				
				Total:
Saturday				
M				
A				
E				
				Total:

Weekly Total R Frequency_____

[a]Specify response strength in terms of frequency/time unit, duration, intensity, and/or latency. Place a vertical mark (|) to indicate each occurrence of the response.
[b]Check (√) the appropriate box for the time of occurrence; morning (M), afternoon (A), evening (E), and record time.

Mr. D.'s *presenting problem* (the problem that he said brought him in to seek help), involved frequent arguments with his wife over financial matters. The Problem Checklist indicated that Mr. D. also had difficulty (1) in disciplining his teenage son and (2) with his employer. After further discussion, Mr. D., a furniture salesman, indicated that his work situation was of most concern because his sales had dropped off and he was in danger of losing his job. Mr. D. has worked for his present employer for six years. When asked to rank his problems, he gave difficulty at work the highest priority. When asked for an example of this problem, Mr. D. reported a recent incident in which his boss criticized him for being too abusive with customers. Mr. D. also reported several occasions that month on which he lost his temper and spoke inappropriately to customers, two of them occurring within the past week. Although Mr. D. feared that he would be fired if he continued to act inappropriately, he said he did not know how to make himself act differently.

The RAC-S schema was applied to obtain the information necessary to carry out a behavioral assessment and formulate behavioral change goals for Mr. D. Since Mr. D. had difficulty describing the circumstances of his last unpleasant encounter with a customer, a behavioral re-enactment was arranged by the therapist to obtain concrete examples of Mr. D.'s behavior in the problematic situation. The therapist role-played a customer and Mr. D. role-played himself in a simulation of a recent incident in which Mr. D. lost his temper with a customer. Mr. D. set up the role-play as follows: He was showing a customer some furniture in the store. The customer (played by the therapist) was difficult to please and complained about the cost of everything she saw. During the behavioral re-enactment, the therapist observed that Mr. D. became "frustrated and angry"; that is, he raised his voice, clenched his fists, frowned, and made rapid arm movements. Mr. D. insulted the customer by telling her she had bad taste in sofas; she didn't know quality furniture when she saw it; she would never find anything that suited her and that no salesman in his right mind would put up with her fussiness. The customer became enraged. Her face turned red; she yelled back at him and said she would report him to the manager. The customer then turned on her heel and left the store. When questioned after the role-play, Mr. D. reported that his behavior pattern was similar during recent incidents that had occurred at the store.

In order to determine discriminative stimuli (controlling antecedents) that set the occasion for Mr. D.'s inappropriate responses, he was asked questions similar to those on the RAC-S schema in Figure 1. For example, where and when did the problem occur? Who was present? What was said? Who said it? In describing the role of the customer for the behavioral re-enactment, Mr. D. had provided possible antecedents to the problematic behaviors. He said that "They (the customers) sometimes say that they've seen the same item for less money at _____'s (another furniture store in town). That really makes me mad. We provide much better service for the price." The target behaviors occurred when Mr. D. was in the store with a customer, with other salesmen nearby. Right before Mr. D. responded inappropriately, the customer said something about the price of the item in relation to a competitor.

We have determined the negative consequences related to Mr. D.'s target behaviors: he will lose his job if he continues to offend customers; his boss criticizes him. Further interviewing or observation is necessary to discover the possible reinforcing consequences that maintain Mr. D.'s problematic behaviors. Again, the RAC-S schema (Figure 1) suggests questions that could be used to elicit information regarding the reinforcing consequences of this behavior. For example, what maintains the responses? What attention or other benefits does the client receive? Mr. D. stated that he did not like his present job, but was afraid that he would not be able to find another one that could support his family. He did not associate much with the other employees, who were mostly younger than he, and felt that he was more intelligent than they. When he "told a customer off," however, the other employees told him what a good job he did. Further information about possible reinforcers could be obtained through a behavioral re-enactment in which the therapist role-played Mr. D. while Mr. D. role-played other employees telling him what a good job he did of "telling off that old witch."

The RAC-S Data Form (Figure 4) and the RAC-S Data Chart (Figure 5) have been filled out using the information from Mr. D.'s problematic situation.

FIGURE 4. RAC-S Data Form.

---

1. State the problem and give an example of its occurrence.
   Mr. D. speaks inappropriately and abusively to customers. A customer came into the store and he raised his voice, clenched his fist, made rapid arm movements, and insulted the customer.

2. Describe in specific terms the negative consequences of this problem for the client and/or significant others.

   1. His boss criticizes him.
   2. He may lose his job.

3. Specify the target response(s) to be observed in precise terms. Be sure that a stranger reading your description would know exactly what the client is *saying* or *doing*.
   Behavioral excesses: Raising his voice, clenching his fists, making rapid arm movements and insulting remarks.
   Behavioral deficits: Mr. D. completes too few sales.

4. Describe below the antecedents and possible reinforcers related to the target response.

   Antecedents:
   1. A customer complains about prices related to a competitor's.

   2. Mr. D. is in the store with a customer with other salesmen nearby.

   Possible reinforcers:
   1. Other employees encourage him to "tell off" fussy customers and praise him for doing so.

   2. Customer quickly stops complaining; leaves the store.

FIGURE 5. RAC-S Data Chart.

Days	Antecedents	Possible Reinforcers	Description of Response	Response[a] Strength
Sunday[b]				
M				
A	Not applicable-	-Client does		
E		not work.		
				Total: 0
Monday 9:30 M	Customer com-	Other employ-	Raises his	|
A	plains about	ees encourage	voice; insults	5 min,
E	price.	Mr. D.	customer;	once
			makes rapid	per day
			arm movements.	Total: 1
Tuesday M				
A				
E				
				Total: 0
Wednesday M				|
3:00 A	Customer asks	Customer	Scowls; insults	2 min,
E	for a reduc-	quickly stops	customer;	once
	tion in price	talking; leaves	clenches fists	per day
		store		Total: 1
Thursday 10:00 M	Customer com-	Other employ-	Insults cus-	|
A	plains about	ees praise	tomer; raises	5 min,
E	quality of	Mr. D.	his voice.	once
	merchandise			per day
	and the high			
	price.			Total: 1

RAC-S Data Chart (continued)

Days	Antecedents	Possible Reinforcers	Description of Response	Response[a] Strength
Friday M				
A				
E				
				Total: 0
Saturday M				
A				
E				
				Total: 0
			Weekly Total R Frequency	3

[a]Specify response strength in terms of frequency/time unit, duration, intensity, and/or latency. Place a vertical mark (I) to indicate each occurrence of the response.

[b]Check (√) the appropriate box for time of occurrence; morning (M), afternoon (A), evening (E), and record time.

In observing human behavior, it is interesting to note that short-term reinforcing consequences often have a stronger effect in maintaining a behavior than long-term negative consequences exert in suppressing that behavior. Sometimes we wonder why certain behaviors continue to occur, in spite of severe negative consequences that eventually follow them. For example, a child steals candy at the grocery store, even though he was beaten by his father the last time he was caught stealing. The immediate benefit of passing a test by cheating may offset the possible negative consequences of being caught and disciplined. Staying in bed a few minutes longer may consistently result in arriving late to work and being criticized by the boss.

Although it was stated earlier that Mr. D.'s problematic behaviors occurred twice during the past week, more specific information was needed regarding response strength. Does the problem occur twice every week? Twice per month? Does it last for five minutes? Twenty-five minutes? Mr. D.'s best estimate was that this problem occurred between one and three times per week, lasted for about five minutes, and had been a problem for about eight months.

There is no set rule for obtaining the RAC-S assessment components. The interview should progress in a systematic manner while allowing the interviewer to make use of relevant information as the client presents it.

After the first interview, Mr. D. was instructed to record the frequency and duration of the target behaviors, their antecedents, and consequences on the RAC-S Behavior Record Form. At the next interview, these data were reported and appeared to be consistent with Mr. D.'s previous descriptions of the problematic situation. The RAC-S Data Chart enables the therapist to compare the client's subjective recall of the problematic situation with a systematic record. A written record also serves to correct subjective estimates of behaviors whose reported frequency may be exaggerated. Sometimes, merely observing and recording behavioral excesses will have the effect of reducing their frequency, although this decrease is often temporary.

When the response, its antecedents, consequences, and response strength (frequency, duration, intensity, and/or latency) are ascertained, behaviorally specific goals or objectives can be formulated. Goals are formulated on various levels—immediate, intermediate, and terminal. When a goal is stated, it should be followed by criteria that will be used to judge its attainment. Wherever feasible the goal should specify the desired *Response* and the conditions—*Antecedents, Consequences,* and *Strength*—under which it will occur. The terminal behavioral change goals for Mr. D., for example, were (1) to decrease and completely suppress his inappropriate verbal and nonverbal responses with complaining customers and (2) to establish and increase the frequency of appropriate responses with complaining customers. When problematic antecedents occur, Mr. D. will refrain from making inappropriate comments or gestures. Instead, desirable responses will include Mr. D. speaking in a normal tone of voice, justifying the cost of the furniture in terms of the guarantee and service that are provided along with the purchase. The probable reinforcers under these circumstances could be the customer's responsiveness and subsequent purchase, as well as positive comments from his employer on his increased sales. During treatment, the therapist could utilize social reinforcers, such as praise and attention to strengthen Mr. D.'s appropriate behaviors.

Whenever possible, the client should actively participate in establishing his treatment goals. The client's participation in goal formulation is important because of its implications for making major changes in his life. One possible goal for Mr. D. could have been to obtain a different job. The decision to leave a problematic situation rather than attempt to modify the problematic behavior or conditions in that situation is ultimately the client's decision. The therapist should point out, however, alternative goals that are available to the client. After discussing alternative goals, Mr. D. decided to attempt to modify the target behaviors he had reported.

In establishing a goal to decrease problematic behavior, the therapist should also specify the appropriate behavior that should occur in that problematic situation, as indicated in Mr. D.'s terminal goals. For example, the data to be recorded in Mr. D.'s RAC-S measurement plan include the number of times per week that Mr. D. speaks insultingly to customers; achievement of the treatment goal should be reflected in a decrease in this measure. The response data also include the number of times per week that Mr. D. behaves appropriately to complaining customers; achievement of this treatment goal should be reflected by an increase in this measure. These data provide feedback to the client and therapist on the extent to which treatment goals are being achieved and the client's problem ameliorated.

Sometimes clients, or significant others, have less difficulty in specifying the target behaviors to be decreased than they do in describing appropriate behaviors to be emitted. For example, a mother complains that her three-year-old son starts screaming when she talks on the phone. The mother states the goal as "Johnny does *not* scream when I'm talking on the phone." The therapist should also ask the mother to specify what Johnny *should do* at that time; for example, play quietly with his toys, look at a picture book, watch television.

Although the client should actively participate with the therapist in formulating treatment goals, there are situations for which the therapist must assume major responsibility. When the client commits acts that are illegal or detrimental to himself, society, or significant others, there exist legal and societal sanctions requiring the modification of such behaviors. If the therapist disagrees with the client's goal, he should discuss the issues involved with the client. If the client's goal is in conflict with the therapist's professional ethics, the therapist should try to persuade the client to modify his goal. For example, the client may wish to attain a goal that would be exploitative of other individuals; the therapist should dissuade the client from selecting such a goal. If the client's goal is in conflict with the therapist's personal moral code, the therapist should consider withdrawing from the case and assist the client in obtaining professional assistance elsewhere. Goal formulation involves consideration of personal, social, and cultural factors necessary in making the goals viable for the client in his environment.

Immediate and *intermediate goals* should also be established that represent successive approximations to the terminal goal. Intermediate goals of increasing difficulty or complexity should be formulated that are attainable by the client as he progresses through treatment. Positive reinforcement should be arranged for the client as he attains immediate, intermediate, and terminal treatment goals. The procedure of shaping via successive approximation applies this approach in developing a terminal behavior through positively reinforcing successive approximations or intermediate behaviors that lead to it. An immediate goal for Mr. D. might be that he respond in a soft voice to critical questions asked of him by the therapist. An intermediate goal for Mr. D. might be to respond appropriately to problematic customers in role-plays that simulate the situations involving complaining customers. Another intermediate goal could involve Mr. D.'s speaking more softly to fussy customers.

Behavioral assessment requires a thoughtful and systematic plan for determining problematic responses and their controlling conditions. Assigning the client an active role in the collection and recording of assessment data helps to ensure that the goals will accurately reflect the client's situation. The client should also be actively involved in goal formulation so that the client's values as well as those of the therapist are incorporated in the plan for behavioral change. The effort expended by the therapist and client in carrying out a behavioral assessment provides the basis for formulating an intervention strategy appropriate for the client.

REFERENCES

Bandura, A., *Principles of Behavior Modification,* Holt, Rinehart, and Winston, Inc., New York, 1969, Chapter 2, pp. 70-117.

Goldiamond, I., "Justified and Unjustified Alarm Over Behavioral Control," in Milton, O. (Ed.), *Behavior Disorders: Perspectives and Trends*, Lippincott, Philadelphia, 1965.

Kanfer, F.H. and Saslow, G., "Behavioral Diagnosis," in Franks, C.M., (Ed.), *Behavior Therapy: Appraisal and Status*, McGraw-Hill, New York, 1969, pp. 417-444.

Lawrence, H. and Sundel, M., "Behavior Modification In Adult Groups," *Social Work,* **17**, No. 2 (1972), pp. 34-43.

Rogers, C.R. and Skinner, B.F., ,"Some Issues Concerning the Control of Human Behavior: A Symposium," *Science,* **124** (1956), pp. 1057-1066.

Schaefer, H.H. and Martin, P.L., *Behavioral Therapy*, McGraw-Hill, New York, 1969.

Thomas, E.J., Carter, R.D., and Gambrill, E.D., "Some Possibilities of Behavioral Modification with Marital Problems Using 'SAM' (Signal System for the Assessment and Modification of Behavior)," in Rubin, R.D., Fensterheim, H., Lazarus, A.A., and Franks, C.M. (Eds.), *Advances in Behavior Therapy*, Academic Press, New York, 1971, pp. 273-288.

POST-TEST QUESTIONS

(4) 1. Using the information from Vignette 8, state four of Mr. L.'s problematic behaviors.

(1) 2. Specify one antecedent related to Mr. L.'s conversation with his employer.

(2) 3. State two negative consequences of Mr. L.'s non-assertive behaviors.

(1) 4. Using the information from Vignette 7, state a probable reinforcer maintaining Harold's drug taking.

(3) 5. State an intermediate treatment goal for Mr. L. based on the above information specifying (1) a desired response, (2) a relevant antecedent, and (3) a potential positive reinforcer.

chapter 10
conditioned reinforcement and chaining

OBJECTIVES

After completing this chapter, you should be able to:
1. describe a procedure you could use to establish something or someone as a generalized conditioned reinforcer,
2. state the advantage of using conditioned reinforcement over primary reinforcement in maintaining behavioral change in a client's natural environment.
3. describe a procedure that can be used to determine if an S^D has become a conditioned reinforcer, and
4. give an example of a problem that can be analyzed as a stimulus-response chain.

The concept of *conditioned reinforcement* is based on the observation that a neutral or nonreinforcing stimulus can become a reinforcer through association with a reinforcing stimulus. Money, for example, is a conditioned reinforcer for most people. Money is only reinforcing, however, because it has been paired with other reinforcers such as food, shelter, and entertainment. Therapists typically dispense *social reinforcers* such as approval, encouragement, and attention, since these conditioned reinforcers are often available for appropriate behavior in the client's natural environment. *Unconditioned reinforcers* such as food and candy are also used to condition desired behaviors, as well as to establish other stimuli such as money, tokens, attention, and approval as conditioned reinforcers. Conditioned reinforcement is also called secondary, acquired, or derived reinforcement.

When presented as a consequence of behavior, *unconditioned or primary reinforcers* increase response strength and do not require prior association with other reinforcers; they are thus considered intrinsically or naturally reinforcing. Unconditioned positive reinforcers include food, sex, water, warmth, and tactile stimulation. Some nonfood items such as certain drugs can also be naturally reinforcing. *Conditioned or secondary reinforcers* are stimuli or events that acquire reinforcing properties only through pairing or association with other reinforcers. Almost anything can become a conditioned reinforcer. Conditioned positive reinforcers include money, points, trading stamps, and attention.

Conditioned reinforcement, as well as unconditioned reinforcement, can be positive or negative. Negative reinforcement, both unconditioned and conditioned, will be covered in Chapter 13.

The paradigm for conditioned positive reinforcement is similar to that for unconditioned positive reinforcement:

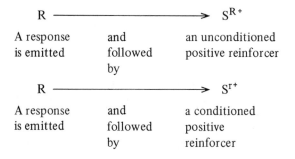

$$R \longrightarrow S^{R+}$$

A response	and	an unconditioned
is emitted	followed	positive reinforcer
	by	

$$R \longrightarrow S^{r+}$$

A response	and	a conditioned
is emitted	followed	positive
	by	reinforcer

The r+ in S^{r+} is the notation for conditioned positive reinforcement just as R+ in S^{R+} is the notation for unconditioned positive reinforcement. When the specific reinforcer has not been identified, S^+ is used, such as in the general paradigm for positive reinforcement $R \rightarrow S^+$. When the reinforcer is known, however, either S^{r+}, or S^{R+} is used to indicate conditioned or unconditioned positive reinforcement.

Conditioned reinforcement follows the same rules that apply to unconditioned reinforcement. As with unconditioned reinforcement, the conditioned reinforcer is most effective when it immediately follows the response. The effectiveness of conditioned reinforcers is also affected by deprivation and satiation. Intermittent schedules of conditioned reinforcement make the response more resistant to extinction than a continuous schedule. When a conditioned reinforcer is withheld continuously from the response it has conditioned, the response strength decreases as extinction takes place. In order to maintain its effectiveness, a conditioned reinforcer requires occasional pairing with another established reinforcer. For example, an individual must occasionally purchase something with the money he accumulates in order for money to continue to be effective as a conditioned reinforcer.

Conditioned reinforcers can be of two types: simple and generalized. *Simple conditioned reinforcers* have been paired with only one reinforcer and are associated only with that reinforcer. For example, a gas station gives coupons that can be traded in only for one kind of drinking glass; a child receives chips for good behavior in school that can be exchanged only for bubble gum. A *generalized conditioned reinforcer*, however, has been paired with a variety of reinforcers. Money is probably the most common generalized conditioned reinforcer because of the many primary and conditioned reinforcers it can obtain. *Deprivation* and *satiation* factors influence the differential effectiveness of simple conditioned reinforcers and generalized conditioned reinforcers. Generalized conditioned reinforcers, such as money and attention, are less likely to become ineffective due to satiation than simple conditioned reinforcers because of the wide variety of reinforcers they are associated with. The effectiveness of a simple conditioned reinforcer relies on the individual's level of deprivation of that particular reinforcer. Generalized conditioned reinforcers, however, are less dependent on deprivation levels of specific reinforcers. If an individual is satiated with regard to one reinforcer, there are other reinforcers of which he is sufficiently deprived to ensure the effectiveness of the generalized conditioned reinforcer. For example, Carlos offers Max a token to run an errand. This token can be exchanged only for a chocolate bar. If Max has just eaten two chocolate bars (low level of deprivation), the probability of his running the errand for a token is less than if Max has not eaten chocolate for several days (high level of deprivation). Carlos would, therefore, be wise to give Max a token that could be exchanged for either chocolate, gum, baseball cards, or soda for running the errand. By using this generalized conditioned reinforcer, the probability that Max would run the errand would, thereby, increase, regardless of whether or not he had eaten chocolate recently, because it is unlikely that he is satiated on all the items available.

As mentioned earlier, in order for a neutral stimulus to acquire reinforcing properties, it must be paired with an established reinforcer. Tokens, money, and trading stamps typically serve as conditioned reinforcers only after the individual has learned that they can be exchanged for other goods. For example, a mother set up a token reinforcement system for her three children whereby they could receive tokens for performing household chores. These tokens could then be exchanged for various privileges such as television, extra spending money, or an extra dessert. The tokens did not serve as reinforcers for the children's performance of chores, however, until they were exchanged for various goods and privileges. The tokens were paired or associated with a variety of established reinforcers and thus became generalized conditioned reinforcers. The previously neutral stimulus, in this case, the token, must be paired with the established reinforcers in a particular manner. The token must first serve as a discriminative stimulus for the response that will produce an established reinforcer. In order for the token to become a conditioned reinforcer, it must serve as an S^D in whose presence the response of giving Mother the token is followed by the delivery of one of the established reinforcers, for example, extra spending money. In paradigm form, this example would look like this:

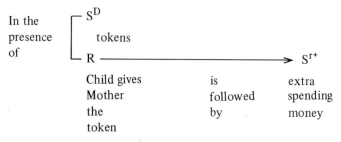

In the presence of	S^D tokens		
	R		$\longrightarrow$ S^{r+}
	Child gives Mother the token	is followed by	extra spending money

Once the token has been established as a discriminative stimulus, it acquires conditioned reinforcing properties because of its association with established reinforcers. The effectiveness of a conditioned reinforcer, like an unconditioned reinforcer, is determined by its ability to increase the strength of behavior it follows. Tokens, if they have become conditioned reinforcers, can increase the strength of other behaviors, in the above example, performing chores.

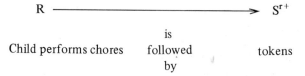

R		S^{r+}
Child performs chores	is followed by	tokens

In establishing a conditioned reinforcer, the therapist should consider the individual's reinforcement history, that is, stimuli that have served as reinforcers in the past and can currently exert control over his behavior. Affection, attention, and approval are social reinforcers that are usually conditioned during infancy and early childhood. These stimuli are called social reinforcers because they become available through interaction with other persons. Social reinforcers, such as a smile, are paired in childhood with the parents' ministering to the child's physical needs; for example, feeding him, changing his diapers, and relieving his discomfort. The parents' social responses become conditioned reinforcers. For example, the mother serves as a discriminative stimulus in whose presence the child eats. The mother (S^D) becomes associated with the food and relief of hunger, as well as with the other caregiving responses associated with feeding, such as cuddling, smiling, and speaking. She thereby becomes a social reinforcer for the child and has tremendous influence in conditioning and strengthening his behavior. Thus, usually by the time a child reaches school age, parental approval, recognition, "very good" and other forms of praise have acquired the ability to increase the strength of many behaviors.

Some children have rarely received praise, affection, or attention contingent upon appropriate behaviors. These children often emit disruptive or inappropriate behaviors to receive attention from parents, teachers, or other adults. The behavioral practitioner should teach these adults to provide social reinforcement for appropriate behaviors and to withhold it for inappropriate behaviors. There are also children for whom social reinforcers are ineffective in conditioning or strengthening behavior. It is possible to establish praise, smiling, approval, and attention as conditioned reinforcers by pairing them with stimuli known to be reinforcing to these children. Previously ineffective verbal stimuli such as "good" can also be established as conditioned reinforcers by pairing them with other reinforcers.

In order to develop an effective relationship with a client, the therapist must become established as a conditioned positive reinforcer. In this way, the therapist can influence the development and maintenance of appropriate behaviors in the client. Therapists commonly establish themselves as conditioned positive reinforcers for clients by listening to their problems and encouraging them to talk about themselves and their situations in a nonpunitive environment. The therapist serves as the S^D in whose presence the client's talking about his problems is followed by established reinforcers such as therapist attention or encouragement. In this way, the therapist is paired with the delivery of established reinforcers and acquires the ability to influence a wide range of client behaviors as a conditioned reinforcer. In paradigm form, the above example would look like this:

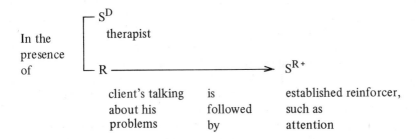

Sometimes coffee or other primary reinforcers are offered to the client by the therapist on a non-contingent basis; that is, these reinforcers are given without requiring the client's performance of any behavior other than his taking and consuming them. The therapist can also pair himself with other reinforcers such as playing games or sports with children, or making soda and candy available to adolescents, on a non-contingent basis. Once the therapist has become established as a conditioned reinforcer, he can selectively reinforce client responses by using his approval, attention, and opinions, thereby shaping appropriate client behaviors. For example, the therapist can strengthen the client's recording of assessment data:

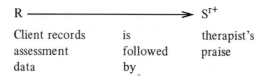

In some situations primary reinforcers are initially more effective than secondary reinforcers in conditioning desired behaviors. Food can be used to teach colors or shapes to an autistic child or to reinstate speech in a chronic mental patient, as in Vignette 4. Speech and appropriate interpersonal behaviors are typically maintained in our society through social reinforcement; therefore, such behaviors conditioned with primary reinforcers should also be paired with and maintained by secondary reinforcers. A social reinforcer, such as praise, should be presented in close temporal association with the primary reinforcer to promote the shifting from primary to conditioned reinforcement. For example, in teaching a retarded child arithmetic, the special education teacher gives him an M & M for each problem he solves. Just before she gives him the M & M, she says "very good." "Very good" thus becomes established as a conditioned reinforcer. The delivery of the M & M is gradually shifted from a continuous to an intermittent reinforcement schedule while the teacher says "very good" after each correct solution. Gradually the primary reinforcer is discontinued until only the social reinforcer, "very good," is presented after each response. The social reinforcer can also be shifted to an intermittent reinforcement schedule that more closely approximates conditions in the child's natural environment. He will not receive an M & M in a regular classroom for each math problem he solves. He should receive approval or praise from the teacher and his parents, however, and he will receive grades for his work. Shifting from M & M's to praise and approval (primary to secondary reinforcement) promotes the generalization and maintenance of his new behaviors. There are two advantages of using generalized conditioned reinforcers over primary reinforcers in behavioral change programs. (1) An individual is less likely to satiate on a generalized conditioned reinforcer. (2) Conditioned reinforcers are more abundantly available in our society contingent upon appropriate behavior. Using reinforcers that closely approximate the type available to the client in his environment, therefore, promotes the generalization and maintenance of newly conditioned appropriate behaviors.

The term *token economy* refers to a planned reinforcement program in which individuals can earn tokens for performing desired behaviors. They can exchange these tokens for a variety of objects or privileges. The tokens serve as generalized conditioned reinforcers for appropriate behaviors, and are given according to values assigned to performance of specific behaviors. For example, a hospitalized mental patient might receive one token each time he makes his bed, two tokens for brushing his teeth, and five tokens for participating in a therapy group. He can exchange these tokens for goods or privileges such as a candy bar (2 tokens), a pack of cigarettes (5 tokens), or a one-half hour walk outside the ward (8 tokens). Similarly, when a teacher gives gold stars for various academic and classroom behaviors, the gold stars are often exchanged by students for privileges such as extended play periods. The token economy system has been implemented in institutions for the mentally retarded, mental patients, and juvenile offenders. Token economies tend to be effective in these settings because the staff have greater control of the individual's reinforcing environment than is possible in the natural environment. The token economy provides incentives for individuals to acquire and perform behaviors that are necessary for their functioning in the community.

As discussed earlier, the procedure for establishing an object or event as a conditioned reinforcer consists of pairing a neutral stimulus with a known reinforcer. This procedure requires that the neutral stimulus serve as a discriminative stimulus (S^D) for a response that is reinforced in its presence. The S^D can subsequently be tested in two ways to determine if it has become a conditioned reinforcer (S^{r+}). One test is to present the S^D following the occurrence of another response. If the S^D can increase the response strength of that other response, it has become a conditioned reinforcer. A second test involves withholding all reinforcers for the discriminated response until the response rate decreases. The S^D is then presented *after* the response occurs. If the response strength increases, the S^D has become a conditioned reinforcer. This procedure tests the ability of the S^D to reinforce the response for which it served as the S^D. This second procedure is usually more appropriate in an experimental situation, as in many applied situations it would be unethical to decrease the strength of an appropriate response in order to test the effectiveness of an S^D as a reinforcer.

We perform many behaviors that initially might appear too complex for behavioral analysis. In analyzing these complex performances, however, we find that frequently they consist of *stimulus-response chains*. *Chaining* is useful in (1) analyzing complex behavior patterns and (2) conditioning complex behavior patterns to replace deviant performances or to enlarge deficient repertoires. One unit of a stimulus-response chain consists of a discriminative stimulus (S^D), a response (R), and a conditioned reinforcer (S^{r+}). The entire chain is composed of many stimulus-response units and usually terminates with a primary or established reinforcer (S^{R+}). Each conditioned reinforcer in the chain also serves as the S^D for the subsequent response, as shown below:

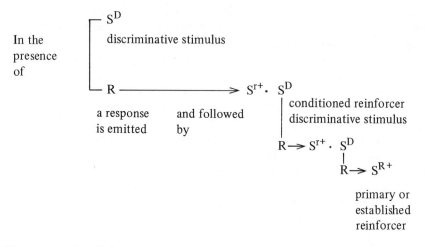

In the presence of

- S^D — discriminative stimulus
- R ⟶ $S^{r+} \cdot S^D$
  - a response is emitted   and followed by
  - conditioned reinforcer
  - discriminative stimulus
  - $R \longrightarrow S^{r+} \cdot S^D$
    - $R \longrightarrow S^{R+}$ — primary or established reinforcer

Many everyday behaviors are controlled by stimulus-response chains. For example, eating between meals for an overweight person can be subjected to a stimulus-response chain analysis. The inappropriate eating can be broken down into a number of behavioral components, each of which is maintained by a conditioned positive reinforcer. One such sequence might look like this:

- S^D — television commercial
- $R \longrightarrow S^{r+} \cdot S^D$
  - get up from couch   sight of kitchen
  - $R \longrightarrow S^{r+} \cdot S^D$
    - walk to kitchen   sight of refrigerator
    - $R \longrightarrow S^{r+} \cdot S^D$
      - walk to refrigerator   sight of refrigerator door
      - $R \longrightarrow$
        - open refrigerator

$$\longrightarrow S^{r+} \cdot S^D$$

| sight of
| cake

$R \longrightarrow S^{r+} \cdot S^D$

take | cake in hand
cake $R \longrightarrow S^{r+} \cdot S^D$

walk to | standing in
couch | front of couch

                        $R \longrightarrow S^{R+}$

                   sit on   eating the
                   couch; put   cake
                   cake in mouth

Each response leads to a conditioned reinforcer that also serves as the S^D for the next response. In the above example, the inappropriate eating became associated with watching television, so that television commercials acquired a discriminative function (S^D) for food-getting responses (R) that led to food intake (S^{R+}). The food was maladaptively paired with watching television, so that the person developed a variety of behavioral sequences, each of which led to eating while watching television. The intermediate behaviors of going to the kitchen and opening up the refrigerator or pantry became routinely conditioned as part of the simulus-response sequence.

In analyzing complex sequences of behaviors like chains, the behavior modifier should determine optimal points at which the chain could be broken to decrease undesirable or maladaptive behaviors. In the inappropriate eating example, the chain could be interrupted at the final unit, that is, when the individual is sitting on the couch putting the cake in his mouth. At this point, however, it is unlikely that the eating behavior can be easily interrupted since the individual is under the direct stimulus control of the cake. If the chain can be interrupted at an earlier point, for example, before the individual walks to the kitchen, the remaining units of the chain that lead to maladaptive eating can be prevented from occurring. The remaining units are not extinguished, however, and could be expected to recur immediately upon reinstatement of any of the S^Ds currently maintaining the responses.

A backward stimulus-response chaining procedure can be used to condition appropriate behavioral patterns as part of the treatment program for a client. In *backward chaining*, the last stimulus-response unit of the chain is conditioned first and the other units are added until the desired chain is complete. For example, in teaching a retarded child to dress himself, the therapist's intermediate goal is to establish a sequence of responses in which the child puts on his shirt and buttons it up. The therapist starts with the shirt on the child, buttoned except for one button that is half-buttoned. The therapist shows the child how he pushes the button through the hole, and asks the child to repeat this response. The child pushes the button through the hole, and the therapist says "good" and gives the child a piece of candy. In the second step, the child's shirt is on him and all buttoned except for one button. The therapist shows the child how to grasp the button in one hand and the buttonhole in the other and push the button through the hole. The third step consists of the child wearing the shirt, all buttoned except for two buttons. The child buttons the first button; the closed button serves as the conditioned reinforcer for having buttoned it and the discriminative stimulus for buttoning the second button. The therapist continues this procedure until the child buttons the entire shirt, puts his arms in each sleeve, and takes his shirt out of the drawer. As each new response is added, the child performs it along with the remaining responses until the chain is completed and he receives the "good" and candy. When the final response of taking his shirt out of the drawer is added, the child takes his shirt, puts each arm in the correct sleeve, and buttons each button, until his shirt is correctly worn. Reinforcement is given only after the last response in the chain is performed. Once the behavioral sequence is established, each response is maintained by the stimuli that it produces. Each response produces a stimulus that serves as (1) a reinforcer for that response and (2) a discriminative stimulus for the next response in the chain.

REFERENCES

Ayllon, T. and Azrin, N., H., *The Token Economy*, Appleton-Century-Crofts, New York, 1968.

Hendry, D.P., *Conditioned Reinforcement*, The Dorsey Press, Homewood, Illinois, 1969.

Kelleher, R. and Gollub, L., "A Review of Positive Conditioned Reinforcement," *Journal of Experimental Analysis of Behavior,* 5 (1962), pp. 543—597.

Krasner, L., "The Therapist As A Social Reinforcement Machine," in Strupp, H.H. and Luborsky, L. (Eds.), *Research in Psychotherapy,* American Psychological Association, Inc., 2 (1962), pp. 61—94.

Lent, J.R., Leblanc, J., and Spradlin, J.E., "Designing A Rehabilitative Culture For Moderately Retarded Adolescent Girls," in Ulrich, R., Stachnik, T., and Mabry, J., *Control of Human Behavior, Vol. 2,* Scott, Foresman and Company, Glenview, Illinois, 1970, pp. 121—135.

Millenson, J.R., *Principles of Behavioral Analysis,* The MacMillan Company, New York, 1967, Chapter 12, pp. 257–285.

O'Leary, K.D. and Becker, W., "Behavior Modification Of An Adjustment Class: A Token Reinforcement Program," *Exceptional Child,* 33 (1967), pp. 637–644.

Phillips, E.L., "Achievement Place: Token Reinforcement Procedures In A Home-Style Rehabilitation Setting For 'Pre-Delinquent' Boys," *Journal of Applied Behavior Analysis,* 1, No. 3 (1968), pp. 213–223.

Schoenfeld, W.N., Antonitis, J.J. and Bersch, P.J., "A Preliminary Study of Training Conditions Necessary For Secondary Reinforcement," *Journal of Experimental Psychology,* 40 (1950), pp. 40–45.

Staats, A.W., *Complex Human Behavior,* Holt, Rinehart, and Winston, New York, 1963, Chapter 8, pp. 321–355.

POST-TEST QUESTIONS

(2) 1. An institutionalized mental patient, Mr. C., was given money during a verbal conditioning study. He dropped one coin on the floor and left the rest of the coins he had earned on the table. The psychologist concluded that money did not function as a generalized conditioned reinforcer for Mr. C. in the way that it does for most adults in our society. What could the psychologist do to establish the reinforcing value of money for Mr. C.?

(4) 2. You are a social worker involved in a community setting, and adolescents who have had one or two contacts with the police and juvenile authorities are referred to you. You station yourself in the low socio-economic neighborhood where these youths live because you plan to engage a group of them in activities that will help them stay out of trouble with the law, improve their academic performances, interview for and successfully hold jobs, and solve various interpersonal and

family difficulties. Give two examples that indicate what you could do to establish yourself as a generalized conditioned reinforcer for these clients.

(1) 3. In Vignette 4, the red light served as an S^D for Mr. C.'s vocalizations. It was paired with candy and praise from the psychologist. How could the psychologist determine whether the red light had become a conditioned reinforcer?

(2) 4. State two advantages of using conditioned reinforcement over using primary reinforcement in maintaining behavioral change in a client's natural environment.

(4) 5. Give an example of a problem that can be analyzed as a stimulus-response chain. Include at least two stimulus-response units and label the appropriate components.

chapter 11
modeling and imitation

OBJECTIVES

After completing this chapter, you should be able to:

1. give an example that describes how a modeling plus reinforcement procedure is used to develop and strengthen imitative behavior,
2. give an example of the use of modeling in developing assertive behaviors in a group treatment setting, and
3. describe the use of a modeling procedure with prompts, reinforcement, and fading, given specific case material.

Modeling and *imitation* play an important role in the acquisition of both appropriate and maladaptive behaviors. Children acquire many of their behavior patterns by observing and imitating their parents, teachers, friends, and other models in their environment. Adults also emit responses that have been learned through imitation of behaviors exhibited by influential individuals. A *model* is an individual whose behavior serves as a cue (modeled stimulus) that sets the occasion for an imitative response to be made by another person. The behavior imitated is similar along some dimension(s) to the behavior of the model. A specific reinforcer may not be evident for the imitative response. Viewing television, for example, provides a variety of models for people to imitate. Cereal, toothpaste, and beer commercials make frequent use of prestigious and influential individuals to promote the purchase of these products by viewers. Maladaptive or deviant behavior can likewise be imitated. For example, Clem, who has never stolen anything, steals a pen from a drug store after observing his friend Hank, an admired athlete, take one.

99

Imitative behavior does not always immediately follow model presentation. For example, a child watching television observes a prestigious actor throw his candy wrapper into a trash container and tell his audience to do the same. The child may *learn* this response, although he does not *perform* it immediately after seeing it. Imitation may, however, occur at some later time, for example when he is eating a candy bar with his friends and throws the wrapper in the trash can telling his friends to do the same.

Model presentation facilitates the acquisition of behaviors or behavior patterns that otherwise would be more difficult to develop. For example, in using a shaping procedure to teach speech to a retarded child, the child typically emits many sounds before he finally emits an appropriate response that can be reinforced. The therapist initially reinforces approximations that may only faintly resemble the terminal verbal response. A shaping procedure focuses on developing one response class at a time, for example, forming the correct vowel sound with the lips. In contrast, a modeling procedure can provide the child with a model who demonstrates the full range of responses involved in a complex behavior pattern, such as speaking a complete sentence. These complex behaviors are frequently acquired more rapidly through modeling than through a shaping procedure. What is referred to here as the imitative response may consist of a small segment of a behavioral sequence such as saying the first letter of a word, or it may consist of a series of responses, such as speaking a complete sentence.

The modeling procedure involves a *modeled stimulus* (S^m) that sets the occasion for an imitative response that is *physically or topographically similar* to or that shares a common quality or attribute(s) with the modeled stimulus. Positive reinforcement can be used to increase the strength of the imitative response. The modeling plus positive reinforcement procedure consists of the presentation of a modeled stimulus (S^m) to set the occasion for a physically similar response (R) that will be followed by a positive reinforcer (S^+).

The modeling plus reinforcement paradigm is as follows:

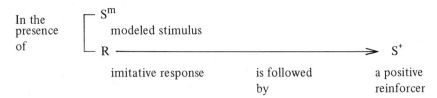

In the presence of

S^m — modeled stimulus

R — imitative response — is followed by — S^+ a positive reinforcer

The effect of the modeling plus reinforcement procedure is an increase in the strength of the imitative response. The term *modeled stimulus* refers to the behavior of the model that sets the occasion for the imitative response to occur. The *imitative response* is topographically or physically similar to the modeled stimulus with regard to an observable dimension(s) such as position or movement through space. Although the imitative response does not have to be an *exact* reproduction of the modeled stimulus in order to be reinforced, it must share a common attribute along a relevant dimension. If close reproduction is the terminal goal, however, the imitative response can be further differentiated by using a shaping procedure in conjunction with modeling.

In Vignette 7, Harold can complete more school assignments by saying "No" when his friends invite him to their homes before he has finished his assignments. The social worker can teach Harold to respond appropriately to his friends' invitations by utilizing a modeling plus reinforcement procedure. In this procedure, the social worker models an appropriate way of saying, "No, I can't visit with you until I finish my assignments," with appropriate tone of voice, gestures, and facial expressions. Harold's imitative response must be physically similar to the modeled stimulus. In paradigm form, the above example would look like this:

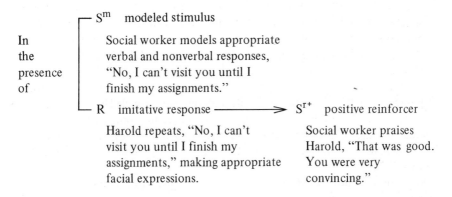

In using a modeling plus reinforcement procedure, the model's behavior serves as the modeled stimulus, S^m. The client observes the model, then imitates that response or sequence of responses and receives a positive reinforcer for appropriate imitation.

The ability to imitate is not shared equally by all people. Some individuals exhibit limited or no imitative repertoires. A severely retarded child, for example, may imitate motor behavior but not verbal behavior. Since imitation is so important in language acquisition, this child probably does not speak. An autistic child may not imitate any behavior that is modeled and, likewise, be mute. On the other hand, some autistic children imitate every sound they hear, or every movement they observe. Such children exhibit this excessive imitative behavior to the extent that they rarely initiate appropriate behaviors; they frequently spend much of their time in the constant repetition of certain words or bizarre actions. These deficient or maladaptive repertoires result in limited or inappropriate behavior patterns.

In teaching cooperative play to a child who has not demonstrated imitative motor responses to modeled stimuli, a general class of imitative motor responses must be shaped and brought under the control of the modeled stimulus. In other words, the first goal is to teach the child how to imitate some modeled motor responses; this usually involves not only modeling and reinforcement procedures, but also shaping, verbal instructions, and prompting techniques. When teaching the child with a limited imitative repertoire, prompts like, "Now you do what I do," "Follow me," or "Do this" often facilitate the child's responding with the appropriate imitative response. If the child does not respond to the modeled stimulus plus verbal prompts, it may be necessary to physically guide the behavior. For instance, to teach a child to move his arms, the therapist may move the child's arms for him in response to the modeled stimulus of arm movement. The procedure then includes the modeled stimulus, the verbal prompt, "Do this," and moving the child's arms, followed by a positive reinforcer. The method of guidance or manipulation of the child's arms can be gradually removed or faded out when the child begins to move his arms after presentation of the verbal prompt. The verbal prompt can also be faded out by progressively reducing the volume of the prompt until the child is imitating arm movements after presentation of just the modeled stimulus. These modeling, prompting, and reinforcement procedures are applied to develop other motor responses until the child appropriately imitates any modeled motor response. Once the child's imitative motor responses are under the control of the modeled stimuli, the motor behaviors that comprise cooperative play can be modeled. The child receives positive reinforcers for correctly imitating the modeled stimuli.

Suppose you now want to teach cooperative play to a child who exhibits excessive imitative motor and verbal responses. When you model an action, such as clapping your hands together and saying, "Do this," he will imitate your hand-clapping. This child, however, not only claps his hands together but also repeats "Do this" over and over. In this case, it is necessary to extinguish the maladaptive imitative responses while (1) selectively reinforcing appropriately imitated responses and (2) reinforcing responses that are incompatible with the repetitive behaviors. Modeling, prompting, and reinforcement are used to establish and strengthen appropriate imitative behaviors, while extinction is applied to excessive imitative behaviors. Since this child does exhibit an imitative repertoire, appropriate behaviors can be conditioned more readily than for the child who does not imitate at all.

Verbal behavior can also be taught through modeling, reinforcement and prompting techniques. For example, in teaching Mr. C. in Vignette 4 to speak appropriately to slides he was shown, visual as well as auditory stimuli were used. The following procedure was used in addition to the experimental procedure described in Vignette 4. Mr. C. was shown a slide of a boy and girl and asked, "What do you see in this slide?" He did not respond. The therapist then modeled the appropriate response by saying, "It's a boy and girl." When Mr. C. imitated the correct response, he received M & M's, points, and praise ("good") from the therapist. The therapist's prompts were faded out by saying them in a progressively softer voice until inaudible. The therapist could also fade out the prompts by omitting one word or syllable from the prompt each time it was given, beginning with the last syllable. If Mr. C. answered before any prompt was given, he would be reinforced immediately.

The preceding discussion was largely based on individuals with severe motor or speech impairments. Although the procedures described are complex, they have been effective in modifying the behaviors of individuals with extreme incapacities. The remainder of this chapter deals with less severe impairments and illustrates applications of imitation and modeling techniques in a variety of clinical situations.

The modeling procedure is applied in the treatment setting to facilitate the acquisition of novel behaviors or sequences of behaviors. The presentation of a reinforcer following the imitative response strengthens it and constitutes an important adjunct to the modeling procedure. Imitative responses are subject to the same kinds of control as are other operant responses; for example, they are influenced by reinforcement and punishment. The client observes a model—the therapist or a group member (if he is participating in group treatment)—perform appropriate behaviors in a role-play relevant to his problematic situation. He is then instructed to imitate the model's behavior in a similar role-play. The client is positively reinforced when he performs appropriate imitations. In Vignette 1, the therapist utilized this procedure to modify Mr. P.'s responses to criticism.

The effectiveness of the model in influencing imitative behavior is determined by such factors as the prestige or attractiveness of the model and the consequences of the model's behavior. Individuals who are perceived as prestigious, influential, or attractive are often effective models. Models are more likely to be imitated when their behaviors are followed by reinforcing consequences. In order to increase the likelihood that modeled behaviors will be imitated by the client, the therapist should be viewed as an attractive, influential person and should reinforce appropriate imitation.

Assertive training is a behavioral change procedure that can be used for treating clients with deficient interpersonal behavioral repertoires. Such response deficits are referred to as *non-assertive behaviors* and are frequently characterized by mumbling, holding one's head down, looking at the floor or ceiling when conversing, speaking in a soft voice, and agreeing with someone rather than stating divergent views or opinions. The non-assertive individual typically fails to verbally express positive or negative sentiments, such as pleasure or anger, in interpersonal situations. Numerous situations exist, however, in which verbal expression of these feelings would be both appropriate and desirable. Failure to verbalize such feelings or thoughts is maladaptive for the client when he experiences negative consequences, physical or social.

Overly-assertive individuals may also incur aversive consequences, because their behaviors exceed appropriate expression of their rights and include verbal and nonverbal responses that demean or humiliate other persons. These clients require assistance in making discriminations necessary for appropriately expressing their grievances.

Non-assertive individuals sometimes have difficulty learning to behave assertively without including some inappropriate verbal or nonverbal behaviors in their initial attempts at being assertive. These inappropriate behaviors may include interrupting someone who is speaking, shouting to get attention, glaring, or sneering at the individual to whom one is speaking. For example, while appropriately stating his right to socialize with a particular woman, a young man might also inappropriately sneer or glare at his father who has forbidden him to see her. The therapist must continuously draw the distinction between appropriate and inappropriate assertion for the client during assertive training, so that both his verbal and nonverbal responses are congruent with appropriate expressions of assertiveness in specific situations.

Appropriate assertiveness includes both verbal and nonverbal behaviors that express legitimate rights of the individual. Some examples of the expression of these rights are: "Sir, I believe I was in line first"; "Mother, I prefer this dress"; "Waiter, this steak is not done the way I asked for it"; or "Excuse me, but you charged me for two drinks and I only had one." We can all think of situations in which it is more appropriate to express one's rights and opinions than to remain silent.

Assertive training is a treatment procedure in which the non-assertive or overly-assertive individual learns to express his opinions and rights in an appropriate manner. Assertive training can be used to reduce the anxiety associated with failure to perform appropriately in interpersonal situations. Anxiety plays an important role in conditioning some maladaptive behaviors, and will be discussed in Chapter 14.

Modeling, prompting, and reinforcement can contribute to the effectiveness of assertive training. For example, Gretchen was 22 years old, yet every time she went shopping with her mother, she bought the clothes her mother selected. She had purchased many dresses this way and rarely wore them. Gretchen paid for her own clothes, and although she sometimes told her mother which dress she liked and wanted to buy, she always bought the dress her mother selected. Gretchen sometimes shopped secretly to buy the clothes she really wanted. Gretchen was dissatisfied with most of her wardrobe and with her failure to purchase the clothes she selected when shopping with her mother. She told the therapist, "I am a weak person because I can't even do a simple thing like tell my mother what I want to buy and buy it in front of her." Through behavioral re-enactment, it was ascertained that the problematic behaviors included

Gretchen's turning her head away from her mother, shuffling her feet, and mumbling, "Do you mind if I try this dress on?" In response to her mother's criticism of her choice, Gretchen frequently said, "Whatever you say, Mother." The negative consequences of this behavior for Gretchen included her buying clothes she did not like and rarely wore. She also had very little money left over to buy the clothes she liked. Gretchen was angry with herself for not standing up to her mother, and this prevented her from discussing other things with her mother.

Assertive training with Gretchen involved various role-play situations. For example, Gretchen was instructed to tell her "mother" that since she was paying for her own wardrobe, she would buy the clothes she wanted. If Gretchen had difficulty following instructions, the therapist would model the appropriate responses for Gretchen, such as, "Mother, I earn money for my wardrobe and I'd like to buy this dress." Gretchen would then imitate the model, after which she would receive feedback from the therapist regarding appropriateness of the tone of her voice, eye contact, posture, facial expressions, and verbal content. Gretchen practiced assertive statements in the therapeutic situation, correcting deficiencies in her verbal and nonverbal behaviors. Gretchen was given behavioral assignments to carry out in her natural environment, such as looking at her mother and speaking in a calm tone of voice while stating a preference. Gretchen reported her experiences in carrying out these assignments to the therapist. The therapist reinforced successful performances and provided additional instruction and training for achievement of difficult assignments.

A *hierarchy* of problematic assertive situations can be constructed in which each situation is ranked by the client according to its behavioral difficulty. For example, Gretchen had most difficulty buying clothes she selected in the presence of her mother. The item lowest on her hierarchy involved stating her preference of a store in which to shop. A middle range item was Gretchen telling her mother what color dress she wanted. The therapist and Gretchen role-played situations involving each item on the hierarchy, from least to most difficult, until Gretchen was able to perform the desired behaviors. If she had difficulty performing in any of the role-plays, the therapist modeled appropriate behaviors and instructed Gretchen in imitating him. Prompting and reinforcement were also used to facilitate the performance of appropriate behaviors.

Assertive training, modeling, and other role-play techniques can also be used in a group setting. Group members observe and identify problematic behaviors, model appropriate behaviors, and provide corrective feedback and reinforcement. The group members participate in the assessment of each other's behaviors and the development of intervention strategies.

Role-playing can be applied throughout the behavioral assessment and intervention stages of treatment. In *behavioral re-enactment*, the therapist or group members assume the roles of the client and/or significant others in order to assess the client's problematic behaviors and their controlling conditions.

Modeling can be used in role-plays in which the therapist or group members appropriately demonstrate behaviors that are problematic for the client. If the client still shows difficulty in performing appropriately, he is provided with S^Ds in the form of prompts or cues. The client is positively reinforced when he emits appropriate behaviors or acceptable approximations.

REFERENCES

Baer, D.M., Peterson, R.F., and Sherman, J.A., "The Development of Imitation by Reinforcing Behavioral Similarity to a Model," *Journal of the Experimental Analysis of Behavior,* 10(1967), pp. 405-416.

Bandura, A., *Principles of Behavior Modification*, Holt, Rinehart, and Winston, Inc., New York, 1969, Chapter 3, pp. 118-216.

Bandura, A. and Walters, R.H., *Social Learning and Personality Development*, Holt, Rinehart, and Winston, Inc., New York, 1963.

Bloomfield, H.H., "Assertive Training in an Outpatient Group of Chronic Schizophrenics: A Preliminary Report," *Behavior Therapy ,* 4 (1973), pp. 277-281.

Butterfield, W. and Parson, R., "Use of Modeling and Shaping by Parents to Develop Chewing Behavior in a Retarded Child," *Journal of Behavior Therapy and Experimental Psychiatry,* 4 (1973), pp. 285-288.

Corsini, R.J., *Roleplaying In Psychotherapy: A Manual*, Aldine Publishing Company, Chicago, Illinois, 1966.

Hingtgen, J.N., Coulter, S.K. and Churchill, D.W., "Intensive Reinforcement of Imitative Behavior in Mute Autistic Children," *Archives of General Psychiatry,* 17 (1967), pp.36-43.

O'Connor, R.D., "Relative Efficacy of Modeling, Shaping, and the Combined Procedures for Modification of Social Withdrawal," *Journal of Abnormal Psychology,* 79, No. 3 (1972), pp. 327-334.

Risley, T. and Wolf, M., "Establishing Functional Speech in Echolalic Children," *Behaviour Research and Therapy,* 5 (1967), pp. 73-88.

Wolpe, J., *The Practice of Behavior Therapy*, Pergamon Press, New York, 1969, Chapter 5, pp. 61-71.

POST-TEST QUESTIONS

(3) 1. Give an example that describes how a modeling plus reinforcement procedure is used to develop and strengthen imitative behavior.

(3) 2. Give an example that describes how a modeling plus reinforcement procedure is used to develop and strengthen imitative behavior.

(4) 3. Describe the use of a modeling procedure with prompts, reinforcement, and fading, given the following information: A therapist is trying to teach a retarded child to answer questions about his family. When the therapist asks the child, "How many brothers do you have?" the child does not answer. The child can talk and has in his repertoire all the words necessary to answer the question.

chapter 12
punishment

OBJECTIVES

After completing this chapter, you should be able to:
1. give an example of each of the two types of punishment procedures and indicate how to evaluate their effectiveness.
2. given a case example, identify the punishment procedure used, and label the relevant components.
3. give an example that contrasts extinction with punishment by response-contingent removal of positive reinforcement,
4. describe ways in which the effectiveness of punishment can be maximized, given a case example, and
5. give an example of punishment applied in a self-control contingency.

Up to now, we have presented several methods of strengthening responses. We have also discussed extinction as a method for reducing the strength of a behavior. Another method for reducing the strength of a response is *punishment*. In common usage, the term punishment is associated with vengeance or retribution. In behavioral terms, however, punishment refers to procedures applied to reduce response strength, rather than to inflict harm or injury on an individual. In this chapter, we discuss two types of punishment procedures: (1) *response-contingent presentation of a punisher* and (2) *response-contingent removal of a positive reinforcer*.

109

The term *punisher* refers to a stimulus that weakens or suppresses a response it follows. The term aversive stimulus has sometimes been confused with the term punisher or punishing stimulus. An *aversive stimulus* is an event that is typically described as unpleasant, annoying, or painful, such as shock, intense noise or light, physical blows (e.g., hitting, pinching, kicking), traffic tickets, fines, or threats. Although aversive stimuli can, and frequently do, serve as punishers, they do not always act to suppress behavior. On the other hand, a punisher, by definition, always acts to suppress behavior, whether or not the punisher is an aversive stimulus.

Punishers can be unconditioned or conditioned stimuli. An unconditioned punisher is intrinsically or naturally punishing, that is, it does not require pairing with another punisher in order to suppress behavior. A conditioned punisher requires prior pairing with an established punisher in order to suppress behavior. Shock, intense light or noise, and physical blows are common examples of unconditioned punishers. (They are also examples of unconditioned aversive stimuli.) Threats, fines, failing grades, and removal of privileges are common examples of conditioned punishers. (These are also examples of conditioned aversive stimuli.)

The procedure for *response-contingent presentation of a punisher* consists of presenting a punishing stimulus immediately after the target response has occurred. The punishment effect involves suppression of the target or punished response and decreased probability that the response will recur under similar conditions. A baseline measure of the strength of the target response should be taken prior to initiating any intervention. The strength of the target response is measured again after the intervention has been applied. If the stimulus has served as a punisher, the strength of the response should have decreased in relation to the baseline measure. A stimulus is not a punisher unless it serves to weaken or suppress a response, just as a stimulus is not a positive reinforcer unless it increases response strength. Thus, shouting "Stop!" to Sally and Jean will suppress Sally's kicking at the dinner table, whereas Jean continues to kick until slapped by her mother. In paradigm form, the procedure for punishment by presentation of a punisher is as follows:

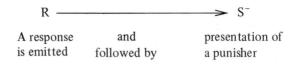

R		$\longrightarrow$	S⁻
A response is emitted	and followed by		presentation of a punisher

Punishment effect: Decreased response strength of the target behavior as compared with the baseline measure.

The S⁻ in the above paradigm indicates a stimulus (S) whose presentation decreases (⁻) the strength of the response it follows. This form of punishment is commonly used in a variety of situations. For example, George starts to track mud into the house and his mother shouts at him (S^{r-}); an autistic child bites himself and receives a slight electric shock (S^{R-}). These examples in paradigm form would look like this:

$$R \longrightarrow S^{r-} \qquad\qquad R \longrightarrow S^{R-}$$

| George tracks mud into the house | Mother shouts at him | Child bites himself | slight electric shock |

Punishment effect: George stops tracking mud into the house.

Punishment effect: Child stops biting himself.

The decision to use a punishment procedure involving presentation of a punisher, particularly when an unconditioned aversive stimulus such as shock is used, should be based on the following considerations: (1) the necessity for immediate effect, (2) the relative potency of other techniques that are available, and (3) the negative consequences for the individual or significant others if the behavior is not suppressed. For example, consider the autistic child whose body was covered with sores as a result of self-mutilation. The child's hands and feet had to be tied to his bed so that he would not bite and scratch himself. Applying a small number of shocks to the child's leg suppressed this behavior, after positive reinforcement of incompatible responses and extinction proved to be unsucessful. When a young child who has been told to stay off the railroad tracks continues to play there, the parents must select a technique that will be effective quickly, preferably on the basis of a single administration. A hard slap on the rear end should suppress the undesired, dangerous behavior and establish the association of playing on the railroad tracks with the punishment.

In the second type of punishment, *removal or withdrawal of a positive reinforcer* is made contingent upon occurrence of the undesired target response. This type of punishment is called *response-contingent removal of a positive reinforcer*. The punishment procedure consists of removing a positive reinforcer immediately after the target response has been emitted. The punishment effect is to suppress the target or punished response in comparison with the baseline measure. The paradigm for punishment by removal of a positive reinforcer is

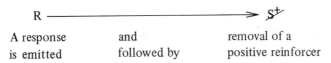

| A response is emitted | and followed by | removal of a positive reinforcer |

The S^{+} in the above example indicates a stimulus (S) whose removal decreases ($-$) the strength of the response it follows. For example, when Sam kicked his sister, his television privileges for the evening were withdrawn; making a mistake on an exam cost a student five points; Kathy threw her clothes on the floor, and she was not allowed to drive the car for a week. In paradigm form, Kathy's situation would look like this:

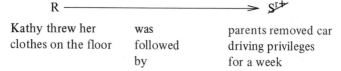

R		$\rightarrow$	S^{r+}
Kathy threw her clothes on the floor	was followed by	parents removed car driving privileges for a week	

Punishment effect: Kathy stops throwing her clothes on the floor.

The extinction procedure is sometimes confused with the procedure of punishment by response-contingent removal of positive reinforcement. In extinction, the reinforcer that conditioned or maintains the response is withheld continuously; that is, each time the response occurs it is not followed by a previously presented positive reinforcer. In punishment by response-contingent removal of positive reinforcement, however, a reinforcer other than the one that conditioned or is maintaining the response is withdrawn. These differences are pointed out in the following paradigms:

A. Extinction

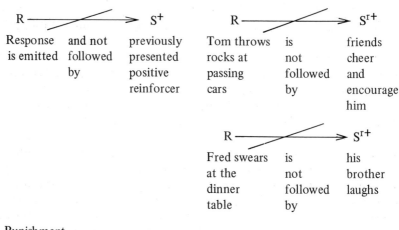

R		$\rightarrow$	S^+	R		$\rightarrow$	S^{r+}
Response is emitted	and not followed by		previously presented positive reinforcer	Tom throws rocks at passing cars	is not followed by		friends cheer and encourage him

R		$\rightarrow$	S^{r+}
Fred swears at the dinner table	is not followed by		his brother laughs

B. Punishment

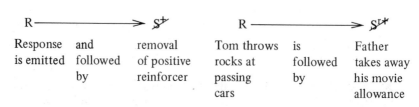

R		$\rightarrow$	S^+	R		$\rightarrow$	S^{r+}
Response is emitted	and followed by		removal of positive reinforcer	Tom throws rocks at passing cars	is followed by		Father takes away his movie allowance

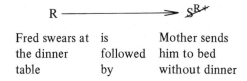

Fred swears at	is	Mother sends
the dinner	followed	him to bed
table	by	without dinner

Under extinction, the response typically decreases gradually in strength; with punishment, suppression of the response is usually more immediate. In order for response-contingent removal of positive reinforcement to be effective, the positive reinforcer removed must exert greater control in suppressing the target response than does the reinforcer in maintaining the target response. The removal of Tom's movie allowance must, therefore, exert greater control in suppressing rock throwing than the social reinforcement he receives from his friends for throwing rocks. Similarly, removal of dinner must exert greater control in suppressing Fred's swearing at the table than the laughter of his brother in maintaining Fred's swearing. The punishment effect can be maximized by introducing an extinction procedure during punishment: Tom's friends are told to ignore Tom when he throws rocks; Fred's brother is told to look away silently when Fred curses.

Time-out is a form of punishment by response-contingent removal of positive reinforcement. In time-out, the individual is removed from the problematic situation immediately after the inappropriate behavior occurs and placed in an environment with minimal availability of reinforcement. The time-out procedure involves removal of discriminative stimuli for the punished response as well as removal of reinforcers in the problematic situation. In Vignette 2, for example, Mrs. D. took Stephen to his room when he beat his sister. Taking Stephen to his room prevented him from responding to S^Ds in the problematic situation (Dianne's teasing, making faces) as well as removed positive reinforcement for his inappropriate behavior (mother's attention). The time-out room must be devoid of reinforcers that would lessen the effect of that environment as a punisher.

When using a time-out procedure, specific behavioral contingencies should be set. For example, the time-out period should be established for a specified, brief period. If the individual resists time-out by kicking, screaming, or cursing, a punishment contingency could be established in which such behaviors extend the time-out period, for five to ten minutes per incident, for example. Release from time-out is made contingent upon passage of the designated time and occurrence of appropriate behaviors in the time-out room. The time-out procedure, therefore, is different from procedures used in some institutions where an individual may remain isolated for extended periods.

Certain factors influence the effectiveness of the punishment procedure. In either type of punishment, the punisher (that is, either the presentation of a punishing stimulus or the removal of the positive reinforcer) should occur *immediately after* the response. If punishment for the target response is delayed, the intended punisher could inadvertently suppress other behaviors it follows instead of, or in addition to, suppressing the target response. For example, a child may be spanked or reprimanded by his father hours after he committed an inappropriate response in the presence of his mother who said, "Wait until your father gets home; then you'll get it!" Even though the father's spanking or reprimand might be associated verbally with the undesired behavior, it can suppress appropriate behaviors emitted by the child immediately prior to punishment. Other factors influencing the effectiveness of punishment are the *intensity* and *frequency* of the punisher. The punishing stimulus should be sufficiently intense to suppress the undesired response. Similarly, the reinforcer removed should exert more control in suppressing the individual's behavior than the reinforcer maintaining the undesired response. The punisher should be arranged to occur on a continuous schedule, that is, each time the target response is emitted. Different schedules of punishment, however, like different schedules of reinforcement, have been shown to generate characteristic patterns of responding.

In order to obtain maximum effectiveness of the punishment procedure, (1) the punisher should occur immediately after the target response, (2) the punisher should be administered each time the response occurs, (3) the punisher should be of sufficient intensity to suppress the target response, (4) alternate appropriate behaviors should be specified, (5) appropriate behaviors should be reinforced, and (6) reinforcement for inappropriate behaviors should be removed or reduced. For example, four-year-old Billy climbs trees after his mother forbade him to do so. She finds him in a tree with other children urging him to climb higher. To maximize the punishment she should send the other children away (removal of positive reinforcement); spank Billy (presentation of an intense punishing stimulus); specify another activity that Billy can engage in; and reinforce him for playing at the appropriate activity.

Several side-effects or disadvantages of response-contingent presentation of a punisher may occur that would limit the overall effectiveness of punishment as a behavioral control technique: (1) The punished response may reappear in the absence of the punisher. For example, if Audrey's mother slaps her hand when she reaches for food across the table, Audrey's food-reaching response will probably decrease at home. She might, however, reach across the table for food in nursery school or at her grandmother's, where Mother is not present and a slap is not administered for food-reaching. (2) Aggression in the form of physical or verbal attacks against the individual administering the punishment may occur. When Stan's sister pinched him after he spilled milk on the floor, he hit her. (3) Aggression may be directed toward someone or something that is in no way responsible for delivery of the punisher. The boss scolded Harry for handing his report in late; when Harry arrived home, he started criticizing his son's hairstyle. (4) The person who administers an aversive stimulus as a punisher can become a conditioned aversive stimulus by association with the aversive stimulus; the punished individual may avoid him. (5) A punisher could suppress appropriate behaviors as well as inappropriate behaviors occurring at the time the punisher is delivered. (6) An intended punisher can serve as an S^D for a response that is subsequently reinforced. It thereby can become a conditioned positive reinforcer that increases, rather than decreases the strength of the target behavior. An intended punisher is a stimulus that is administered to decrease response strength but may be unable to do so. For example, Mrs. G. is busy cooking dinner and her son, Ken, starts playing with the telephone receiver. Although she tells him to leave it alone, he persists until she finally yells at him. He begins to cry and she then goes over to him, soothes him, and plays with him until he stops crying. The child may learn from this example that the way to get Mommy's attention (yelling) is to play with the telephone receiver. Mother will yell, but if he cries, she will play with him. In paradigm form, the example would look like this:

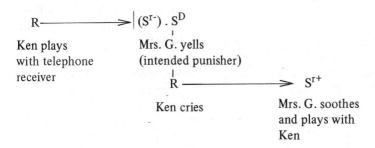

The effect of this stimulus chain is that Mrs. G.'s yelling (S^{r-}) can become a conditioned positive reinforcer through association with the reinforcers of playing with and soothing Ken. Mrs. G.'s yelling, therefore, will increase the response strength of Ken's playing with the telephone; it also serves as an S^D for crying. Furthermore, Mrs. G.'s yelling can also reinforce other inappropriate behaviors.

Another example of an intended punisher serving as a conditioned positive reinforcer involves a marital argument. Mrs. F. criticizes her husband. He swears at her and she begins to cry. He then begins to comfort her, they make up, and have sexual intercourse. The stimulus-response chain in paradigm form looks like this:

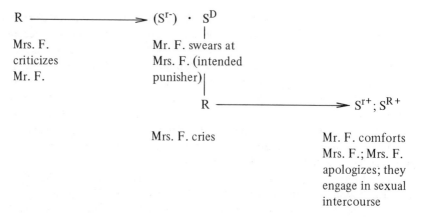

Arguments can become conditioned reinforcers if they have served as S^Ds for responses that lead to sexual reinforcement. Mrs. F.'s criticism or Mr. F.'s swearing can strengthen other agumentative behaviors, because of their previous association with positive reinforcers.

Punishment can be self-administered to suppress undesirable behavior. If a punishment contingency is established and followed, it can be an effective way for an individual to control his own behavior. For example, a Republican might establish the following contingency for himself: If I complete less than two reports each day this week, I will send $5.00 for each incomplete report to the National Democratic Committee. Another individual might establish the following contingency for himself: Every time I eat between meals, I will give away my ticket to the nontelevised basketball game. Another example of a self-controlled contingency is: "If I bite my fingernails, I will put Epsom salt (unpleasant taste) on them." Of course, to maximize punishment, self-administered reinforcement contingencies can be added: For every report I complete this week, I will leave work fifteen minutes early; for each day I eat only during mealtimes, I will play one extra record album. Although self-contingency management programs lack the control provided by an external behavior modifier, these self-control procedures offer an effective system for individuals to modify undesirable behaviors.

In spite of the disadvantages of punishment and the stringent requirements for ensuring its effectiveness, punishment is still commonly used as a behavioral control technique. One reason for this involves its typically immediate effect in suppressing undesired behavior. The short-term consequences, therefore, are reinforcing for the individual who administers the punishment. For example, mother's spanking three-year-old Tommy for saying "hell" suppresses Tommy's undesired speech at that time. She is thus reinforced for spanking him, although Tommy might well repeat this word the next day, or even later that day when he is alone or with his friends. Because the behavior of individuals is so frequently governed by short-term consequences, punishment will probably continue to be used for suppressing undesirable behaviors.

REFERENCES

Azrin, N.H., "Some Effects of Two Intermittent Schedules of Immediate and Non-immediate Punishment," *Journal of Psychology,* **42** (1956), pp. 3-21.

Azrin, N.H., and Holz, W.C., "Punishment," in Honig, W.K., *Operant Behavior: Areas of Research and Application,* Appleton-Century-Crofts, New York, 1966, pp. 790-826.

Baer, D.M., "Laboratory Control of Thumbsucking by Withdrawal and Re-presentation of Reinforcement," *Journal of the Experimental Analysis of Behavior,* **5** (1962), pp. 525-528.

Boe, E.E. and Church, R.M., *Punishment; Issues and Experiments,* Appleton-Century-Crofts, New York, 1968.

Church, R.M., "The Varied Effects Of Punishment on Behavior," *Psychological Review* **70** (1963), pp. 369-402.

Kazdin, A.E., "The Effect of Response Cost and Aversive Stimulation in Suppressing Punished and Nonpunished Speech Disfluencies," *Behavior Therapy,* **4** (1973), pp. 73-82.

Solomon, R.L., "Punishment," *American Psychologist,* **19**(1964), pp. 239-253.

Tyler, V.O. and Brown, G.D., "The Use Of Swift, Brief Isolation As a Group Control Device For Institutionalized Delinquents," *Behaviour Research and Therapy,* **5**, No. 1 (1967), pp. 1-10.

POST-TEST QUESTIONS

(3) 1. Give an example of each of the two types of punishment procedures and indicate how you would evaluate their effectiveness.

(2) 2. Give an example that contrasts extinction with punishment by response-contingent removal of positive reinforcement.

(5) 3. Given an example showing how you could maximize the effectiveness of punishment with a client who gets off the subject during your interviews and rambles on another topic.

(3) 4. Using the information from Vignette 2, name the punishment procedure instituted as treatment by Mrs. D. with Stephen. Draw a paradigm of an incident that would lead her to use this procedure. Label the appropriate components.

(1) 5. Give an example of punishment applied in a self-control contingency.

chapter 13
negative
reinforcement

OBJECTIVES

After completing this chapter, you should be able to:
1. contrast the effects of punishment and negative reinforcement,
2. give an example of escape behavior conditioned by negative reinforcement,
3. describe the involvement of positive and negative reinforcement, given a case example, and
4. describe avoidance behavior, given a case example.

In this chapter, we discuss the role of *negative reinforcement* in conditioning *escape* and *avoidance* behavior. In negative reinforcement, a response is made that terminates, removes, or reduces the effects of a stimulus. The removal of this stimulus, or negative reinforcer, *increases* the probability that the response will recur under similar circumstances. The term *negative reinforcement* is used because the *reinforcement* function is to increase response strength; the word *negative* indicates the *removal or reduction* of the effects of the stimulus. A stimulus is defined as a negative reinforcer only if its termination or reduction increases the strength of the response that removes or reduces its effect. A negative reinforcer, therefore, is a stimulus in whose presence an escape or avoidance response is made.

Negative reinforcers can be unconditioned (primary) or conditioned (secondary) stimuli, as is the case with positive reinforcers and punishers. *Unconditioned negative reinforcers* include shock, intense light, noise, or a physical blow. *Conditioned negative reinforcers* include threats, fines, bad grades, frowns, or a harsh word such as "stupid." These stimuli can also serve as unconditioned or conditioned punishers; that is, their presentation can decrease the strength of responses they follow. The terms punisher and negative reinforcer have often been used interchangeably in the literature. For our purposes, however, we will restrict the use of punisher to a stimulus whose administration *decreases* response strength and the use of negative reinforcer to a stimulus whose removal *increases* response strength.

Aversive stimuli may act as negative reinforcers when their removal increases response strength, or as punishers when their presentation decreases response strength. Aversive stimuli, like rewards, are influenced by individual, societal, and cultural characteristics. A stimulus that is unpleasant, annoying, or painful to one individual may not be "aversive" to another. An individual may not make a response in the presence of an aversive stimulus that terminates the stimulus. In this case, the aversive stimulus is not a negative reinforcer.

Escape behavior terminates or reduces the effects of the negative reinforcer. The escape conditioning procedure consists of the presentation of a stimulus (S^-) that remains in effect until a specific response is emitted (R) that terminates or reduces the effect of that stimulus ($\mathcal{S}^-$). The S^- acts as a discriminative stimulus that sets the occasion for a response made in its presence to be reinforced, in this case, negatively reinforced. The escape conditioning paradigm is as follows:

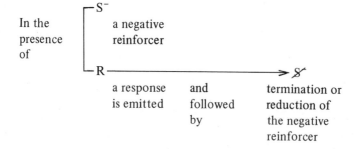

The $\mathcal{S}^-$ in the above paradigm indicates a stimulus (S) whose removal (−) increases response strength. The effect of the escape conditioning procedure is strengthening of the escape response.

Examples of escape conditioning can be found in a wide variety of situations. When your belt feels tight around your waist (S^{R-}), you loosen it a notch or two (R). This response terminates the pressure around your waist ($\mathcal{S}^{R-}$). The probability that you will perform this response on future occasions when your belt is tight has increased. John's wife, Karen, complains that he never takes her anywhere (S^{r-}), and he goes to a neighborhood bar (R) to escape her complaining ($\mathcal{S}^{r-}$). The probability is thereby increased that on future occasions when Karen complains, John will go to the neighborhood bar. In paradigm form, the above example would look like this:

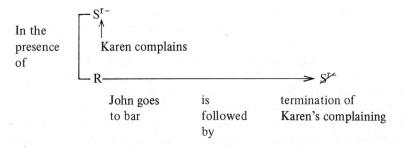

In the presence of

Karen complains

John goes to bar   is followed by   termination of Karen's complaining

In the above example, John's going to the bar was negatively reinforced and thereby strengthened. The negative reinforcer also strengthens other responses that have the same or similar effect on the environment as the reinforced response. Thus, not only is a single response, going to the bar, reinforced, but a class of responses, each of which terminates his wife's complaining, is also strengthened. For example, driving to the bowling alley, bicycling to a friend's home, and walking around the block, are all members of the operant defined as responses that terminate Karen's complaining.

The reinforcement and punishment paradigms are reproduced in Figure 1 for review and comparison.

One potential pitfall of a punishment procedure not mentioned in the previous chapter involves escape from the punishment situation. An inappropriate escape response made during punishment will reduce the effectiveness of the punishment and increase the probability that this response will recur in similar situations. For example, in Chapter 12, Fred was sent to bed without dinner for swearing at the table. If Fred sneaked down the stairs to the kitchen and made

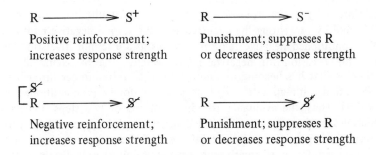

Positive reinforcement; increases response strength

Punishment; suppresses R or decreases response strength

Negative reinforcement; increases response strength

Punishment; suppresses R or decreases response strength

FIGURE 1. **Reinforcement and punishment paradigms.**

himself a sandwich, the escape response of secretly eating the sandwich would be negatively reinforced by reducing the punishing effect of being sent to bed without dinner.

A response that has been negatively reinforced in the presence of one stimulus can generalize to other, similar stimuli. For example, Ted's excessive alcohol drinking is negatively reinforced by escape from his father's criticisms. This escape response generalizes to other situations in which he is criticized by his mother or employer. The more similar the situation or person is to the original stimulus, the greater the effects of stimulus generalization.

Escape behavior may be related to an accidental or superstitious contingency. In this case, a response is made and the effects of the stimulus are also reduced or terminated. The response, however, is only accidentally or coincidentally associated with removal of the stimulus, and is not functionally related to the event. For example, Mike is driving his car and suddenly the horn begins to honk loudly (S^{R-}). He pushes and pulls various knobs on the dashboard and steering wheel but the noise persists. Finally, he jiggles the turn signal (R) and the horn stops honking ($S^{R\sim}$). The turn signal is not functionally connected to the horn, and the relationship between jiggling the turn signal and the termination of the honking is accidental. Some other event, such as shifting of contact wires under the hood, terminated the honking. Since Mike was negatively reinforced for jiggling the turn signal, it is likely that he will emit this behavior on similar occasions in the future.

In the escape paradigm, a stimulus is presented and remains in effect until the individual emits a response that is negatively reinforced by removal or reduction of that stimulus. Negative reinforcement is also involved in *avoidance conditioning*. In avoidance conditioning, the individual can avoid presentation of a negative reinforcer by emitting a specific response that prevents its occurrence. A conditioned negative reinforcer (S^{r-}) is presented that serves as a discriminative stimulus or cue indicating that a second negative reinforcer (S^-) will follow unless a specific response (R) is made. The response is negatively reinforced by termination or reduction of the conditioned negative reinforcer (S^{r-}) and by preventing the occurrence of the second negative reinforcer ($\nrightarrow S^-$). The conditioned negative reinforcer serves as a discriminative stimulus since it sets the occasion for negative reinforcement. The S^{r-} is initially a neutral stimulus that has become a conditioned negative reinforcer through pairing or association with an established negative reinforcer (unconditioned or conditioned). Thus, the avoidance paradigm consists of two steps: (1) pairing of a neutral stimulus with an established negative reinforcer in whose presence an escape response is negatively reinforced; (2) presentation of the conditioned negative reinforcer (formerly the neutral stimulus) as a discriminative cue in whose presence an avoidance response terminates the conditioned negative reinforcer and prevents the occurrence of the established negative reinforcer. The avoidance conditioning paradigm looks like this:

(1)

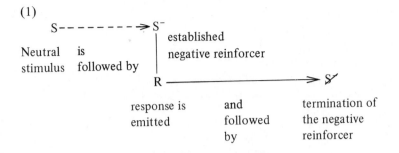

(2)

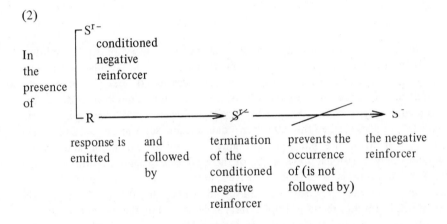

The effect of avoidance conditioning is an increase in the strength of the avoidance response. For example, Jerry said to his father, "If you don't buy me that toy, I'll scream right here in the store." Jerry's father, preoccupied with his shopping, ignores Jerry. Jerry starts screaming and his father buys him a toy. The father's avoidance response of buying Jerry a toy is strengthened and more likely to occur in the future when Jerry threatens to scream. In paradigm form, the above example would look like this:

(1)

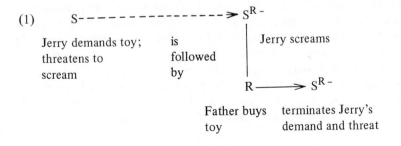

(2)

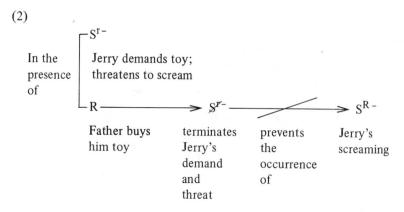

Avoidance behavior usually requires occasional delivery of the established negative reinforcer. If Jerry's father fails to perform the avoidance response (buying a toy) and the negative reinforcer (screaming) does not follow, the avoidance response may extinguish. If Jerry's father does not perform the avoidance response and Jerry does scream, however, this one episode can reinstate and strengthen the father's avoidance response. A response conditioned through an avoidance paradigm is highly resistant to extinction and usually requires only occasional presentation of the established negative reinforcer.

A relationship is sometimes observed between two people in which one person's behavior is positively reinforced while the other's is negatively reinforced. In the above example, Jerry's demand and threat were positively reinforced by his father's buying him the toy. His father's buying him a toy was negatively reinforced by the termination of Jerry's demand and threat.

In traumatic avoidance conditioning an aversive stimulus of high intensity is involved in conditioning the avoidance response. In an elevator phobia, for example, an intense aversive stimulus was initially paired or associated with the elevator. On subsequent occasions, the person turns away from the elevator, thus escaping the presence of the elevator (conditioned negative reinforcer) and avoiding the intense aversive stimulus previously associated with the elevator (established negative reinforcer). The person behaves as though remaining in or near the elevator will lead to the feared aversive stimulus. A response conditioned through such a traumatic avoidance paradigm is highly resistant to extinction, even on the basis of a single pairing of the elevator with the aversive stimulus. The intense aversive stimulus may never again occur, yet the avoidance behavior persists. In this situation, turning away from the elevator is considered maladaptive because there is no objective basis for fear of riding the elevator.

In assessing problematic situations, it is important to determine if the client's target behavior is negatively reinforced through escape or avoidance conditioning. Fear of elevators, doctors, or dentists, for example, can prevent the client from carrying out certain activities that are required for appropriate functioning—taking elevators at work, or getting medical or dental examinations. When a client spends considerable time in avoidance responding, he has less opportunity to perform behaviors that can be positively reinforced.

REFERENCES

Heckel, R.V., Wiggins, S.L., and Salzberg, H., "Conditioning Against Silence In Group Therapy," *Journal of Clinical Psychology,* **28** (1962), pp. 216-221.

Jones, M.R. (Ed.), *Miami Symposium On The Prediction Of Behavior, 1967: Aversive Stimulation,* University of Miami Press, Coral Gables, Florida, 1968.

Lovaas, O.I., Schaeffer, B. and Simmons, J.Q., "Experimental Studies In Childhood Schizophrenia: Building Social Behavior In Autistic Children By Use Of Electric Shock," *Journal of Experimental Research In Personality,* **1** (1965), pp. 99-109.

Lovibond, S.H., *Conditioning and Enuresis,* Pergamon Press, New York, 1964.

MacCulloch, M.J., Birtles, C.J., and Feldman, M.P., "Anticipatory Avoidance Learning for the Treatment of Homosexuality: Recent Developments and an Automatic Aversion Therapy System," *Behavior Therapy,* **2** (1971), pp. 151-169.

Patterson, G.R. and Reid, J.B., "Reciprocity and Coercion: Two Facets Of Social Systems," in Neuringer, C. and Michael, J., *Behavior Modification In Clinical Psychology,* Appleton-Century-Crofts, New York, 1968.

Solomon, R.L. and Wynne, L.C., "Traumatic Avoidance Learning: The Principles of Anxiety Conservation and Partial Irreversibility," *Psychological Review,* **61** (1954), pp. 353-385.

POST-TEST QUESTIONS

(2) 1. Give an example contrasting the effects of punishment and negative reinforcement. Specify relevant responses and stimuli involved in each procedure.

(3) 2. Give an example of escape behavior conditioned by negative reinforcement. Label relevant responses and stimuli.

(2) 3. Using the information from Vignette 3, describe the involvement of positive and negative reinforcement in the interaction between Carla and her mother prior to the social worker's intervention.

(4) 4. Sylvia told her husband Harold, "Buy me a new car or I want a divorce." Harold bought her a new car and she stopped threatening to divorce him. Draw a paradigm that describes the avoidance behavior, labeling relevant components.

chapter 14
respondent conditioning

OBJECTIVES

After completing this chapter, you should be able to:
1. draw a paradigm showing respondent conditioning of a phobia,
2. describe an operant procedure for treating both operant and respondent features of a phobia,
3. identify operant and respondent behaviors, given case material, and
4. describe a respondent procedure for suppressing a maladaptive behavior, given a case example.

As we mentioned earlier in the book, there are two broad classes of behavior, operant and respondent. Up to now, we have focused on operant behavior. Operant behavior is *emitted* and controlled by its *consequences. Respondent* or *classically conditioned* behavior comprises the second class of behavior. Respondents differ from operants in that the stimulus controlling the occurrence of the respondent *precedes* it, whereas in operant behavior the reinforcing stimulus *follows* the response. Respondents are typically simple reflexes or responses mediated by the autonomic nervous system. These responses have usually been considered to be outside the control of the individual. Tears caused by dirt in the eye, palms perspiring while taking a difficult exam, rapid breathing, shaking, or choking during a horror scene in a movie, and pupillary constriction upon emerging into bright sunlight are all examples of respondents. These responses are *elicited* by a preceding or *antecedent* stimulus.

It is sometimes difficult to ascertain if a behavior is under operant or respondent control. In order to do so, it is necessary to determine whether the response is elicited by an antecedent or controlled by its consequences. For

129

example, crying can be operant or respondent. If Betsy's crying is elicited by an inoculation or a slap, it is respondent crying. If, however, Betsy's crying is observed to increase as a result of reinforcing consequences (parents comply with Betsy's demands), it is operant crying.

The respondent or classical conditioning paradigm can be used to explain the acquisition of behaviors frequently referred to as "emotional." Various labels of emotional behavior, such as anger, anxiety, or frustration, are insufficient descriptions in themselves. Behavioral correlates of these labels should be delineated for specific individuals so that others observing the behavior or reading a description of it could accurately identify the behavior. Emotional behavior is usually accompanied by physiological changes in heart rate, blood pressure, perspiration, and muscle tension. Individuals learn to identify their own feeling states early in life when a verbal label is associated with certain physiological changes by parents or significant others. For example, if a child is shaking uncontrollably, breathing rapidly, and tears are streaming down his flushed face, his mother might ask him what's wrong or what is he *afraid* of. The child replies that a big dog knocked him down, and the mother says, "You are *afraid* of the dog." The operant and respondent behaviors of the child's encounter with the dog, therefore, become associated with the word "afraid." When experiencing similar physiological changes on future occasions, the child will be more likely to label them as being afraid or fear.

Many maladaptive behaviors involve anxiety as a central component. The anxiety is maladaptive or inappropriate because it is not currently associated with an objective source and remains resistant to extinction in spite of its maladaptive features. Anxiety involves respondents such as changes in heart rate, blood pressure, glandular secretions, respiration, muscle tension, and skin resistance. Operant components of anxiety may include escape or avoidance behaviors such as making excuses, lying, rapid pacing, repetitive motor responses such as handwashing, and agitated speech patterns.

When maladaptive anxiety is attached to a specific object, the term *phobia* is typically used. Phobias are acquired through classical conditioning in which a neutral stimulus acquires the ability to elicit anxiety through pairing with an unconditioned aversive stimulus. The unconditioned stimulus (UCS) is a stimulus capable of eliciting an unconditioned response (UCR) without requiring prior association with another stimulus. For example, food in the mouth elicits salivation; a freshly peeled onion elicits tears. Through repeated association with the UCS, a neutral stimulus (S) can become a conditioned stimulus (CS) capable of eliciting a conditioned response (CR) similar to the unconditioned response (UCR). Frequently, this conditioning is accidental. For example, a painful unconditioned stimulus, such as a dog bite (UCS), elicits anxiety responses without prior conditioning. Anxiety responses such as those mentioned above are unconditioned responses (UCRs). The UCS (bite) is paired with the sight of the dog who administered the bite. The sight of the dog is initially a neutral or nonaversive stimulus, but acquires the ability to elicit anxiety. In paradigm form, the example would look like this:

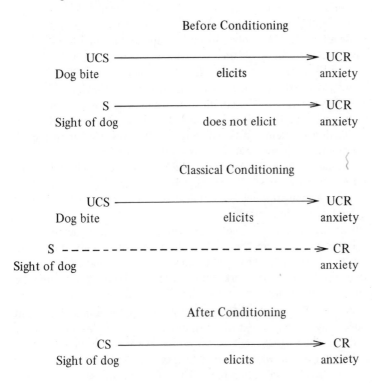

Before Conditioning

UCS ⟶ UCR
Dog bite   elicits   anxiety

S ⟶ UCR
Sight of dog   does not elicit   anxiety

Classical Conditioning

UCS ⟶ UCR
Dog bite   elicits   anxiety

S ------------------------ ⟶ CR
Sight of dog   anxiety

After Conditioning

CS ⟶ CR
Sight of dog   elicits   anxiety

During conditioning, the neutral stimulus (S) is presented immediately prior to the UCS. The broken line indicates that the neutral stimulus is paired with the UCS and is acquiring the ability to elicit a conditioned response. The strength of a conditioned respondent is measured by (1) the magnitude of the CR and (2) the latency or interval between presentation of the CS and elicitation of the CR. The magnitude of a classically conditioned response is measured by contraction of a muscle or blood vessel or secretion of a gland. For example, heart rate is measured by counting the pulse; skin resistance by measuring the galvanic skin response (GSR); salivation, by measuring drops of saliva. Latency is measured by the amount of time that passes between presentation of the CS and elicitation of the CR. The shorter the latency, the stronger the response. The greater the magnitude, the stronger the response.

Many phobic responses eventually extinguish when the individual remains in the presence of the conditioned stimulus without making an escape response.

Conditioned respondents, like operants, can be weakened by extinction. The extinction procedure consists of presenting the CS repeatedly until it fails to elicit the CR. Since the unconditioned stimulus no longer follows the conditioned stimulus, the conditioned response weakens until it extinguishes. The phobias that are difficult to extinguish, however, (1) have been conditioned by a very intense UCS and (2) involve operant escape and avoidance responses that are negatively reinforced. Avoidance behavior prevents the individual from finding out that the UCS is no longer presented. The effect of the UCS presented during conditioning is so strong that it maintains avoidance behavior even when the UCS is no longer presented. The conditioned response is likely to generalize to other stimuli similar to the CS along some dimension or characteristic. A stimulus generalization gradient exists whereby stimuli most similar to the CS elicit the strongest CRs. As stimuli become less similar to the CS, weaker CRs are elicited. For example, if the experience with the dog was extremely painful or fearful, other furry animals or small animals with four legs might elicit a high amount of anxiety. As the stimulus became less similar to the original dog, its ability to elicit anxiety would decrease.

Other stimuli in the conditioning situation can also become associated with anxiety, such as the place where the incident occurred, other individuals who were present, or the dog's bark. These stimuli can become CSs that elicit anxiety CRs. In addition, the CS of a dog's bark, for example, can serve as an S^D for the operant response of running into the house. A stimulus can, therefore, serve the function of both a CS and an S^D in relation to respondent and operant behaviors, respectively. When we eat in a restaurant, for example, the presence of meat on the tongue (UCS) elicits salivation (UCR). Through previous conditioning, the sight of the waiter approaching (CS) or a picture of a steak on the menu (CS) can also elicit salivation (CR). These CSs can also serve as S^Ds for the operant responses of reaching for the steak or ordering the steak from the menu, since these stimuli set the occasion for operant responses to be followed by positive reinforcement.

Many situations involve both operant and respondent behaviors. For example, in Vignette 1, Mr. P. emitted the operant responses of rapping his knuckles together and making excuses in criticism situations. The criticism also elicited the following respondent behaviors: Mr. P. perspired heavily, his hands trembled, his face turned red, and his breathing became more rapid. In assessing problematic situations, respondent as well as operant behaviors should be identified so that an appropriate treatment plan can be formulated.

The behavioral assessment format presented earlier can be applied to problematic situations involving respondent behaviors. For respondent behaviors, the RAC-S schema focuses on the response (R), its eliciting antecedents (A), and response strength (S). As mentioned earlier, the strength of respondent behavior is measured by latency and/or magnitude. The negative consequences of the problematic behavior for the individual or significant others are examined, although analysis of the respondent behavior focuses on the relationship between the eliciting antecedent(s) (CS, UCS) and the response (CR, UCR).

Both operant and respondent techniques can be used to modify phobic behaviors. These methods involve the conditioning of behaviors that are incompatible with anxiety in the phobic situation. Successful treatment involves modification of both operant and respondent behaviors that constitute "anxiety" for the client. One operant method for modifying phobic responses involves shaping via successive approximation. This procedure includes the following steps: (1) identify the feared stimulus, (2) identify positive reinforcers that can be used to condition incompatible responses, (3) identify the desired terminal behavior, (4) establish a hierarchy of items or graded situations related to the feared stimulus, ranking them according to their ability to elicit anxiety; for example, distance from the feared object (one mile, two blocks, one block, within arm's length, etc.), (5) introduce the feared stimulus at the lowest item on the hierarchy (for example, at a great distance) while reinforcing the individual for responses incompatible with escape or anxiety responses, and (6) following the hierarchy, gradually introduce successive approximations to the feared stimulus and reinforce the individual for making approach responses incompatible with anxiety or escape responses.

For example, in treating a child with school phobia, the therapist observed that as soon as the child entered the schoolyard, he trembled, began to stammer, his face turned white, and his body became tense and rigid. When the child approached the classroom, he quickly turned and ran away. The therapist also observed that as the child got further and further from the school, he became calmer and his physiological responses returned to normal. The therapist established a hierarchy based on distance from the school and his classroom. The following intermediate goals based on the hierarchy were established for the child: talking about various aspects of school; walking toward the school from two blocks away; walking toward the school from one block away; walking across the street from the school; crossing the street toward the school; standing in the schoolyard; walking up the steps into the school; walking in the halls of the school; entering the classroom; sitting at his desk. The therapist used attention and comic books as well as jelly beans as positive reinforcers. The desired terminal behaviors were that the child walks to school, enters the building and his classroom, and stays the whole day. To treat the problem, the therapist used the following procedure: When the child walked in the direction of the school with the therapist from two blocks away, the therapist showed the child a comic book and they laughed at the characters. When they were across the street from the school, the therapist took him to the drugstore and bought a bag of jelly beans, the child's favorite candy. The therapist walked closer and closer to the school with the child, reinforcing his approach behaviors with jelly beans. This procedure was continued until the child exhibited little or no anxiety when talking about school and walked up to the school, went inside, entered the classroom, and remained at school for the entire day. This procedure treats both operant and respondent features of the problematic behavior by reinforcing approach responses incompatible with escape and fear. The child gradually became calmer and able to move closer to the feared stimulus. The positive reinforcement gradually exerted greater control over his approach behavior than the previous negative reinforcement had exerted in maintaining the avoidance behavior.

Systematic desensitization. is a respondent method for treating phobias. It involves deep muscle relaxation in a procedure that suppresses anxiety by counterposing phobic or anxiety-evoking stimuli with relaxation stimuli. The premise of systematic desensitization is that an individual who is deeply relaxed cannot be anxious and tense at the same time. The first step in this procedure is to teach the client deep muscle relaxation. The client is given instructions in progressive relaxation procedures and is assigned relaxation exercises to practice at home.

The second step in systematic desensitization involves the formulation of a hierarchy of the feared stimulus and situations in which the client feels anxious. The hierarchy begins with the least anxiety-producing situation, progressing to the most anxiety-producing event. Here is an example of a hierarchy that a client complaining of an airplane phobia developed:

1. calling an airline to make plane reservations for her boss
2. calling an airline to make plane reservations for herself
3. seeing a plane take off or land
4. sitting in a taxi on the way to the airport
5. walking into an airport terminal
6. waiting in the lounge before boarding a plane
7. walking up the stairs to the plane
8. stepping into the plane
9. sitting in her seat on the plane.

Prior to treatment, this client had never actually gotten past step 5. She usually became so anxious that she canceled her reservations and took a train or drove.

Some highlights of the desensitization procedure are briefly mentioned here; the procedure has been more elaborately described elsewhere (see Wolpe, 1958; 1969; Wolpe and Lazarus, 1966). In desensitization, the client imagines one item or scene at a time from the hierarchy while relaxed, beginning with the least anxiety-producing item. The client is instructed to imagine the scene presented by the therapist; for example, calling for airplane reservations for her boss. The client reports her subjective level of anxiety after each scene. If she indicates anxiety, the therapist tells the client to relax again and then presents a weaker scene. The previous anxiety-arousing scene is presented when the client indicates no anxiety while imagining the weaker scene. The next scene on the hierarchy is presented again and repeated until the client no longer experiences anxiety while imagining this scene. The following item on the hierarchy is presented in the same manner, and the procedure is followed until the entire hierarchy is completed. The scenes are usually presented for approximately twenty to thirty minutes at each session. Although the client is not treated in the actual problematic situation, the effects of relaxation in the presence of imagined anxiety-arousing stimuli usually transfer to the real situation once the client has achieved relaxation capable of suppressing or inhibiting anxiety-evoking stimuli. It has been found that discovering the original conditioning stimulus (UCS) is usually not essential for successful treatment of phobias. Awareness of or "insight" into the originally conditioned phobic situation usually does not extinguish the client's autonomic anxiety responses nor does it affect the client's movement toward the feared stimulus or situation.

As described, phobias can be treated by operant or respondent procedures, both of which attempt to modify operant and respondent elements of the phobia. The operant procedure focuses on conditioning motor and verbal behaviors incompatible with escape and avoidance in the feared situation, while lowering the individual's anxiety as he approaches. The respondent procedure focuses on conditioning physiological responses incompatible with anxiety in the phobic situation, while developing imaginal approach responses that generalize to the actual situation.

Covert sensitization (Cautela, 1967; 1969) is a technique using imaginal stimuli to elicit anxiety. Instead of inhibiting anxiety with relaxation as in systematic desensitization, covert sensitization is used to elicit anxiety in situations in which the client exhibits behavioral excesses that are maladaptively reinforced. This technique is particularly appropriate for treating behavioral excesses such as stealing, overeating, sexual deviations, drug addiction, and alcoholism. In covert sensitization, the maladaptive behavior is described in great detail and paired—in the client's imagination—with highly aversive stimuli. A typical aversive scene used in covert sensitization includes a vivid description of nausea and vomiting induced by approaching the attractive but inappropriate object. The "pleasant" respondents associated with the maladaptive behavior are thereby suppressed by the anxiety response elicited by the imaginal aversive stimuli. In implementing this treatment technique, the therapist should specify appropriate escape and avoidance responses that can be negatively reinforced by termination or reduction of the imaginal aversive stimuli. The client is taught to imagine an appropriate response he can make in the presence of the maladaptive situation that will be reinforced. This increases the likelihood that the client will emit appropriate avoidance responses in the actual problematic situation.

Other respondent conditioning techniques have involved the use of aversive stimuli such as electric shock and nausea-inducing drugs (emetics). These techniques have been used to treat drug addiction, alcoholism, and sexual deviations. Their function is to elicit anxiety in the presence of the conditioned stimulus (CS) that elicits the inappropriate conditioned response (CR). For example, in treating a child molester, the following paradigms could be operative:

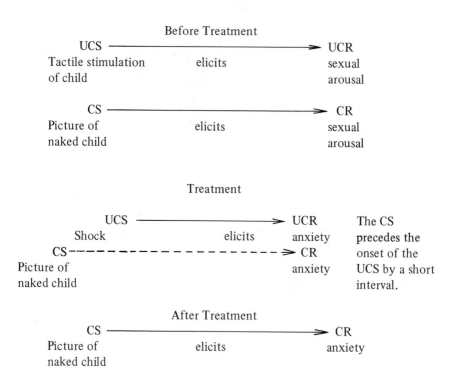

Before Treatment

UCS		UCR
Tactile stimulation of child	elicits	sexual arousal

CS		CR
Picture of naked child	elicits	sexual arousal

Treatment

UCS		UCR	The CS
Shock	elicits	anxiety	precedes the
CS		CR	onset of the
Picture of naked child		anxiety	UCS by a short interval.

After Treatment

CS		CR
Picture of naked child	elicits	anxiety

Covert sensitization can be utilized in conjunction with avoidance conditioning in which the CS acquires a discriminative function for an avoidance response. The avoidance response is negatively reinforced by termination of the S^{r-} (CS) (picture of the naked child) and avoidance of the S^{R-} (UCS) (shock). The therapist should specify an appropriate avoidance response for the client to make, such as changing the picture to one of an adult female. In this way, the client can learn responses incompatible with the maladaptive responses in the problematic situation. For example,

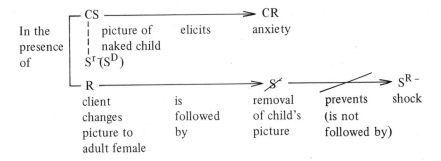

By arranging for the client to practice appropriate avoidance responses in the treatment situation, the likelihood is increased that he will emit these responses in the actual problematic situation.

Until recently, operant and respondent behaviors were typically regarded as comprising two completely separate and distinct classes of behavior. Behavioral principles applicable to one class of behavior were not considered applicable to the other. Operant behaviors were restricted to the so-called voluntary or striated, skeletal muscles. Respondent behaviors were restricted to elicited "involuntary" autonomic responses involving smooth muscles, glands, and simple reflexes. Current research has made these distinctions more difficult to maintain. Recent technology, particularly in *biofeedback*, is gaining widespread interest for its applications in the treatment of insomnia, migraine, high blood pressure, and other psychosomatic complaints. Behaviors categorized as respondents, previously thought to be exclusively under autonomic or involuntary control, such as brain waves, blood pressure, and heart rate, have been operantly conditioned. The strength of these behaviors can be increased or decreased by manipulation of reinforcing consequences. Biofeedback technology has widespread implications for the treatment of cardiac, visceral, and psychosomatic disorders previously considered to remain outside the individual's control.

REFERENCES

Barber, T., DiCara, L.V., Kamiya, J., Miller, N.E., Shapiro, D., and Stoyva, J. (Eds.), *Biofeedback and Self-Control, 1970*, Aldine-Atherton, Chicago, 1971.

Cautela, J.R., "Behavior Therapy And Self-Control: Techniques and Implications," in Franks, C.M. (Ed.), *Behavior Therapy: Appraisal and Status*, McGraw-Hill Book Company, New York, 1969, pp. 323-340.

Cautela, J.R., "Covert Sensitization," *Psychological Reports*, **20** (1967), pp. 459-468.

Cautela, J.R. and Wisocki, P.A., "Covert Sensitization for the Treatment of Sexual Deviations," *Psychological Record,* 21 (1971), pp. 37-58.

Franks, C.M., Conditioning and Conditioned Aversion Therapies In the Treatment Of the Alcoholic," *International Journal of Addictions,* 1 (1966), pp. 61-98.

Homme, L.E., "Perspectives in Psychology: XXIV. Control of Coverants, the Operants of the Mind," *Psychological Record,* 15 (1965), pp. 501-511.

Jones, M.C., "Elimination Of Children's Fears," *Journal of Experimental Psychology,* 7 (1924), pp. 383-390.

Paul, G.L., *Insight Versus Desensitization In Psychotherapy,* Stanford University Press, Stanford, California, 1966.

Pavlov, I.P., *Conditioned Reflexes,* Oxford University Press, London, 1927.

Rachman, S. and Teasdale, J.D., "Aversion Therapy: An Appraisal," in Franks, C.M. (Ed.), *Behavior Therapy: Appraisal and Status,* McGraw-Hill Book Company, New York, 1969, pp. 279-320.

Rescorla, R.A. and Solomon, R.L., "Two-process Learning Theory: Relationship between Pavlovian Conditioning and Instrumental Learning," *Psychological Review,* 74 (1967), pp. 151-182.

Shapiro, D., Barber, T.X., DiCara, L.V., Kamiya, J., Miller, N.E., and Stoyva, J. (Eds.), *Biofeedback and Self-Control, 1972: An Aldine Annual on the Regulation of Bodily Processes and Consciousness,* Aldine, Chicago, 1973.

Shapiro, D. and Schwartz, G.E., "Biofeedback and Visceral Learning: Clinical Applications," *Seminars in Psychiatry,* 4 (1972), pp. 171-184.

Watson, J.B. and Rayner, R., "Conditioned Emotional Reactions," *Journal of Experimental Psychology,* 3 (1920), pp. 1-14.

Wolpe, J., *The Practice of Behavior Therapy,* Pergamon Press, New York, 1969.

Wolpe, J., *Psychotherapy By Reciprocal Inhibition,* Stanford University Press, Stanford, California, 1958.

Wolpe, J., and Lazarus, A., *Behavior Therapy Techniques: A Guide To The Treatment Of Neuroses,* Pergamon Press, New York, 1966.

POST-TEST QUESTIONS

(3) 1. Using the information from Vignette 5, state one operant behavior and two possible respondent behaviors involved in Mrs. M.'s "being upset."

(7) 2. The following include examples of operant behaviors and respondent behaviors. Place an "O" in the space for those italicized behaviors that are operant, and an "R" for those that are respondent.

    a. (1) _____ One teenager in a treatment group *swears* at another boy. The second boy's face

       (2) _____ *turns* red.

    b. (1) _____ You *ask* a client a question about his brother; you observe that his

       (2) _____ breathing *quickens* and perspiration

       (3) _____ *appears* on his forehead.

    c. (1) _____ You *give* Janet a piece of candy for completing her assignment. Carol

       (2) _____ observes this and *starts whining.*

(2) 3. (1) Draw a paradigm showing respondent conditioning of the following phobia: A child is afraid of dentists. When he approaches a dentist's office, he begins to tremble, turns pale, breathes rapidly, then turns and runs away. This child has some dental problems that must be taken care of soon, or he may lose many of his teeth.

    (2) Describe an operant procedure for treating both operant and respondent features of this phobia.

(2) 4. Mr. F. is an alcoholic. He typically takes his first drink at 10:00 a.m. and drinks on and off during the day at work. When he comes home, he has three or four drinks before dinner, a few while watching television, and "a nightcap or two" before bed. Mr. F. is in danger of losing his job and his wife is threatening to leave him unless he stops drinking. Describe a respondent procedure that could be used to suppress Mr. F.'s excessive drinking.

chapter 15
transfer of change

OBJECTIVES

After completing this chapter, you should be able to:
1. state three obstacles to generalization of desired responses from the therapy situation to the client's environment,
2. state three ways to maximize successful generalization of desired responses from therapy to the client's environment.
3. give an example of behavioral rehearsal in therapy and the rationale for its use, and
4. give an example of the use of behavioral assignments in a therapy situation and the rationale for their use.

Therapeutic or treatment goals delineate behaviors that the client should perform in his *natural environment*, that is, the people and physical surroundings in which both adaptive and maladaptive behaviors are conditioned and maintained. Frequently, however, therapy takes place in another environment, such as a social agency or institution. An individual may perform the desired behaviors in the therapeutic environment, but not in his natural environment. *Transfer of change* refers to the generalization or transfer of behavioral change from the treatment setting to the client's natural environment. Several obstacles can be identified in attempting to transfer desired behaviors from the treatment setting to the client's environment. The therapist should anticipate these potential obstacles in formulating a strategy with the client for maximizing generalization of desired behaviors.

One major obstacle to generalization is the lack of reinforcement for desired

141

responses in the client's natural environment for which he had received positive reinforcement in therapy. If an appropriate response is not reinforced, the response will undergo extinction until it is unlikely to occur. For example, in the treatment setting, an alcoholic has learned alternative non-alcohol-drinking responses he can make in typical drinking situations. When he makes the alternative responses in those actual situations, however, he is not reinforced. His friends do not support his non-alcohol-drinking behaviors and the latter can, therefore, be expected to extinguish.

A second obstacle involves reinforcement in the client's environment for inappropriate, maladaptive responses; moreover, the client may receive reinforcement only for performing these undesired responses. For example, the therapist has extinguished Debbie's tantrum behaviors (kicking, screaming, and banging her head on the floor) and has conditioned quiet, solitary play behaviors in his office. At home, however, Debbie's mother is busy with her painting and does not pay attention to Debbie when she plays quietly. The mother inappropriately gives Debbie attention by scolding or pleading with her when she is disruptive. This increases the probability that Debbie's tantrum behaviors will be reinstated, because positive reinforcement is given only after undesirable, disruptive behaviors.

A third obstacle to successful generalization involves dissimilarity between the therapeutic environment and the client's environment. Stimuli in the client's environment are not similar enough to stimuli in the treatment environment for the client to generalize his newly acquired responses to the novel stimuli. The therapist conditions desired responses to occur in the presence of certain S^Ds or CSs in the treatment situation. He must also consider the extent to which stimuli in the client's environment are similar to treatment S^Ds and CSs in their ability to set the occasion for and elicit desired responses. A therapist conditioning heterosexual behaviors in an adult male—for example, eye contact with women, conversational behaviors—must determine the availability of women in the client's environment who could set the occasion for these desired behaviors to occur. If during his normal activities the client did not have opportunities to meet females, the therapist should consider modifying the client's environment so that the desired behaviors could be reinforced. Similarly a drug addict may perform and practice alternative behaviors to drug taking and copping (procuring) in the therapist's office. The situation on the street may be so different from the treatment setting, however, that it fails to provide S^Ds or cues that would set the occasion for performance of the newly-acquired behaviors. The desired behaviors, therefore, would have a low probability of occurring in the client's natural environment.

The sight of a neon sign saying "BAR" is an S^D for Mr. A., an alcoholic, to enter the bar and order a drink. It may also serve as a CS that elicits emotional responses (CRs) associated with drinking alcohol. The therapist, therefore, must assess the drinking situations in order to isolate stimuli that control Mr. A.'s drinking.

A fourth obstacle to generalization occurs when the desired responses are not sufficiently conditioned in the therapeutic environment. Although appropriate stimuli are present in the client's environment, the desired responses are less likely to occur in the natural environment because the client has not practiced them sufficiently. For example, a client has been instructed by the therapist to state his opinions to a colleague instead of remaining silent when he disagrees on an issue. Although the client said that he understood the therapist's instructions, when an issue arose the next day, he did not perform the appropriate opinion-stating behaviors.

The transfer of change problem requires formulation of strategies to promote generalization. The generalization of desired responses can be optimized by identifying likely obstacles and designing an intervention program to take these factors into consideration. It is often advantageous to involve significant others in the client's environment, such as family and friends, in the treatment process. These significant others can serve both as S^Ds and as reinforcing agents for desirable behaviors. In order to maximize generalization of desired behaviors, these significant others must learn (1) to establish and carry out reinforcement contingencies, and (2) to be consistent in reinforcing desired behaviors, and withholding reinforcement from undesirable behaviors. These individuals should receive positive reinforcement for their efforts, although frequently the newly performed appropriate behaviors of the client will themselves serve as reinforcers for the responses of significant others.

One method of coping with insufficient reinforcement for appropriate behaviors is to maintain the desired behaviors on an intermittent reinforcement schedule after conditioning. As described earlier, intermittent reinforcement can be employed to generate consistent response rates that are highly resistant to extinction. Usually, intermittent reinforcement more closely approximates the reinforcement schedules characteristic of a client's environment than does continuous reinforcement.

In order to deal with the problem of stimulus dissimilarity between the treatment setting and the client's natural environment, it may be advisable to condition the desired behaviors in the client's environment instead of in the therapist's office. If this is not feasible, various elements of the client's environment can be introduced into the treatment setting, such as involving friends or relatives in conditioning desired behaviors. By conducting treatment in the client's natural environment, the therapist minimizes the transfer problem; the client learns appropriate behaviors under the actual environmental conditions. The therapist can condition appropriate behaviors in the presence of S^Ds or CSs that previously supported maladaptive responses. In some situations, it is preferable to remove the client from his environment for treatment in order to effectively establish appropriate behaviors in a controlled situation. In these cases, it is also important to work concurrently with significant individuals in the environment to which the client will return so that changes in the client's behavior will be maintained. The use of more than one therapist to condition desirable behavior can also help to maximize transfer of change by allowing the client to practice and perform appropriately in the presence of more than one individual.

Behavioral rehearsal and *behavioral assignments* can be employed to promote generalization of behavior change. Advice or suggestions for behaving appropriately are often insufficient to enable a client to perform those behaviors. Clients are frequently told by friends, relatives, or authorities to "shape up" or to behave in one way or another; such exhortative methods may be ineffective in achieving behavioral change. Often an individual can state that his behaviors are inappropriate; he may even be able to indicate what would constitute appropriate behaviors in his situation. He does not perform the appropriate responses, however; these responses may not exist in his behavioral repertoire, or they may exist at a very low probability of occurrence. For this reason, *behavioral rehearsal* is an effective method used to increase the probability of a client's performing appropriate behaviors by having him practice them with corrective feedback before he tries them out in the actual problematic situation. Behavioral rehearsal is a role-playing technique in which the client practices or rehearses desired behaviors that have been suggested and/or modeled by the therapist or group members. The client is given instructions on how to behave in a role-play that closely resembles his problematic situation. After the role-play begins, he may require further instructions, prompting, and reinforcement in order to perform appropriately. As the client gains skill and confidence, the likelihood is increased that he will perform the behaviors appropriately in his natural environment. The client practices appropriate behaviors until he has achieved the criterion performance specified in the treatment plan. Additional practice sessions conducted after initial behavior change has occurred may be held to ensure sufficient conditioning of the behaviors. This method of *overlearning* or *overtraining* increases the probability that the client will perform the appropriate behaviors in his natural environment.

Behavioral assignments are given to systematically direct the client toward treatment goals. They structure the client's activities between therapy sessions to ensure that progress toward treatment goals occurs in the client's natural environment as well as in the treatment environment. After each session, the client usually receives a behavioral assignment that specifies a task that he is to perform in his natural environment. Behavioral assignments should be realistic, in that there should be a reasonable likelihood that the client can carry it out in his environment. This task may include behaviors that he has practiced during a treatment session. The client reports his success or failure in carrying out the assignment at the following session. The therapist may request that the client demonstrate the behaviors that were to be performed in order to determine both appropriate and/or deficient responses. Deficient performances are rehearsed with additional instructions, prompts, and feedback provided to the client until he performs appropriately. The client may then be given the same or a modified assignment, depending on the difficulty he experienced in performing the previous assignment.

In Vignette 1, behavioral rehearsal and behavioral assignments were used to maximize transfer of change from the group setting to Mr. P.'s natural environment. Behavioral rehearsal, behavioral assignments, and overlearning are ways of maximizing successful generalization of desired responses from the treatment setting to the client's natural environment.

REFERENCES

Baer, **D.M.** and **Wolf, M.M.**, "The Entry Into Natural Communities Of Reinforcement," in Ulrich, R., Stachnik, T., and Mabry, J. (Eds.), *Control of Human Behavior, Volume Two*, Scott, Foresman and Company, Glenview, Illinois, 1970, pp. 319–324.

Goldstein, **A.P.**, **Sechrest, L.B.**, and **Heller, K.**, *Psychotherapy and the Psychology Of Behavior Change*, John Wiley and Sons, Inc., New York, 1966, Chapter 5, pp. 212–259.

Hawkins, **R.P.**, **Peterson, R.F.**, **Schweid. E.**, and **Bijou, S.W.**, "Behavior Therapy In The Home: Amelioration Of Problem Parent-Child Relations With The Parent In A Therapeutic Role," *Journal of Experimental Child Psychology*, **4**, No. 1 (1966), pp. 99-107.

Lovaas, **O.I,,** **Koegel, R.**, **Simmons, J.Q.**, and **Long, J.S.**, "Some Generalization and Follow-up Measures on Autistic Children in Behavior Therapy." *Journal of Applied Behavior Analysis*, **6** (1973), pp. 131-165.

McFall, **R.M.** and **Lillesand, D.B.**, "Behavior Rehearsal with Modeling and Coaching in Assertion Training," *Journal of Abnormal Psychology*, **77**, No. 3 (1971), pp. 313-323.

Patterson, **G.R.**, **McNeal, S.**, **Hawkins, N.**, and **Phelps, R.**, "Reprogramming The Social Environment," *Journal Of Child Psychology and Psychiatry*, **8** (1967), pp. 181-195.

POST-TEST QUESTIONS

(3) 1. List three common obstacles to generalization of desired responses from the therapy situation to the client's environment.

(3) 2. In Vignette 4, Mr. C.'s verbal behavior was conditioned in a laboratory-like situation. (1) State one reason the conditioned behaviors might not generalize from the treatment situation to his on-the-ward behavior. (2) State two ways you could maximize successful generalization for Mr. C.

(4) 3. (1) State two behavioral assignments the marriage counselor gave Mrs. M. in Vignette 5. (2) State two reasons for a therapist's use of behavioral assignments in implementing an intervention program.

(2) 4. Using the information from Vignette 5, how could behavioral rehearsal be used to help Mrs. M. discuss a movie with Mr. M.? What is the rationale for using behavioral rehearsal?

chapter 16
treatment
planning

OBJECTIVES

Given a case example, you should be able to:
1. identify environmental and client resources and barriers to goal attainment,
2. identify a relevant intervention strategy including two behavioral techniques and state the rationale for their use,
3. describe a method for evaluating the chosen intervention techniques, and
4. describe a behavioral contract you could negotiate between members of a family in treatment.

The treatment planning process starts at intake and continues throughout treatment until the client's treatment goals have been achieved. The term *treatment planning* is used to represent the therapist's pre-treatment and ongoing preparation in working with the client from intake to termination, including follow-up contacts necessary to ensure maintenance of treatment gains.

The assessment process has been completed: controlling antecedents and consequences for the target response(s) have been delineated, wherever possible, and the strength of the target response(s) has been determined. A terminal treatment goal(s) has been formulated that specifies the desired behaviors to be performed by the end of treatment, along with supporting antecedents and consequences. This terminal treatment goal may be modified during the course of treatment if additional information is obtained that changes the assessment of the client's problem. Immediate and intermediate treatment goals that approximate the terminal treatment goals are also formulated in observable terms. Immediate, intermediate, and terminal treatment goals provide the basis for selection of appropriate intervention techniques. Thus, a behavioral assessment and modification sequence includes the following components:

1. Establish a treatment contract with the client and obtain the informed consent of the client for treatment.
2. List all client problems.
3. Order the problems according to their priority; select one problem for immediate attention.

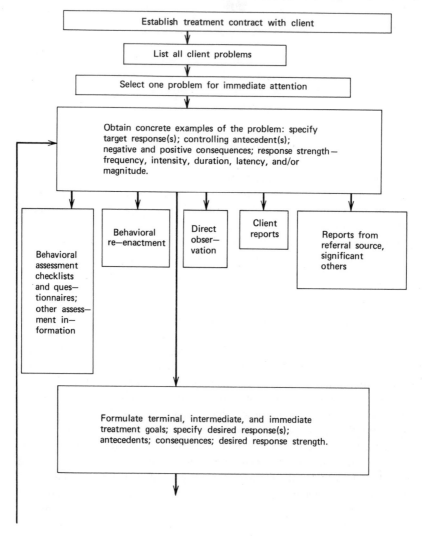

FIGURE 1.   Flow chart of behavioral assessment and modification sequence.

4. Obtain concrete examples of the problem selected: include descriptions of (a) target *response*(s), (b) eliciting and/or discriminative *antecedent*(s) (c) *negative consequences* and/or punishers, (d) potential *positive* and/or *negative reinforcers*, and (e) *response strength*–frequency, intensity, duration, latency, and/or magnitude–of the target behavior(s).

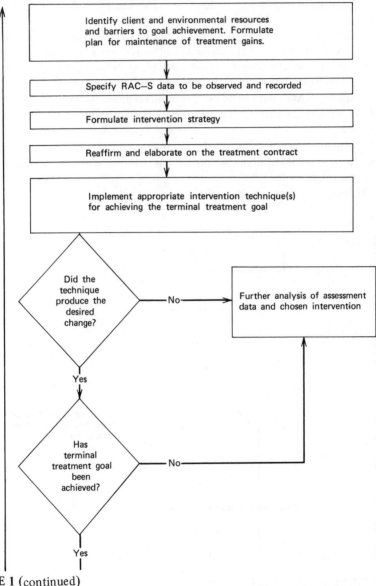

FIGURE 1 (continued)

5. Formulate terminal, intermediate, and immediate behavioral change or treatment goals, specifying (a) the desired *response*(s), (b) the *antecedent*(s), (c) the potential *reinforcers*, and (d) the desired *response strength*—frequency, intensity, duration, latency, and/or magnitude; one or more of these dimensions are used in establishing criteria for goal achievement. A target date for achievement of each goal should be set. This can be modified later if necessary. A date for case review should also be established.

6. Identify client and environmental resources and barriers to goal achievement. Identify reinforcers that are available and individuals who control the delivery of reinforcers for the client. Formulate plan to maximize generalization of treatment gains to the client's natural environment.

7. Specify RAC-S data to be observed and recorded throughout treatment.

8. Formulate an intervention strategy including appropriate behavioral techniques.

9. Reaffirm and elaborate on the treatment contract, specifying modifications in the behavioral requirements for the client and/or therapist in order to achieve the treatment goals.

10. Implement intervention technique(s).

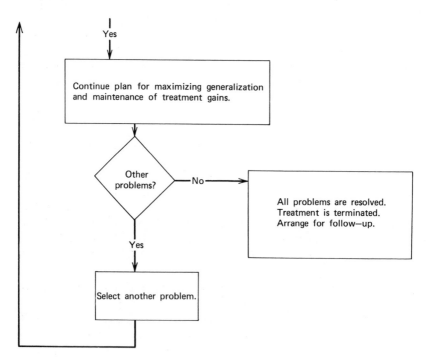

FIGURE 1. (continued)

11. Evaluate the effects of the intervention technique(s) by comparing the response strength of the target behavior(s) before, during, and after treatment. The measures or criteria for evaluating progress should be explicit in the statement of the treatment goals, as indicated in Step 5.

12. When the terminal treatment goal has been achieved, continue the plan for maximizing generalization and maintenance of treatment gains in the client's environment.

13. Select another problem. Repeat the sequence starting with step 4 above. If all problems are resolved, treatment is terminated. Make arrangements for follow-up where indicated.

14. If the terminal treatment goal has not been achieved, subject the target behavior to further analysis. It is possible that the original assessment was inaccurate; therefore, gather the data necessary to reassess the problem. If the assessment was accurate, select and implement another intervention technique(s).

15. Repeat the sequence starting with step 11 above.

Figure 1 is a flow chart of the behavioral assessment and modification sequence.

Behavioral intervention techniques can be classified according to their effects in altering response strength. As stated earlier there are five treatment outcomes or directions in which a target behavior can be modified. Behavioral techniques can be applied so that a response is (1) acquired or developed, (2) increased in strength, (3) maintained at a particular strength or pattern of occurrence, (4) decreased in strength, or (5) completely suppressed. Behavioral techniques are applied as *interventions* to influence the frequency, intensity, duration, latency, and/or magnitude of target behaviors. The technique chosen should be based on the requirements of the immediate, intermediate, or terminal treatment goal. That is, if the treatment goal states that a behavior is to be decreased in strength, the technique should be selected from among those in Figure 2 in the column, "Decrease Response Strength."

Figure 2 is a chart of behavior techniques classified according to their applicability in modifying response strength in a particular direction. Some of these techniques can be combined in more complex behavioral procedures. For example, assertive training may include positive reinforcement, model presentation and differential reinforcement. Covert sensitization involves a combination of operant and respondent techniques including respondent conditioning and negative reinforcement.

Besides frequency, intensity, duration, latency, and magnitude, other factors must be taken into consideration when choosing a behavioral intervention technique. These include cost (expense involved), efficiency (time), client and environmental resources and barriers, relative effectiveness of available techniques, comfort to the client, and ethical considerations. For example, although a punishment technique involving aversive stimuli may be more immediately

FIGURE 2. A classification of behavioral techniques.

Acquire or Develop a Response	Increase Response Strength	Maintain Response Strength	Decrease Response Strength	Completely Suppress Response
Shaping via successive approximation	Positive reinforcement	Schedules of reinforcement	Punishment	Punishment
Negative reinforcement	Negative reinforcement	Negative reinforcement	Extinction (operant and respondent)	Extinction (operant and respondent)
Model presentation (Modeling)	Differential reinforcement	Differential reinforcement	DRO schedule	Respondent conditioning
Stimulus fading	Respondent conditioning	Respondent conditioning	Respondent conditioning	
Respondent conditioning				

effective and efficient, a positive reinforcement shaping technique may have greater long-term effectiveness with fewer detrimental side-effects. In addition, the use of positive reinforcement techniques may encounter fewer objections from the community than techniques utilizing aversive stimuli.

Behavioral techniques should be used in accordance with the ethical codes and values adopted by the human services professions. Like other therapeutic modalities, treatment utilizing behavioral techniques should be implemented only with informed consent of the client. With children or institutionalized populations such as the mentally retarded, delinquents, prisoners, or mental patients, however, special care should be exercised to ensure that the individual is not subjected to cruel or harsh interventions. Interventions that cause severe discomfort to the client should be employed only where the benefits of using such a technique clearly outweigh the consequences to the client or significant others of not using that technique.

After a systematic assessment is made of the client's situation, the therapist should formulate an intervention *strategy* for resolving the client's problem(s). The rationale for the intervention strategy is developed from treatment goals that are mutually established, wherever feasible, by the therapist and the client. One or more behavioral techniques may be included as part of the intervention strategy for achievement of the client's goals. The intervention strategy provides a framework in which behavioral change leading to goal attainment can be systematically planned. Without an explicit strategy, application of an isolated behavioral technique can be ineffective in achieving treatment goals. For example, positive reinforcement could be applied to increase the frequency of arm raising in an institutionalized mental patient, Mr. W., who spends most of his time sitting in a chair in a corner by himself, unshaven and unkempt. Although positive reinforcement may be effective in increasing the frequency of a motor activity such as arm raising, this activity in itself may not be beneficial for Mr. W. if conditioned outside the context of a treatment plan. If the treatment goals for Mr. W. include the development of self-care skills such as shaving, washing, brushing his teeth, and combing his hair, the therapist's plan to increase arm raising could be an intermediate goal. The intervention strategy for developing self-care skills might include the following behavioral techniques: positive reinforcement, shaping, and chaining. Shaping and chaining can be used to develop low-frequency behaviors; positive reinforcement is used to increase and maintain the strength of the desired behaviors once they occur.

In order to evaluate the effectiveness of the interventions, it is necessary to obtain baseline measures of Mr. W.'s self-care skills. Before the intervention plan is implemented, Mr. W. is given an electric shaver and instructed to shave every morning. The therapist observes him daily over a two-week period to record the frequency of his shaving. Other ward staff such as aides or nurses could also record the frequency of his shaving. The data recorded include (1) the number of days Mr. W. appears clean-shaven, and/or (2) the number of times Mr. W. makes attempts to shave. Mr. W. may pick up the shaver and put it to his face, for example, but be ineffective in removing the hairs from his face. Similarly, baseline measures should be obtained for other self-care behaviors, including hair combing, washing, and brushing his teeth.

In the above example, the criterion for attainment of the shaving goal stated that Mr. W. be clean shaven at least five times a week. Achievement of this goal, therefore, required that Mr. W. appropriately shave five out of seven days each week. When observed during the initial weeks of treatment, Mr. W. shaved part of his face once or twice a week. Further along in treatment, Mr. W. appeared clean shaven three or four times a week. By the end of treatment, the shaving goal was achieved so that Mr. W. appropriately shaved himself at least five times a week. If the behavior had not changed from its baseline rate after the intervention had been employed for a reasonable amount of time, the problematic situation would have been reassessed and another technique(s) implemented.

Performance of desired behaviors should be evaluated not only in the therapeutic situation, but also in the client's natural environment. It may be necessary to develop the desired behaviors initially in the treatment environment. The success of treatment, however, rests on the client's ability to perform these behaviors in the actual problematic situation. The Treatment Evaluation Form (Figure 3) can be given to the client to obtain his or her evaluation of treatment. The form includes a statement of the client's problems and goals. In instances where the client lacks the skills required to fill out the form, it can be filled out by significant others such as parents, teachers, or relatives. This form can also be sent to the client at periodic intervals following termination, such as three months, six months, or one year. The therapist can also schedule periodic interviews with the client either at the therapist's office or the client's home to evaluate the extent to which treatment gains have been maintained. Arrangements for follow-up contacts should be made prior to termination of treatment.

FIGURE 3.   Lawrence-Sundel treatment evaluation form.*

The following are the problems which you worked on in therapy and the goals you wished to achieve through therapy. Please correct or add any problems or goals if you had a different understanding of problems or goals that you worked on.

If the statements are correct, please initial your O.K.

Problems and goals worked on in therapy:

Problems	Goals
1	1
2	2
3	3

To what extent are the above listed problems solved?

	Much Worse	Worse	The Same	Better	Much Better	Completely Solved
Problem 1						
Problem 2						
Problem 3						

To what extent, if any, has there been a change in these problems since the last session? Date of last session:

	Much Worse	Worse	The Same	Better	Much Better	Completely Solved
Problem 1						
Problem 2						
Problem 3						

To what extent were the above listed treatment goals achieved?

	Not At All Achieved	Small Gain	Moderate Gain	Mostly Achieved	Goal Achieved
Goal 1					
Goal 2					
Goal 3					

*Reprinted with permission of Macmillan Publishing Co., Inc. from "Behavioral Group Treatment with Adults in a Family Service Agency," by Martin Sundel and Harry Lawrence, in *Individual Change Through Small Groups* by P. Glasser, R. Sarri, and R. Vinter (Eds.). Copyright © 1974 by The Free Press, a Division of Macmillan Publishing Co., Inc.

The client's *commitment* to solving his problem(s) through the treatment program can be an essential factor in achieving a successful outcome. The term *treatment contract* is used to denote the commitment of both the client and therapist to perform certain behaviors that can lead to resolution of the client's problem(s). The contract also helps to ensure client involvement and partici-pation in the treatment process. Initially, the treatment contract specifies the behaviors required of the client and therapist in problem selection, assessment, and goal formulation. In other words, the therapist will carry out a behavioral assessment of the client's problem(s) and formulate appropriate goals with him, and the client agrees to participate in relevant data-gathering procedures. After goals are established and an intervention strategy is formulated, the treatment contract is expanded to specify the behaviors to be performed in order to achieve the treatment goals. The client agrees to carry out behavioral assignments made by the therapist and regularly report their outcomes.

A behavioral contract can be established between members of a family in which the desired behaviors of each person are specified along with the consequences of those behaviors. The therapist typically negotiates the conditions of such a contract. For example, a contract between a mother and son might require that the son feed and clean up after his dog daily before his mother allows him to play with his friends. For each day he fails to perform the chores, his mother deducts 25¢ from his weekly allowance. Behavioral contracts are often signed by the persons involved as a means of formalizing their commitment to the treatment plan.

A systematic procedure for planning a client's treatment is essential in formulating an appropriate intervention strategy and determining its effective-ness. The responsible therapist should establish and follow a systematic record keeping plan that (1) delineates the client's problems and goals, (2) describes the interventions that have been employed, and (3) indicates and/or charts the client's progress toward or away from treatment goals. Each problem should be listed separately along with specification of the target response(s), controlling conditions, and a corresponding behavioral goal(s). Relevant client and environ-mental resources and barriers should be described in relation to each goal. The intervention strategy should identify behavioral techniques appropriate for achieving the client's goals. These components of the treatment planning sequence are listed below as they might appear in a client's chart or case record:

1. problem(s): concrete examples; assessment information; target responses; controlling conditions; response strength
2. goals: immediate, intermediate, terminal
3. treatment contract in which the client is involved in problem selection, assessment, and goal formulation; the client states a commitment to work toward achieving treatment goals
4. personal/environmental resources and barriers to goal achievement
5. formulation of intervention strategy and specification of behavioral tech-niques to be employed; include plan for generalization and maintenance of desired behavioral change.

Progress toward each goal should be recorded by date. The effects of the various interventions employed should be described. When the client's goals are reached, follow-up contacts should be arranged, where indicated, to ensure the maintenance of treatment goals.

The following is an excerpt from a sample record based on the information in Vignette 8:

1. Problem: Mr. L. has difficulty in establishing and maintaining satisfying relationships with women.

Typical example: When Ms. Jones approached him last week and asked him how his work was going, Mr. L. looked at the floor, mumbled, "O.K. I guess," covering his mouth with his hand and speaking in a monotone.

Controlling conditions: Antecedent: Ms. Jones began a conversation with Mr. L. Responses: Mr. L. looked at the floor, mumbled, "O.K. I guess," covered his mouth with his hand and spoke in a monotone. Consequences: Ms. Jones made an excuse and immediately left his company. Potential negative reinforcer: Ms. Jones's presence. Response strength: three times last week.

2. Goals: Terminal: Mr. L. approaches a woman, appropriately converses with her and asks her for a date; she accepts the date and they discuss topics of mutual interest. Desired response strength: at least once per week. Target date: 3 months. Case review date: 8 weeks. Intermediate: When a woman initiates conversation with Mr. L., he maintains eye contact, speaks clearly with his hands at his side; the woman continues to speak with him. Immediate: decrease mumbling, decrease Mr. L.'s talking with his hand over his mouth; increase the volume of his voice and vary the pitch in conversation.

3. Treatment contract: Mr. L. agrees to engage in data-gathering procedures in order to assess his problematic situation and formulate goals. A measurement plan is formulated in which Mr. L. records the number and type of contacts he has with women, his responses, and their consequences. He also agrees to carry out the behavioral assignments the therapist gives him and to report back to the therapist on their outcomes. The therapist agrees to carry out a behavioral assessment to select problems and formulate goals. He also agrees to design and implement intervention strategies and to evaluate client progress toward goals.

4. Resources and barriers: Resources: Mr. L. earns a steady income and is self-supporting; Mr. L.'s stated cooperation and desire to improve his situation. Barriers: Mr. L. has few opportunities to meet eligible women; Mr. L. has few friends.

5. Intervention strategy for immediate goal: verbal instructions, differential reinforcement and behavioral rehearsal will be used. to (1) decrease Mr. L.'s mumbling and speaking with his hand in front of his mouth and (2) to increase the volume of his voice and vary the pitch.

The client will be given verbal instructions in raising the volume of his voice and in varying the pitch. The therapist will provide social reinforcement such as "good," "that's better," and smile when the client emits desired behavior patterns. The therapist will reinforce approximations to the desired speech. Behavioral rehearsal will be used to allow the client to practice the desired behaviors in the presence of the therapist and to increase the likelihood of generalization. The client will be instructed to practice various exercises into a tape recorder at home and to bring the tape to the next session.

Therapist's signature _____ Date _____

Sample Progress Note

2/11/75 Mr. L.'s mumbling has decreased in the presence of the therapist. He no longer places his hand in front of his mouth while talking. Mr. L. reported a conversation with a woman at work during which he kept his arms folded across his chest instead of over his mouth. Mr. L. continues to speak in a monotone although the volume of his voice has increased when speaking into the tape recorder. Plan for next contact—Mr. L. was given an assignment to continue practicing the speaking exercises on his tape recorder. Mr. L. will rehearse a role-played conversation at the next session.

REFERENCES

Grant, R.L. and Maletzky, B.M., "Application of the Weed System to Psychiatric Records," *Psychiatry in Medicine,* **3** (1972), pp. 119–129.

Houts, P.S. and Scott, R.A., *Goal Planning In Mental Health Rehabilitation,* Hershey, Pennsylvania, 1972.

Kanfer, F.H. and Phillips, J.S., "A Survey Of Current Behavior Therapies And A Proposal For Classification," in Franks, C.M. (Ed.), *Behavior Therapy: Appraisal And Status,* McGraw-Hill Book Company, 1969, pp. 445–475.

Stuart, R.B., "Behavioral Contracting Within the Families of Delinquents," *Journal of Behavior Therapy and Experimental Psychiatry,* **2** (1971), pp. 1–11.

Sulzer, E.S., "Research Frontier: Reinforcement And The Therapeutic Contract," *Journal Of Counseling Psychology,* **9**, No. 3 (1962), pp. 270–276.

Wolpe, J. and Lazarus, A.A., *Behavior Therapy Techniques,* Pergamon Press, New York, 1966, Chapter 3, pp. 24–37.

ADDITIONAL REFERENCES

Behavior Therapy in Psychiatry, A Report of the APA Task Force on Behavior Therapy, American Psychiatric Association, Washington, D.C., 1973.

Brown, D.G., *Behavior Modification in Child, School and Family Mental Health: An Annotated Bibliography*, Research Press. Champaign, Illinois, 1972.

POST-TEST QUESTIONS

(2) 1. State one possible resource and one barrier to goal attainment given the following treatment goal for Mr. L. in Vignette 8: Mr. L. appropriately asks his employer to consider his promised pay raise.

(2) 2. Identify an intervention strategy including two behavioral techniques; state the rationale for their use given the following treatment goals for Mr. L. in Vignette 8: establish and increase interpersonal skills such as (1) eye contact, (2) increased volume and frequent changes in pitch of voice, (3) staying on one topic at a time, and (4) appropriately responding to another person's comments.

(4) 3. Describe a behavioral contract that you could negotiate between the parents and two children of the Z. family based on the goals of decreased fighting between the children and increased rate of performance of specific chores.

(2) 4. Describe a method for evaluating the effectiveness of an assertive training procedure that could have been used with Mr. L.

course
post - test

(2) 1. State the inappropriate behaviors emitted by Mr. P. during criticism.

(3) 2. How could a modeling plus reinforcement procedure have been used to help Mr. P. obtain a new job?

(2) 3. What reinforcement was arranged for Mr. P. in the treatment situation, and what were the conditions for its delivery?

(4) 4. List Mr. P.'s respondent behaviors elicited by criticism.

(2) 5. Describe the behavioral procedures that were used to promote generalization of desired behavior change from the group treatment setting to Mr. P.'s natural environment.

Questions for Vignette 2

(5) 1. List five contingencies Mrs. D. carried out with Stephen and Dianne.

(3) 2. Name the behavioral principle that was the basis for both time-out used with Stephen and the punishment used with Dianne. Name the reinforcers involved for Stephen and Dianne.

(2) 3. The therapist told Mrs. D. to spend time with Stephen in the evenings, and to read to him twice a week. His goal was to increase social behaviors emitted by mother and son that would be positively reinforced by each other. Describe two possible situations that would indicate that the therapist's goal was being achieved.

(6) 4. Describe a shaping procedure Mrs. D. could have used to establish cooperative play behaviors for Stephen and Dianne.

Questions for Vignette 3

(2) 1. Specify the two measures used to determine movement toward the treatment goals.

(2) 2. State two factors that could operate during conditioning or extinction that would slow the rate of decrease of Carla's screaming.

(4) 3. Describe the interaction between Carla and her mother in terms of positive and negative reinforcement. Draw a paradigm and label relevant components.

(2) 4. Name the operant procedure used to decrease Carla's screaming when she was asked to put her toys away. Describe how it was implemented; that is, to which of Mrs. H.'s actions does the procedure refer?

(1) 5. What was the social worker's rationale for instructing Mrs. H. to praise Carla for putting her toys away?

Questions for Vignette 4

(2) 1. In the vignette, no goal is explicitly stated for treatment. State a possible treatment goal for Mr. C. and specify a measure that could be used to determine whether it was achieved.

(1) 2. What data should be collected before implementing the treatment described in the vignette?

(3) 3. Describe the function of the red light. Name and briefly state the purpose of the operant procedure involving the red light.

(2) 4. Apply the concept of conditioned reinforcement to explain how Mr. C.'s vocalizations could have generalized to the ward from the treatment setting even though the unconditioned reinforcer, candy, was not given to him on the ward. What specifically did the psychologist do to promote the transfer of Mr. C.'s vocalizations to the ward?

(3) 5. Describe how the psychologist could use a DRO schedule to determine if the M & M's and points served as reinforcers for Mr. C.'s increased vocalizations, rather than the reinforcers being primarily the attention he received in the treatment situation.

Questions for Vignette 5

(4) 1. State four possible desired behaviors that could be included in treatment goals for Mrs. M. Indicate measures that could be used to evaluate movement toward those goals.

(2) 2. In behavioral terms, describe the rationale for the procedure involved in Mrs. M.'s drawing up two lists of topics.

(2) 3. State two measures that could be used to evaluate the effectiveness of the discrimination training procedure employed by the counselor.

(1) 4. How was Mr. M.'s leaving the house negatively reinforced?

Questions for Vignette 6

(4) 1. Specify the target behaviors and their negative consequences for Mrs. G. and Mr. T.

(3) 2. State three measurable goals of the procedure carried out by the psychiatric nurse.

(2) 3. Describe two behavioral techniques the psychiatric nurse could use to help Mrs. G. and Mr. T. generalize appropriate verbal behavior outside the group.

(2) 4. Describe (a) a reinforcer that was given in the group to Mrs. G. and Mr. T. contingent on appropriate speech and (b) a possible reinforcer that would maintain their appropriate speech outside the group.

Questions for Vignette 7

(3) 1. Specify three antecedents to Harold's drug taking.

(2) 2. State two negative consequences possibly related to Harold's drug taking.

(4) 3. State four negative consequences of Harold's failing grades.

(2) 4. Specify two measures that could be used to evaluate movement toward treatment goals.

(3) 5. State three possible reinforcers (positive or negative) maintaining Harold's drug taking.

Questions for Vignette 8

(2) 1. State two desired behaviors that could be included in treatment goals appropriate to Mr. L.'s problem of non-assertion.

(2) 2. Describe two role-playing techniques that could be used as part of Mr. L.'s treatment if he were participating in group therapy.

(2) 3. Describe a procedure that Mr. L. could use to establish himself as a conditioned reinforcer for his dates.

appendix 1
vignettes

VIGNETTE 1

Developing Appropriate Behaviors in Group Treatment

At a group therapy meeting, Mr. P. complained of frequent "anxiety and depression." He had recently been laid off from his job, was bored, and had no outside interests. He spent most of his time sleeping or watching television.

In asking Mr. P. to specify the behavioral components of his anxiety and depression, it was found that Mr. P. felt "anxious" in situations where he was criticized by his wife or employer. He often felt "depressed" after these encounters. In a role-play of these situations, Mr. P. perspired heavily, his face turned red, his breathing became more rapid, and he rapped his knuckles against each other. His hands trembled and he made excuses as he replied to the criticism.

Mr. P. and members of the·group role-played situations in which Mr. P. was criticized by his employer and wife in order to assess his current behavior patterns. When Mr. P. disagreed with the group members' analysis of his situation, role reversal was used to allow Mr. P. to observe someone else demonstrating his typical behaviors and their effects on others.

In order to demonstrate appropriate responses to criticism, several group members played the part of Mr. P. in role-plays and responded appropriately to criticism. Afterwards, Mr. P. played himself in role-plays of the criticism situations. When Mr. P. experienced difficulty imitating the appropriate behaviors, the therapist prompted him in making the appropriate responses. Mr. P. practiced responding appropriately in role-plays and received praise from the therapist and group members as soon as he demonstrated appropriate behavior. Assignments were given to Mr. P. to perform the behaviors practiced in the group in his natural environment.

Similar procedures were used to help Mr. P. prepare for an interview for a new

175

job. He soon completed a successful job interview and was hired as a bus driver.

To deal with Mr. P.'s "boredom," the group assigned him to pursue an outside interest or hobby. Mr. P. decided to reestablish his interest in bowling. The therapist instructed Mr. P. to go to a bowling alley, to observe people bowling, and to discuss his experience with two persons. Shortly thereafter, he and his wife joined a bowling league.

VIGNETTE 2

The Parent as a Behavior Modifier

Mrs. D. complained to a therapist at a Community Mental Health Center that she found it impossible to discipline her nine-year-old son, Stephen. He frequently beat his younger sister Dianne, making her cry and inflicting bruises. He also broke her toys during these episodes. When Mrs. D. intervened to stop Stephen from beating Dianne, Stephen cursed and kicked Mrs. D. Verbal reprimands and attempts to physically punish Stephen failed to eliminate his undesirable behaviors.

After instructing Mrs. D. to monitor situations in which the beatings occurred, it was found that Dianne often teased or made faces at Stephen prior to his beating her. Mrs. D.'s report also indicated that she spent most of her time in the evenings trying to discipline Stephen.

Treatment consisted of Mrs. D. instructing Dianne to stop teasing and making faces at Stephen with the contingency arranged that if she teased and made faces, privileges for the day such as ice cream or watching television would be removed. On two subsequent occasions, Dianne lost television privileges and ice cream. After these two experiences, Dianne stopped teasing and making faces at Stephen.

Treatment further consisted of instructing Mrs. D. to request that Stephen go to his room when he beat Dianne. If he refused to obey, Mrs. D. would physically carry or move Stephen to his room, where he was required to remain by himself for 15 minutes. If he kicked and cursed Mrs. D., the time was extended five minutes. If he screamed or made loud noises while in his room, the time was also extended five minutes.

The first time Mrs. D. moved Stephen to his room, he kicked and cursed. He also screamed while in his room. Stephen remained in his room for 25 minutes. After the third time Mrs. D. instituted the treatment procedure, Stephen stopped cursing and kicking her. By the fourth time the procedure was applied, Stephen went to the room by himself and quietly remained there until his time was up. After the fifth time the procedure was employed, Stephen no longer beat his sister.

Mrs. D. was also instructed to spend leisure time with Stephen in the evenings.

Since Stephen enjoyed when Mrs. D. read to him, Mrs. D. was instructed to read to him twice each week.

VIGNETTE 3

Decreasing Tantrum Behaviors

In a group of welfare mothers who were learning child management skills, Carla's mother, Mrs. H., told the social worker that almost every time she told Carla to put her toys away, Carla screamed. Mrs. H. would attempt to placate her by promising to buy her new clothes and by putting Carla's toys away herself.

Mrs. H. was instructed to refrain from making promises to Carla when she screamed about putting away her toys, and to walk away from Carla under these circumstances. She was informed that Carla's screaming might increase in severity at first, but if she held firm, Carla's screaming would gradually decrease. Mrs. H. carried out these instructions for five days, during which time Carla's screaming gradually decreased. By the sixth day, Carla no longer screamed when told to put her toys away. The social worker had also instructed Mrs. H. to praise Carla and give her concrete rewards, such as gum or cookies, when she did put her toys away. Mrs. H. followed these instructions and Carla began putting her toys away more frequently.

VIGNETTE 4

Conditioning Verbal Behavior

Mr. C. was a 45-year-old patient who had been on a back ward of a mental hospital for eleven years. He was described by ward staff as mute and withdrawn. He spent much of the day sitting in a chair looking at the floor or pacing up and down the halls of the ward. Mr. C. remained silent when spoken to and did not initiate conversation with patients or staff.

The treatment procedure consisted of placing Mr. C. in a room where slides of animals, people, and landscapes were shown to him through a slide projector. Mr. C. was asked to talk about the pictures when he saw a red light appear on a panel. When the red light was off, the psychologist spoke about the pictures and Mr. C. was asked to silently look at them. When the red light was turned on, Mr. C. was instructed to speak. When Mr. C. made any vocalization, M & M's fell through a chute into Mr. C.'s left hand. A counter registered one point for each vocalization that Mr. C. made. In addition, the psychologist said "good" immediately after each vocalization. An automatic recorder counted each second of speech as one vocalization response.

Mr. C. made no vocalizations during the initial treatment session, only 5 responses the second session, and 48 responses during the fifth session. During the tenth treatment session, Mr. C. made 76 monosyllabic responses such as "boy and girl," "cat," "house and yard." During the next five sessions, the psychologist asked Mr. C. specific questions about the content of the slides and gave Mr. C. hints that facilitated correct responding. On the fifteenth session Mr. C. appropriately described a slide as follows: "A boy and girl are playing on the swing."

After 15 sessions, ward staff reported that for the first time in many years Mr. C. had spoken to several persons, and had made short replies to comments directed to him by staff.

VIGNETTE 5
Stimulus Control of Marital Interaction

Mrs. M. consulted a marriage counselor with regard to marital difficulties. Her husband refused to see the counselor with her. Mrs. M. complained that her husband ran around town drinking with his male friends during the evenings and spent little time with her and their children. They rarely went to the movies or to other entertainment, and Mrs. M. did all the food shopping by herself. She had stopped making his breakfast as a result of their frequent arguments before he left for work. Mrs. M. berated her husband for going out with his friends, for not helping her around the house, and for not spending time with her and their children. Mr. M. responded to her criticism by cursing her and telling her to mind her own business. Mrs. M. became so upset during these arguments that she ran into her room and locked the door, remaining there until Mr. M. left the house.

In his interviews with Mrs. M., the counselor determined that Mr. and Mrs. M. rarely discussed topics of mutual interest. Their conversations revolved around Mrs. M.'s complaints and Mr. M.'s abusive responses to them. Mrs. M. said that she would like to have more satisfying conversations with her husband and felt that improvement in this area was her primary concern. As part of the treatment plan, the counselor instructed Mrs. M. to make a list of topics that she should discuss with her husband (List A). These topics included his work, the two children, and fishing. Mrs. M. made a second list of topics that she should not discuss with her husband (List B). Topics on the second list included his staying out late at night, watching television at his friends' homes, not taking Mrs. M. shopping or to the movies, and not spending time with his family. Mrs. M. was also instructed to greet Mr. M. with a kiss when he came home from his job and to ask him how his work had gone.

The counselor praised Mrs. M. during role-plays in which she discussed topics from List A and ignored Mrs. M. when she discussed topics on List B. Mrs. M.'s talking about topics on List A increased in frequency while her talking about topics on List B decreased in frequency.

VIGNETTE 6
Developing Appropriate Conversation

Mrs. G. and Mr. T. were both elderly residents of a nursing home. In social situations, they often asked questions and made comments that were unrelated to the topic being discussed. For example, when several residents were discussing a recent film shown at the home, Mr. T. asked the person speaking if he liked the pancakes served that morning. In addition, Mrs. G. and Mr. T. were frequently observed to talk continuously for five minutes or more without pausing for responses from others. These speech patterns resulted in their being ridiculed and excluded from many conversations held by other residents.

The psychiatric nurse devised a conversational exercise to be played by the six members of a group in which Mrs. G. and Mr. T. participated. The nurse began the exercise by making a statement and each of the other group members added a statement to her introduction. Each statement was required to bear logical connection to the previous statement.

At first Mrs. G. and Mr. T. both added inappropriate statements to the previous ones. On these occasions they were stopped by the nurse or group members, who required them to make appropriate statements and complimented or praised them for doing so. Group members prompted Mrs. G. and Mr. T., offering hints and suggestions for correct statements. As they practiced the exercise on subsequent occasions, both Mrs. G. and Mr. T. made fewer inappropriate remarks and increasingly more appropriate ones. The frequency of their appropriate remarks during conversation outside the group was also observed to increase. Appropriate speech was reinforced by staff and other residents.

VIGNETTE 7
Behavioral Assessment of Drug Abuse

Harold, a fifteen-year-old high school sophomore, started smoking marijuana six months ago at a party given by one of his friends. He enjoyed that experience and continued his experimentation with other drugs, including amphetamines and barbiturates. During the past few months, Harold has failed to complete his class assignments, sometimes handing in a blank sheet of paper. His midterm report card showed four Fs and one C in a crafts course. Harold's parents, Mr. and Mrs. T., were concerned that he might drop out of school or not pass to the next level. About this time, Mrs. T. found a marijuana cigarette and some of her diet pills in Harold's desk drawer. When confronted with this evidence, Harold admitted to taking drugs, but argued that they did not interfere with his functioning in school or at home.

Shortly after the midterm grades came out, a school counselor referred Harold to the school social worker, describing Harold as being "inattentive in the classroom and poorly motivated," as well as having a "negative attitude toward learning," and failing grades.

Harold complained to the school social worker that his parents frequently grounded him, nagged him, withheld his allowance, and denied him privileges such as watching television and going out with his friends. Upon further questioning, Harold revealed that his parents' disciplinary measures were applied because of his failing grades. Harold admitted that he, too, was worried about flunking out of school, and conceded that his drug taking might be interfering with his studying. When asked to describe his drug taking, Harold indicated that he smoked pot regularly with his friends and ingested pep pills and downers occasionally. Harold indicated that when he started studying, his friends often invited him over to listen to records and get stoned. He also spent many evenings at his girlfriend's home and they usually began the evening by taking some pills. When he was home alone, Harold would look in his notebook for his class assignments, smoke two or three joints before beginning them, and complete only part of his assignments or none of them at all.

After several sessions, Harold said that he was beginning to recognize the relationship between his poor school performance and drug taking.

VIGNETTE 8

Behavioral Assessment of Non-Assertiveness

Mr. L. is a 30-year-old unmarried man who seeks assistance for his difficulty in establishing and maintaining satisfying relationships with women. He complains that women find him unpleasant to be around, and he never knows what to say in their presence. Of the last four women Mr. L. has taken out, all have refused a second date. Mr. L. only has one male friend.

Mr. L. is a bookkeeper for a clothing manufacturer. He has worked for the same firm for nine years. Although he was promised a promotion and raise two years ago, he still earns the same salary and is at the same position he was in when he first began with the company. He has never discussed his feelings about being treated unfairly with his boss, although other employees in similar circumstances have benefited from doing so.

The therapist asked Mr. L. to describe his experience on the last date he had. Mr. L. said that they were having coffee in a restaurant after seeing a movie, and he could not think of interesting things to say to the girl he was with. He concluded that he just "bored her to death" talking about his work. When the therapist asked Mr. L. to describe his date's conversation, Mr. L. said he couldn't remember much about what she said, since he was so concerned about making a good impression. On one occasion, Mr. L. said a young woman fell asleep while he was trying to explain a complicated bookkeeping procedure. The therapist observed that Mr. L. kept his head down during the interview, and often held his hand in front of his mouth when speaking so that his speech was difficult to understand. He sometimes drifted from one topic to another without waiting for the therapist's response to what he had said, and frequently spoke in a monotone.

The therapist asked Mr. L. to describe his last conversation with his boss. Mr. L. was seated across the desk from his boss who asked him what he wanted. Mr. L. mumbled, looked down at the floor, and began to talk about his financial problems. When the boss responded by asking Mr. L. why he could not manage his finances properly, Mr. L. stammered and tried to defend his way of managing money. Finally, Mr. L. mumbled, "I'm sorry," and walked out, without raising the issue of his salary increase.

Upon further questioning, Mr. L. indicated that he often found himself being taken advantage of in situations in which he should have stated his opinions or defended his rights. Mr. L. said that he hoped to improve this situation through therapy and would cooperate with the therapist's recommendations. The therapist gave Mr. L. an assignment to record significant information about the situations in which he felt exploited.

appendix 2
course pre-test

Questions for Vignette 1

(2) 1. State the inappropriate behaviors emitted by Mr. P. during criticism.

(3) 2. How could a modeling plus reinforcement procedure have been used to help Mr. P. obtain a new job?

(1) 3. What was the rationale for the bowling assignment as a way to treat Mr. P.'s boredom?

(2) 4. What type of reinforcement was planned for Mr. P. in the treatment situation and what were the conditions for its delivery?

(2) 5. Describe the behavioral procedures that were used to promote generalization of desired behavior change from the group treatment setting to Mr. P.'s natural environment.

Questions for Vignette 2

(5) 1. List five contingencies Mrs. D. carried out with Stephen and Dianne.

(3) 2. Name the procedure that describes Mrs. D.'s interventions with Dianne. Describe an incident in which this procedure might be used.

(2) 3. The therapist told Mrs. D. to spend time with Stephen in the evenings, and to read to him twice a week. His goal was to increase social behaviors emitted by mother and son, which would be positively reinforced by each other. Describe two possible situations that would indicate that the therapist's goal was being achieved.

Questions for Vignette 3

(2) 1. What were the two goals of the program carried out by Mrs. H.?

(2) 2. What were the measures used to determine movement toward the goals?

(1) 3. What phenomenon was the social worker describing when he told Mrs. H. that Carla's screaming might increase in severity at first?

(2) 4. What two conditions were maintaining Carla's screaming prior to treatment?

appendix 3
course pre-test
answers

Answers for Vignette 1

(2) 1. State the inappropriate behaviors emitted by Mr. P. during criticism.
Answers: During criticism, Mr. P. (1) rapped his knuckles against each other and (2) made excuses. (Note: The other behaviors were elicited, not emitted; they constitute incorrect answers if included.)

(3) 2. How could a modeling plus reinforcement procedure have been used to help Mr. P. obtain a new job?
Answer: Group members modeled appropriate behaviors for Mr. P. in role-plays of job interviews. When Mr. P. imitated these appropriate behaviors in role-plays, he received positive reinforcement from the group members and therapist.

(1) 3. What was the rationale for the bowling assignment as a way to treat Mr. P.'s boredom?
Answer: The bowling assignment was a way to establish appropriate behaviors that could be reinforced in Mr. P.'s natural environment. These behaviors would be incompatible with boredom, that is, sleeping and watching television all day.

(2) 4. What type of reinforcement was planned for Mr. P. in the treatment situation and what were the conditions for its delivery?
Answers: The therapist and group members praised Mr. P. as soon as he responded appropriately in role-plays.

(2) 5. Describe the behavioral procedures that were used to promote generalization of desired behavior change from the group treatment setting to Mr. P.'s natural environment.
Answers:
  1. Behavioral rehearsal was used in the group treatment setting to provide Mr. P. with an opportunity to become more skillful in his

ability to perform appropriate behaviors in his natural environment.

2. Behavioral assignments were given to Mr. P. so that he would practice appropriate behaviors learned in the group setting in his natural environment.

Answers for Vignette 2

(5) 1. List five contingencies Mrs. D. carried out with Stephen and Dianne.

Answers: (1) If Dianne teased and made faces at Stephen, the day's privileges such as ice cream and watching TV would be removed. (2) If Stephen beat Dianne, he was told to go to his room. (3) If Stephen refused to go to his room, Mrs. D. would physically move Stephen to his room where he was to remain for 15 minutes. (4) If Stephen kicked and cursed Mrs. D., the time in the room was extended by 5 minutes. (5) If he screamed or made loud noises while in the room, his time was extended by 5 minutes.

(3) 2. Name the procedure that describes Mrs. D.'s interventions with Dianne. Describe an incident in which this procedure might be used.

Answer: Response-contingent punishment by removal of positive reinforcers was the procedure used by Mrs. D. with Dianne. If Dianne teased or made faces at Stephen, the day's privileges such as ice cream and television were removed.

(2) 3. The therapist told Mrs. D. to spend time with Stephen in the evenings, and to read to him twice a week. His goal was to increase social behaviors emitted by mother and son, which would be positively reinforced by each other. Describe two possible situations that would indicate that the therapist's goal was being achieved.

Criterion for correct answers: Your answers should include information that some behaviors related to time spent together by Mrs. D. and Stephen have increased over their previous rate. The behaviors should be positive or rewarding, in contrast to the verbal reprimands and physical punishment by Mrs. D. and the cursing and kicking by Stephen that characterized their past interactions.

Sample answers: (1) Mrs. D. reports that Stephen is telling her many things about his school activities that he never talked about before. (2) Stephen asks for more nights of reading. (3) Mrs. D. reports speaking in a mild tone of voice to Stephen more often. (4) Mrs. D. reports that she puts her arm around Stephen more often.

Answers for Vignette 3

(2) 1. What were the two goals of the program carried out by Mrs. H.?

Answers: The goals of the program were (1) to decrease the frequency of Carla's screaming about putting her toys away and (2) to increase the frequency of Carla's putting her toys away.

(2) 2. What were the measures used to determine movement toward the goals?
Answers: The measures used to determine movement toward the goals were (1) the decrease in frequency of Carla's screaming and (2) the increase in the frequency of Carla's putting her toys away.

(1) 3. What phenomenon was the social worker describing when he told Mrs. H. that Carla's screaming might increase in severity at first?
Answer: The social worker informed Mrs. H. about a typical *extinction* phenomenon, the increase in severity of a target behavior when the extinction procedure is first instituted.

(2) 4. What two conditions were maintaining Carla's screaming prior to treatment?
Answers: Carla's mother was maintaining Carla's screaming by (1) promising to buy her new clothes and (2) putting her toys away.

Total possible: 27.
Criterion score: 24.

appendix 4
chapter pre - tests

CHAPTER 1

(2) 1. State two essential criteria to be used in specifying a response.

(6) **2-A.** Indicate with a (+) which of the following statements are written in behaviorally specific terms and with a (−) statements which are vague and require further specification.

2-B. After completing 2-A above, rewrite in specific terms only those statements in which the responses are not described behaviorally.

a. Ted saw three clients today and made four phone calls.

b. Bob is becoming a drug addict.

c. Bruce kicked Sally in the shins.

d. She acted out her anger toward him.

CHAPTER 2

(1) 1. In order to maximize the effectiveness of a positive reinforcer for a specific response, what temporal condition is required in its association with the response?

(2) 2. When a client presents his problem in vague terms, what are two major assessment steps you should take?

(5) 3. List the five treatment outcomes or directions in which a target behavior can be modified.

(1) 4. It has been empirically demonstrated that presentation of certain events following a behavior can increase the probability that the behavior will recur. Name the behavioral principle to which this statement refers.

CHAPTER 3

(5) 1. Re-number the following steps so that they are in the correct order to carry out the procedure that you would use to empirically determine if a given stimulus served as a positive reinforcer for a target behavior:

_____ 1. Withhold given stimulus continuously, that is, each time the target response occurs.

_____ 2. Determine strength of target behavior.

_____ 3. Observe decrease in strength of target behavior.

_____ 4. Present stimulus after the target behavior occurs and observe an increase in its strength.

_____ 5. Observe consequences of target behavior.

(2) 2. What are two practical difficulties in applying an extinction procedure to decrease an undesired response?

(3) 3. In Vignette 3, what behavior(s) did Carla's mother positively reinforce before treatment? What were the reinforcers?

CHAPTER 4

(2) 1. Which of the following are probably statements of positive reinforcement contingencies? (Circle the correct ones.)

    a. Finish your math assignment and you may play outside.
    b. If you don't make your bed, watch out!
    c. If you wash the dishes, I'll give you an ice cream cone.
    d. If you fight with your brother, you will get a spanking.
    e. He completed his chores in three hours.

(1) 2. Briefly describe how "superstitious" behavior is conditioned.

(3) 3. Give an example of a positive reinforcement contingency you could establish.

(1) 4. Intermittent reinforcement makes a well-learned response more resistant to extinction. (Circle one.)

    a. True
    b. False

CHAPTER 5

(1) 1. What is the effect of increasing a ratio too quickly on a fixed-ratio schedule?

(2) 2. In fixed-interval and variable-interval schedules, what two events are required in order for reinforcement to be delivered?

(2) 3. State two characteristics of responses maintained on ratio schedules.

(1) 4. State one way in which fixed-ratio and variable-ratio schedules generate different behavior patterns.

CHAPTER 6

(1) 1. In Vignette 4, Mr. C.'s verbal behavior could be developed by (circle one correct answer):

a. extinction
b. bribery
c. shaping via successive approximation
d. reinforcing approximations of incompatible responses

(1) 2. In order to shape a new behavior, you would not need to utilize differential reinforcement. (Circle one.)

a. True
b. False

(2) 3. For the operant, "responses that a child can make to get his mother to buy him a toy," name two members.

(2) 4. How are positive reinforcement and extinction involved in differential reinforcement?

CHAPTER 7

(2) 1. What is an S^D for a response? What is an S^Δ?

(1) 2. What behavior typically results from discrimination procedures involving two stimuli (S^D and S^Δ) and one response?

(1) 3. In Vignette 4, what function did the red light serve?

(6) 4. In the following examples, identify the discriminative stimulus, the response, and the reinforcer by labeling them with S^D, R, and S^+, respectively in the paradigms.

a. Bob sees Joe walking down the street. Bob says "hello," and Joe says, "good morning."

b. Shirley hears the ice cream truck, asks her aunt for a quarter, and buys the ice cream.

(1) 5. True or False. When a response is conditioned in the presence of one discriminative stimulus, it will not occur in the presence of other similar discriminative stimuli.

CHAPTER 8

(2) 1. Rewrite the following sentences so that the strength of the response is stated in measurable terms.

   a. Hortense screamed for a long time.

   b. Roger rarely mows the lawn.

(4) 2. In Vignette 6, what were the behavioral excesses shown by Mrs. G. and Mr. T.?

   What were the negative consequences of these behaviors?

(3) 3. From the information given in the following paragraph, identify Henry's problematic response, its antecedent condition, and its negative consequences.

   When someone comes over to talk to Henry or ask a question, he mutters and speaks in a low voice so that the person has difficulty understanding what he is saying. The person typically stops talking and walks away from Henry soon after he begins to mutter.

(2) 4. State two criteria that can be used in establishing problem priorities for treatment.

CHAPTER 9

(1) 1. Which of the following statements best describes the objective(s) of behavioral assessment? (Circle the correct answer.)

    a. Reconstruct an individual's personality.

    b. Help a person learn to accept himself.

    c. Specify appropriate behaviors.

    d. Identify target behaviors and their controlling environmental conditions, and formulate behavioral change goals.

(3) 2. Using the information from Vignette 2, state (a) two of Stephen's problematic responses, (b) the probable positive reinforcer that maintained them, and (c) the antecedent to the problematic responses.

(1) 3. In order to determine relevant antecedents to the problematic behavior, an appropriate question to ask a client is (Circle a or b):

    a. Where does this problem occur?

    b. Why do you continue to engage in this behavior if you don't like yourself afterwards?

(3) 4. Using the information from Vignette 8, state an intermediate treatment goal for Mr. L. specifying (a) a desired response and (b) a relevant antecedent.

CHAPTER 10

(2) 1. Which is usually more effective, a simple conditioned reinforcer or a generalized conditioned reinforcer? Support your answer.

(1) 2. What is the difference between an unconditioned reinforcer and a conditioned reinforcer?

(4) 3. Give two examples of generalized conditioned reinforcers and two examples of unconditioned reinforcers.

(1) 4. True or False. In order for a neutral stimulus to function as a conditioned reinforcer, it must also serve as a discriminative stimulus.

(3) 5. Label the components of one unit of a stimulus-response chain.

CHAPTER 11

(2) 1. How can discriminative stimuli (S^Ds) and positive reinforcers be involved in a modeling procedure? Use a paradigm to illustrate your answer.

(3) 2. Indicate True (T) or False (F) beside each of the following statements:

    a. _____ If an individual does not perform a response after he has observed someone else perform it, he has not learned it.

    b. _____ It is more difficult to teach a song to a child who has no imitative skills than to a child who imitates excessively.

    c. _____ Imitative behavior cannot be conditioned through reinforcement when the client has no imitative skills as, for example, a severely retarded child.

(3) 3. Using the information from Vignette 1, how could modeling and reinforcement have been used to help Mr. P. obtain a new job?

CHAPTER 12

(2) 1. Name two types of punishment procedures that can be used to suppress a response.

(1) 2. Briefly describe a time-out procedure.

(2) 3. Briefly describe two disadvantages of punishment procedures.

(4) 4. Mrs. Kelly asks Sharon to fold the laundry after it has been washed and dried. When Mrs. Kelly returns, Sharon is talking to her friend on the phone and the laundry has not been folded. What should Mrs. Kelly do to demonstrate her knowledge of the necessary conditions to maximize the effectiveness of punishment?

CHAPTER 13

(1) 1. What is a major advantage of avoidance conditioning in maintaining a conditioned response?

(3) 2. Give an example of a procedure that results in escape behavior.

(4) 3. Give an example of a procedure that results in avoidance behavior.

(2) 4. Give an example of an unconditioned negative reinforcer and one of a conditioned negative reinforcer.

CHAPTER 14

(1) 1. Describe a procedure for extinguishing a classically conditioned response.

(8) 2. Given the following information, specify operant and respondent behaviors: A man gets in his car and drives home. As he walks in the door, the aroma of dinner cooking makes his mouth water. He runs to the kitchen, panting, kisses his wife, and sits down at the table.

(1) 3. Explain the persistence of emotional respondent behavior in the absence of identifiable reinforcing consequences for the individual.

(1) 4. How can a phobia be eliminated?

CHAPTER 15

(2) 1. You are treating an alcoholic client. As part of the treatment program to decrease his drinking, you suggest several nondrinking behaviors appropriate in the social situations where he usually drinks. These behaviors are new to him, but he agrees to try them out. What is the most likely obstacle to success for this part of therapy?

What can you do to counteract this effect or to plan for this problem?

(1) 2. Using the information from Vignette 1, describe how behavioral rehearsal was used with Mr. P. to facilitate generalization of appropriate responses to criticism.

(1) 3. Behavioral assignments are given [circle the correct answer(s)] :

    a. to structure the client's activities between therapy sessions.

    b. to help the client apply in his natural environment what he has learned in treatment.

    c. so the client can receive feedback from the therapist based on a specific task he has attempted to accomplish.

    d. all of the above.

(1) 4. True or False: It is usually more difficult for a desirable behavior to generalize beyond the treatment situation when more than one therapist is involved in conditioning it.

CHAPTER 16

(2) 1. Name two behavioral techniques that can be used to decrease the strength of a problematic behavior.

(1) 2. State the main purpose of a treatment contract.

(1) 3. Identify the next step you would take if a client's treatment goal has not been achieved after a selected behavioral technique has been applied.

(2) 4. State the behavioral techniques involved in an assertive training procedure.

appendix 5
chapter pre-test
answers

CHAPTER 1

(2) 1. State two essential criteria to be used in specifying a response.
Answers:
Two essential criteria used in specifying a response are:
(1) that the response is stated in *positive terms* and
(2) that it refers to *observable* actions; that is, what the individual says or does.

(6) 2-A. Indicate with a (+) which of the following statements are written in behaviorally specific terms and with a (-) statements that are vague and require further specification.
Criteria for correct answers:
Responses describe what the person *says* or *does* in *positively stated, observable* terms. Responses stated negatively are incorrect. Sample answers follow those statements that required further specification.
Answers: Statements a and c are correct as written; statements b and d require further specification.

2-B. After completing 2-A above, rewrite in specific terms only those statements in which the responses are not described behaviorally.

+ a. Ted saw three clients today and made four phone calls.
– b. Bob is becoming a drug addict.
   Sample answer:
   Bob injects heroin into his veins daily.
+ c. Bruce kicked Sally in the shins.
– d. She acted out her anger toward him.
   Sample answer:
   She hit him in the face with a bottle.

The total point value of this test is 8. Score one point for each of the two parts of question one; score one point for each correctly identified statement in question 2-A and one point for each correctly rewritten statement in question 2-B.

Criterion score for this test is 7. If your score is at least 7, you may take the post-test for this chapter. If you score less than 7, refer to the teaching material in the chapter before you take the post-test.

CHAPTER 2

(1) 1. In order to maximize the effectiveness of a positive reinforcer for a specific response, what temporal condition is required in its association with the response?

    Answer: The reinforcer should be delivered *immediately after* the response.

(2) 2. When a client presents his problem in vague terms, what are two major assessment steps you should take?

    Answers:
    1. Specify the problem in observable (behaviorally specific) terms.
    2. Obtain a baseline of the problematic behavior you have identified.

(5) 3. List the five treatment outcomes or directions in which a target behavior can be modified.

    Answers:
    Modification techniques can be applied so that a behavior is (1) acquired or developed, (2) increased in strength, (3) maintained at a particular strength or pattern of occurrence, (4) decreased in strength, or (5) completely suppressed.

(1) 4. It has been empirically demonstrated that presentation of certain events following a behavior can increase the probability that the behavior will recur. Name the behavioral principle to which this statement refers.

    Answer: Positive reinforcement.

The total point value of this test is 9. The distribution of points is indicated next to each question.
Criterion score: 8

CHAPTER 3

(5) 1. Re-number the following steps so that they are in the correct order to carry out the procedure that you would use to empirically determine if a given stimulus served as a positive reinforcer for a target behavior:

Answers:

    _____3_____ 1. Withhold given stimulus continuously, that is, each time the target response occurs.

    _____2_____ 2. Determine strength of target behavior.

    _____4_____ 3. Observe decrease in strength of target behavior.

    _____5_____ 4. Present stimulus after the target behavior occurs and observe an increase in its strength.

    _____1_____ 5. Observe consequences of target behavior.

(2) 2. What are two practical difficulties in applying an extinction procedure to decrease an undesired response?

Answers:
1. Withholding the reinforcer each time the response occurs.
2. Making sure that the client is not getting reinforced for that behavior by someone else.

(3) 3. In Vignette 3, what behavior(s) did Carla's mother positively reinforce before treatment? What were the reinforcers?

Answers: Before treatment, Carla's mother reinforced Carla's screaming about putting her toys away. The reinforcers were (1) promises to buy new clothes and (2) Mrs. H. putting the toys away.

Criterion Score: 9.

CHAPTER 4

(2) 1. Which of the following are probably statements of positive reinforcement contingencies? (Circle the correct ones.)

    (a.) Finish your math assignment and you may play outside.
    b. If you don't make your bed, watch out!

(c.) If you wash the dishes, I'll give you an ice cream cone.

d. If you fight with your brother, you will get a spanking.

e. He completed his chores in three hours.

(1) 2. Briefly describe how "superstitious" behavior is conditioned.

Answer: "Superstitious" behavior is the result of an accidental relationship between a response and a reinforcer. An individual makes a response that is associated with a reinforcer on one occasion, but the response has no effect on the availability of that reinforcer on subsequent occasions.

(3) 3. Give an example of a positive reinforcement contingency you could establish.

Criteria for correct answer: (1) Your answer must be stated in positive terms; (2) the desired behavior must be specified; (3) a reinforcer must be specified that is available immediately after the occurrence of the desired behavior.

Sample Answers: Rake the yard and then you may play baseball with your friends. When you finish writing your reports today, you may go home.

(1) 4. Intermittent reinforcement makes a well-learned response more resistant to extinction. (Circle one.)

(a.) True

b. False

Criterion score: 6.

CHAPTER 5

(1) 1. What is the effect of increasing a ratio too quickly on a fixed-ratio schedule?

Answer: The response will extinguish.

(2) 2. In fixed-interval and variable-interval schedules, what two events are required in order for reinforcement to be delivered?

Answers:

1. Passage of designated time, followed by

2. the individual making the appropriate response.

(2) 3. State two characteristics of responses maintained on ratio schedules.

Answers: Ratio schedules are characterized by (1) high rates of responding and (2) minimal hesitation between responses.

(1) 4. State one way in which fixed-ratio and variable-ratio schedules generate different behavior patterns.

Answer: Fixed-ratio schedules generate a post-reinforcement pause and variable-ratio schedules do not.

Criterion score: 5.

CHAPTER 6

(1) 1. In Vignette 4, Mr. C.'s verbal behavior could be developed by (circle one correct answer):

    a. extinction
    b. bribery
    ⓒ shaping via successive approximation
    d. reinforcing approximations of incompatible responses

(1) 2. In order to shape a new behavior, you would not need to utilize differential reinforcement. (Circle one.)
    a. True
    ⓑ False

(2) 3. For the operant, "responses that a child can make to get his mother to buy him a toy," name two members.
    Criterion for correct answers: Each member of the operant must be a response of the child's that has the same effect, that is, the mother's buying the toy.
    Sample answers:
    The child screams and his mother buys him a toy.
    The child cries and his mother buys him a toy.
    The child asks for a toy and his mother buys it.

(2) 4. How are positive reinforcement and extinction involved in differential reinforcement?
    Answer: Responses that meet specific criteria are *positively reinforced*, while reinforcement is withheld continuously from other responses, that is, they are *extinguished.*

Criterion score: 5.

CHAPTER 7

(2) 1. What is an S^D for a response? What is an $S^\triangle$?
    Answers: An S^D is a discriminative stimulus that sets the occasion for a response made in its presence to be followed by a reinforcer. An $S^\triangle$ is a

stimulus that sets the occasion for a response made in its presence not to be followed by a reinforcer.

(1) 2. What behavior typically results from discrimination procedures involving two stimuli (S^D and $S^\triangle$) and one response?

Answer: The response rate in the presence of S^D increases and the response rate in the presence of $S^\triangle$ decreases.

(1) 3. In Vignette 4, what function did the red light serve?

Answer: Mr. C.'s verbal responses in the presence of the red light were reinforced, and in the absence of the red light his verbal responses were not reinforced. The red light, therefore, served as a discriminative stimulus (S^D) for Mr. C.'s verbal responses.

(6) 4. In the following examples, identify the discriminative stimulus, the response and the reinforcer by labeling them with S^D, R, and S^+, respectively in the paradigms.

a. Bob sees Joe walking down the street. Bob says, "hello" and Joe says, "good morning."

Answer:

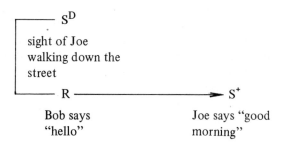

b. Shirley hears the ice cream truck, asks her aunt for a quarter, and buys the ice cream.

Answer:

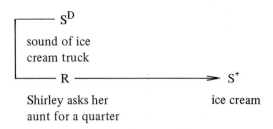

(1) 5. True or False. When a response is conditioned in the presence of one

discriminative stimulus, it will not occur in the presence of other similar discriminative stimuli.
Answer: False

Criterion score: 10.

CHAPTER 8

(2) 1. Rewrite the following sentences so that the strength of the response is stated in measurable terms.
Criterion for correct answers: The sentence must be written so as to state the strength of the response in measurable terms, such as frequency, duration, latency, or intensity.
a. Hortense screamed for a long time.
Sample answer: Hortense screamed for 15 minutes.
b. Roger rarely mows the lawn.
Sample answer: Roger mowed the lawn once last month and once the month before.

(4) 2. In Vignette 6, what were the behavioral excesses shown by Mrs. G. and Mr. T.?
Answers: The behavioral excesses shown by Mrs. G. and Mr. T. were (1) Asking questions and making comments unrelated to topics being discussed, and (2) talking continuously for 5 minutes or more without pausing for responses from others.
What were the negative consequences of these behaviors?
Answers: Mrs. G. and Mr. T. were (1) ridiculed and (2) excluded from many conversations.

(3) 3. From the information given in the following paragraph, identify Henry's problematic response, its antecedent condition, and its negative consequences.
When someone comes over to talk to Henry or ask a question, he mutters and speaks in a low voice so that the person has difficulty understanding what he is saying. The person typically stops talking and walks away from Henry soon after he begins to mutter.
Answers:
Henry's problematic response(s): Henry mutters and speaks in a low voice.
Antecedent: Someone starts talking to Henry or asks him a question.
Negative consequences: The person stops talking and walks away.

(2) 4. State two criteria that can be used in establishing problem priorities for treatment.

Answers: The following four criteria can be used in establishing problem priorities for treatment:

1. the problem that is the most immediate expressed concern of the client or significant others,
2. the problem that has extensive negative consequences for the client, significant others, or society if not handled immediately,
3. the problem that can be corrected most quickly, considering resources and obstacles, and
4. the problem that requires handling before other problems can be treated.

Criterion score: 10.

CHAPTER 9

(1) 1. Which of the following statements best describes the objective(s) of behavioral assessment? (Circle the correct answer.)

a. Reconstruct an individual's personality.
b. Help a person learn to accept himself.
c. Specify appropriate behaviors.
(d.) Identify target behaviors and their controlling environmental conditions, and formulate behavioral change goals.

(3) 2. Using the information from Vignette 2, state (a) two of Stephen's problematic responses, (b) the probable positive reinforcer that maintained them, and (c) the antecedent to the problematic response.

Answers:

a. Undesirable responses: Stephen beat Dianne; Stephen broke Dianne's toys.
b. Probable reinforcer: Mrs. D's attention; that is, she spent most of her time trying to discipline Stephen.
c. Antecedent: Dianne teased, made faces at Stephen.

(1) 3. In order to determine relevant antecedents to the problematic behavior, an appropriate question to ask a client is (Circle a or b):

(a.) Where does this problem occur?
b. Why do you continue to engage in this behavior if you don't like yourself afterwards?

(3) 4. Using the information from Vignette 8, state an intermediate treatment goal for Mr. L. specifying (a) a desired response and (b) a relevant antecedent.

Criteria for correct answers: Your answers must indicate that Mr. L. makes an alternative response in the presence of an antecedent condition that previously served as an S^D for non-assertive behaviors.
Sample answers:
Treatment goal: Mr. L. makes a legitimate request of his boss.
Desired response: Mr. L. looks directly at his boss and makes the request.
Relevant antecedent: Mr. L. is seated across the desk from his boss.

Criterion score: 7.

CHAPTER 10

(2) 1. Which is usually more effective, a simple conditioned reinforcer or a generalized conditioned reinforcer? Support your answer.
Answer: Generalized conditioned reinforcers are more effective than simple conditioned reinforcers because they are associated with a wide variety of reinforcers, while simple conditioned reinforcers are associated with just one reinforcer. (Generalized conditioned reinforcers are less susceptible to the effects of satiation. If an individual is satiated with regard to one reinforcer, there are usually other reinforcers of which he is sufficiently deprived to ensure the effectiveness of the generalized conditioned reinforcer.)

(1) 2. What is the difference between an unconditioned reinforcer and a conditioned reinforcer?
Answer: An unconditioned reinforcer is one that increases response strength without prior association with other reinforcers. A conditioned reinforcer is a neutral or nonreinforcing stimulus that becomes a reinforcer through association with a reinforcing stimulus.

(4) 3. Give two examples of generalized conditioned reinforcers and two examples of unconditioned reinforcers.
Answers: Examples of generalized conditioned reinforcers include praise ("That was very good."), money, affection (kisses, hugs, "I love you."), tokens. Examples of unconditioned reinforcers include food, water, sex, warmth, tactile stimulation.

(1) 4. True or False. In order for a neutral stimulus to function as a conditioned reinforcer, it must also serve as a discriminative stimulus.
Answer: True.

(3) 5. Label the components of one unit of a stimulus-response chain.
Answer: The components of one unit of a stimulus-response chain include a discriminative stimulus (S^D), a response (R), and a conditioned

reinforcer (S^{r+}) that also serves as the S^D for the following response in the chain.

Criterion score: 10.

CHAPTER 11

(2) 1. How can discriminative stimuli (S^Ds) and positive reinforcers be involved in a modeling procedure? Use a paradigm to illustrate your answer.

Answer: A model demonstrates a specific behavior that serves as the modeled stimulus (discriminative stimulus) that sets the occasion for performance of an imitative response to be followed by a positive reinforcer.

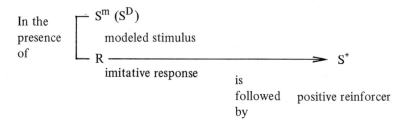

In the presence of

S^m (S^D)
modeled stimulus

R ⟶ S^+
imitative response

is followed by   positive reinforcer

(3) 2. Indicate True (T) or False (F) beside each of the following statements:

a. ___F___ If an individual does not perform a response after he has observed someone else perform it, he has not learned it.

b. ___T___ It is more difficult to teach a song to a child who has no imitative skills than to a child who imitates excessively.

c. ___F___ Imitative behavior cannot be conditioned through reinforcement when the client has no imitative skills as, for example, a severely retarded child.

(3) 3. Using the information from Vignette 1, how could modeling and reinforcement have been used to help Mr. P. obtain a new job?

Answer: Group members could model appropriate job interview behaviors which Mr. P. observes. He then imitates their appropriate behaviors. The therapist and group members praise Mr. P. when he appropriately imitates desired behaviors.

Criterion score: 7.

CHAPTER 12

(2) 1. Name two types of punishment procedures that can be used to suppress a response.
Answers:
1. Response-contingent presentation of a punishing stimulus.
2. Response-contingent removal of a positive reinforcer.

(1) 2. Briefly describe a time-out procedure.
Answer: A time-out procedure consists of removing an individual from a reinforcing situation immediately after inappropriate behavior occurs and placing him in an environment with minimal availability of reinforcement.

(2) 3. Briefly describe two disadvantages of punishment procedures.
Answers: Any two of the following are acceptable:
1. The punished response is likely to reappear in the absence of the punisher.
2. Aggression against the punisher.
3. Aggression toward someone or something that is in no way related to the delivery of the punishment.
4. Punishment could also suppress appropriate behavior occurring immediately prior to its delivery.
5. The person administering the punishment can become a conditioned aversive stimulus through association with the punisher.
6. The punishing stimulus can serve as an S^D for responses that are positively reinforced.

(4) 4. Mrs. Kelly asks Sharon to fold the laundry after it has been washed and dried. When Mrs. Kelly returns, Sharon is talking to her friend on the phone and the laundry has not been folded. What should Mrs. Kelly do to demonstrate her knowledge of the necessary conditions to maximize the effectiveness of punishment?
Criteria for correct answer: Your answer must include the following points: (1) delivery of a punisher immediately after the inappropriate response occurs; (2) a punisher of sufficient intensity to suppress the inappropriate response; (3) specification of appropriate responses; and (4) positive reinforcement for appropriate responses.
Sample answer: Mrs. Kelly tells Sharon to get off the phone and immediately punishes her by telling her that she cannot visit her friends that afternoon. Mrs. Kelly then tells Sharon to fold the laundry and praises her for making the appropriate responses.

Criterion score: 8.

CHAPTER 13

(1) 1. What is a major advantage of avoidance conditioning in maintaining a conditioned response?
Answer: A response that is conditioned through an avoidance procedure is highly resistant to extinction.

(3) 2. Give an example of a procedure that results in escape behavior.
Criteria for correct answer: Your answer must include (1) a negative reinforcer that remains in effect until (2) a response is made that (3) terminates or reduces the effect of that stimulus (negative reinforcer).
Sample answer: When Jane dialed Ann's telephone number and got a busy signal, she hung up.

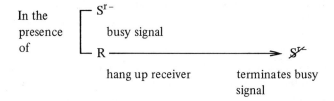

(4) 3. Give an example of a procedure that results in avoidance behavior.
Criteria for correct answer: Your answer must include (1) a conditioned negative reinforcer that is presented as a cue for (2) a response made in its presence that (3) terminates the conditioned negative reinforcer and (4) avoids or prevents the occurrence of another negative reinforcer.
Sample answer: Father tells Jimmy that he will spank him unless he tells him where he got the candy. Jimmy then tells him that Bob gave it to him.

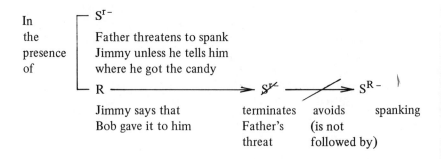

(2) 4. Give an example of an unconditioned negative reinforcer and one of a conditioned negative reinforcer.

Answers:

1. Unconditioned negative reinforcers: shock, physical blows (e.g., hitting, kicking, pinching), intense light, noise, or temperatures. The stimulus does not require prior pairing or association with another stimulus.

2. Conditioned negative reinforcers: threats, fines, demerits, failing grades, harsh or demeaning words, such as "idiot." The stimulus requires pairing or association with another stimulus before it can act as a negative reinforcer.

Criterion score: 9.

CHAPTER 14

(1) 1. Describe a procedure for extinguishing a classically conditioned response.

Answer: Present the conditioned stimulus repeatedly without presenting the unconditioned stimulus until the conditioned stimulus no longer elicits the conditioned response.

(8) 2. Given the following information, specify operant and respondent behaviors: A man gets in his car and drives home. As he walks in the door, the aroma of dinner cooking makes his mouth water. He runs to the kitchen, panting, kisses his wife and sits down at the table.

Answers: Operants: gets in his car; drives home; walks in; runs to the kitchen; kisses his wife; sits down.

Respondents: mouth waters; panting.

(1) 3. Explain the persistence of emotional respondent behavior in the absence of identifiable reinforcing consequences for the individual.

Answer: Respondent behavior is not controlled by its consequences as is operant behavior. It is controlled by antecedents and, therefore, persists regardless of consequences, as long as the conditioned stimulus is occasionally paired with the unconditioned stimulus.

(1) 4. How can a phobia be eliminated?

Answer: By pairing relaxation stimuli with the conditioned stimuli that elicit fear until the relaxation stimuli are capable of eliciting physiological responses incompatible with fear (systematic desensitization).

Criterion score: 10.

CHAPTER 15

(2) 1. You are treating an alcoholic client. As part of the treatment program to decrease his drinking, you suggest several nondrinking behaviors appropriate in the social situations where he usually drinks. These behaviors are new to him, but he agrees to try them out. What is the most likely obstacle to success for this part of therapy?

Answer: Since he has not yet performed these alternative behaviors in the actual drinking situations, there may be few occasions when these behaviors are reinforced under those conditions. The behaviors are, therefore, likely to extinguish.

What can you do to counteract this effect or to plan for this problem?

Answer: You can use behavioral rehearsal and reinforce alternative behaviors to maximize successful generalization from the treatment situation to the problematic social situations. Behavioral assignments, beginning with simple ones, can also be used to introduce these alternative behaviors gradually into the client's actual problematic situations.

(1) 2. Using the information from Vignette 1, describe how behavioral rehearsal was used with Mr. P. to facilitate generalization of appropriate responses to criticism.

Answer: The therapist and group instructed Mr. P. in making appropriate responses in situations in which he was criticized. Mr. P. role-played situations where he received criticism from his employer and his wife, demonstrating appropriate behaviors. He was praised by the therapist and group members for performing appropriately in these role-plays.

(1) 3. Behavioral assignments are given [circle the correct answer(s)]:
   a. to structure the client's activities between therapy sessions.
   b. to help the client apply in his natural environment what he has learned in treatment.
   c. so the client can receive feedback from the therapist based on a specific task he has attempted to accomplish.
   d. all of the above.

(1) 4. True or False: It is usually more difficult for a desirable behavior to generalize beyond the treatment situation when more than one therapist is involved in conditioning it.

Answer: False.

Criterion score: 5.

CHAPTER 16

(2) 1. Name two behavioral techniques that can be used to decrease the strength of a problematic behavior.

Answer: The following behavioral techniques can be used to decrease the strength of behavior: punishment and extinction.

(1) 2. State the main purpose of a treatment contract.

Answer: The main purpose of a treatment contract is to formalize the commitment of the client and therapist to treatment and to specify the behaviors each will perform to achieve the client's treatment goals.

(1) 3. Identify the next step you would take if a client's treatment goal has not been achieved after a selected behavioral technique has been applied.

Answer: If the client's treatment goal has not been achieved, you must reassess the client's problematic situation. (If the original assessment is accurate, try another intervention technique.)

(2) 4. State two behavioral techniques involved in an assertive training procedure.

Answers: Assertive training involves modeling, positive reinforcement, and differential reinforcement.

Criterion score: 5.

appendix 6 chapter post-test answers

CHAPTER 1

(10) **1-A.** Indicate with a (+) which of the following statements are written in behaviorally specific terms, and with a (−) statements which are vague and require further specification.

Criteria for correct answers: Responses describe what the person *says* or *does* in *positively stated, observable* terms. Responses stated negatively are incorrect. Sample answers follow those statements that required further specification.

Answers: Statements a and f are correct as written; statements b, c, d, and e require further specification.

1-B. After completing 1-A above, rewrite in specific terms only those statements in which the responses are not described behaviorally.

+ a. Eddy took two cans of beer from the refrigerator.

− b. Johnny expressed his feelings of inadequacy at the ball game.
Sample answer: After striking out, Johnny threw down his bat and ran home.

− c. Norman showed hostile feelings toward his probation officer this week.
Sample answer: Every time Norman's probation officer asked him a question about school, Norman said, "Mind your own business."

− d. Mr. Smith asserted his authority over use of the car.
Sample answer: Mr. Smith kept both sets of keys to the car in his pocket.

− e. He thinks of his girlfriend often.
Sample answer: He writes letters to his girlfriend daily.

+ f. Susan placed dirty dishes in the sink.

(1) 2.   In Vignette 7, Harold is described as having a "negative attitude toward learning." Specify a behavior that might have led the counselor to describe him in that way.

Criterion for correct answer: Your answer must state an observable behavior emitted by Harold.

Sample answers:

1. Harold turns in incomplete assignments or blank sheets of paper.
2. Harold throws paper airplanes at other students.

(1) 3.   Rewrite the following statement so that it includes a frequency per time unit measure of response strength: Emily read the story to her brother.

Criterion for correct answer: Your answer must state the number of times Emily read the story to her brother within a specified time period.

Sample answers:

1. Emily read the story to her brother four times this week.
2. Emily read the story to her brother twice this morning.
3. Emily read the story to her brother once in the past hour.

The total point value of this test is 12. Score one point for each correctly identified statement in question 1-A, one point for each correctly rewritten statement in question 1-B, one point for a correct answer to question 2, and one point for a correct answer to question 3.

Criterion score for this test is 11. If your score is at least 11, you have mastered this chapter and should go on to Chapter 2. If you score less than 11, refer back to the teaching unit to answer the questions correctly.

CHAPTER 2

(2) 1.   Describe the positive reinforcement procedure and its effect on the strength of a response.

Answer: The presentation of an object or event following a behavior (procedure) that increases the strength of that behavior (effect).

(2) 2.   Give one example of an object or event that you think acts as a positive reinforcer for yourself. State your proof.

Criteria for correct answer: Any object or event is correct provided that evidence is given that the immediately preceding behavior increased in strength after presentation of the stimulus.

Sample answer: You go to a new service station to buy gasoline and when you pay for the gas, you get trading stamps (positive reinforcer), not given at other service stations. You now go only to the new gasoline station twice a week to fill up with gas.

(3) 3. From Vignette 7, draw a paradigm showing how positive reinforcement could be used to increase the frequency of Harold's completing his class assignments, labeling the appropriate components. What evidence could be used to evaluate the effectiveness of this procedure?

Criteria for correct answer: The positive reinforcement paradigm should be given, labeling the specific reinforcer. Evidence for the effectiveness of the procedure must show that the rate of the response increased over its baseline rate.

Sample answer:

$$R \longrightarrow S^+$$

Harold shows	is followed	Harold receives
his Mother	by	television privileges
one completed		for the evening
assignment		

The reinforcer of watching television is effective if the rate of Harold's completing his assignments increases over the baseline rate.

(4) 4. Rewrite the following statements, specifying the target behavior and indicating a baseline measure.

Criteria for correct answers: Responses must be specified in positively stated, observable terms along with a measure of response strength.

a. Hank is always annoying his brother.

Sample answer: Three times last week, Hank read the newspaper aloud while his brother practiced the violin.

Target response: reading the newspaper aloud.

Baseline measure: three times last week.

b. Mary was often depressed.

Sample answer: Mary sat alone in her room four nights this week.

Target response: sitting alone.

Baseline measure: four nights this week.

(2) 5. Correct these statements so that the effectiveness of the candy bar and the movies as positive reinforcers can be maximized.

Criteria for correct answers: The candy bar and the movies must follow the desired responses (walking the dog and washing the car) immediately.

a. Mrs. Jones gave Edward a candy bar and told him to take the dog for a walk.

Sample answer: As soon as Edward returned from walking the dog, Mrs. Jones gave him a candy bar.

b. Harvey washed his father's car and his father took him to the movies three weeks later.
Sample answer: Harvey washed his father's car and his father took him to the movies immediately after he finished.

(1) 6. Describe how baseline data can be used in determining if going shopping immediately after doing housework served as a positive reinforcer for Lillian's doing housework.
Answer: The baseline rate of Lillian's doing housework without going shopping can be compared with the rate of her doing housework when going shopping immediately after. If going shopping is a positive reinforcer, Lillian will do housework more frequently than during the baseline period, when housework is not followed by going shopping.

The total point value of this test is 14. The point distribution is indicated next to each question.

Criterion score: 13.

CHAPTER 3

(3) 1. Describe the procedure for extinguishing a response by giving an example in which you specify a response and its reinforcer.
Criteria for correct answer:
An observable response and a specific reinforcer must be stated. Your answer must state that this reinforcer is withheld each time the response is emitted.
Sample answer:
Response: client stares at the ceiling while talking to you.
Positive reinforcer: attention in the form of talking to him, conversing with him.
Extinction procedure: Each time the client stares at the ceiling while talking to you, you withhold your response of talking with him.

(4) 2. After observing a mother's response to her son's crying, what would you do to determine whether or not the child's crying was conditioned by his mother?
Answer:
1. Determine the rate of the child's crying.
2. Tell the mother to continuously withhold her response to her son's crying.

3. If the child's crying decreases (even after an initial increase), it is likely that the mother conditioned the crying. If the child's crying remains the same over a number of extinction sessions, it is unlikely that the mother conditioned her son's crying.
4. Tell the mother to reinstate her response to her son's crying. If the crying increases (after having decreased), the mother conditioned the son's crying.

(1)   3. Describe the effects of extinction on the rate of a target response.
Answer: There is usually an initial increase or burst in the rate of responding and then a gradual decrease until the rate of the target response is at the preconditioning or operant level.

(2)   4. Using the information from Vignette 3, indicate how positive reinforcement played a part in the following:
(a) In conditioning an undesired behavior.
Answer: Mother provided positive reinforcement—promises to buy new clothes and puts the toys away—for Carla's undesired behavior of screaming when told to put her toys away.
(b) In conditioning desired behavior.
Answer: Mother provided positive reinforcement—praise and concrete rewards—for Carla's desired behavior of putting her toys away.

(1)   5. In what way is spontaneous recovery considered in a treatment plan?
Answer: The behavior modifier can anticipate the possible recurrence of the target response at a later date when the client is in a situation that is similar to the one in which the target response was conditioned. With this foreknowledge, the behavior modifier, client, and/or significant others can arrange for reinforcement to be consistently withheld, should the target behavior recur.

The total point value of this test is 11. The point distribution is indicated next to each question.

Criterion score: 10.

CHAPTER 4

(2)   1. State a positive reinforcement contingency related to Vignette 7 that you might use with Harold in relation to completing his class assignments.
Criteria for correct answer: A specified amount of school work to be completed in order for Harold to receive a specified positive reinforcer must be stated. The response and reinforcer must be stated in positive terms.

Sample answer: You might tell Harold, "If you complete one of your assignments, I will give you 50¢ of your allowance."

(2) 2. As described in this chapter, self-control of contingencies is more desirable than accidental contingencies. What is the difference between an accidental contingency and self-controlled reinforcement?
Answer: In self-controlled reinforcement, an individual arranges conditions so that his response is predictably followed by reinforcement; that is, the response produces, or is functionally related to, the reinforcement. In an accidental contingency, an individual makes a response that is associated with a reinforcer on one occasion, but the response has no effect on the availability of that reinforcer on subsequent occasions.

(1) 3. When is it more appropriate to use a continuous reinforcement schedule rather than an intermittent reinforcement schedule?
Answer: During conditioning of the response, that is, when it occurs with low frequency.

(1) 4. What evidence indicates that intermittent reinforcement makes a response more resistant to extinction than continuous reinforcement?
Answer: If a response is maintained on an intermittent schedule, an individual will emit a greater number of responses during extinction of that conditioned response than if the response had been maintained on a continuous schedule of reinforcement.

(2) 5. State two advantages of using an intermittent reinforcement schedule rather than a continuous reinforcement schedule.
Answers:
  1. Intermittent reinforcement requires fewer reinforcements to maintain the behavior at a regular frequency and pattern after it has been conditioned.
  2. An intermittent schedule makes the response more resistant to extinction.
  3. Intermittent reinforcement more closely approximates reinforcement schedules that maintain behavior in the natural environment.

(3) 6. Define the Premack Principle and give an example of its use and effect.
Answers: The Premack Principle states that any behavior that occurs more frequently than another behavior can serve as a reinforcer for the behavior that occurs less frequently.
Criteria for correct example: Your example must specify two behaviors, one occurring with greater frequency than the other. The relationship between the two is that the higher-frequency behavior is made contingent on the performance of the lower-frequency behavior. The effect is an increase in the frequency of the less frequently occurring behavior.

Sample answer:
Betty frequently invites her friends over for coffee during the day but rarely gives her children breakfast. She can increase the frequency of giving her children breakfast if inviting her friends in is made contingent upon making breakfast for the children. The effects of using the Premack Principle should indicate an increase in the frequency of giving the children breakfast.

Criterion score: 10.

CHAPTER 5

(1) 1. Give an example of "straining the ratio."
Criterion for correct answer: Your example must show that a response has extinguished because the number of responses required for reinforcement was increased too rapidly.
Sample answer: A teacher established a positive reinforcement contingency for a child who scribbled on his math work sheets instead of solving the problems. On the first day of the procedure, she gave the child a gold star immediately after each math problem that he completed. The child earned twelve gold stars. The second day of this procedure, she required that he complete ten math problems in order to receive one gold star. On that day, the child completed three problems and scribbled on the rest of the work sheet.

(3) 2. Using the information from Vignette 4, how could you schedule reinforcement to maintain Mr. C.'s increased vocalizations after session ten?
Criteria for correct answer: Your answer must include the following three points:
1. A gradual shift from a continuous reinforcement schedule (CRF) to a small fixed-ratio schedule, FR 2, for example.
2. FR 2 shifted progressively to larger FR schedules, such as FR 3, FR 4, FR 6, FR 8 ... .
3. A gradual shift from FR to VR schedules (VR 4, VR 7, VR 10 ...) to better approximate the natural environment.

(7) 3. Match the various schedules in Column A with their characteristics from Column B. (Items from Column B can be used 0, 1 or more times in Column A and each schedule in Column A can have 1 or more characteristics from Column B.)

Column A	*Column B*

Column A
Fixed-Interval ___1, 6___

Variable-Interval ___3___

Fixed-Ratio ___2, 5___

Variable-Ratio ___4, 5___

Column B
1. Initial low rate of responding, terminal high rate of responding.
2. Post-reinforcement pause.
3. Consistent, moderate rate of responding; no post-reinforcement pause.
4. Characteristic slot machine schedule.
5. Very high response rate with minimal hesitation between responses.
6. Scallop.
7. Initial burst of responding, tapering off to low rate of responding.

Criterion score: 10.

CHAPTER 6

(3) 1. Define an operant and give an example of one, describing two of its members.
Criterion for correct example: Members of the operant specified must have the same or similar effect on the environment.
Sample answer:
Operant: Cooking responses a woman can make to receive praise from her husband.
Member: She prepares a special gourmet salad.
Member: She makes his favorite coconut cream pie.

(6) 2. The steps involved in shaping a behavior are indicated below. Fill in the specific responses and/or reinforcers related to each step, using your own example of shaping a motor (nonverbal) behavior.

Fill in with examples

a. Specify terminal response.

    a. An autistic child throws a ball.

b. Specify reinforcer(s).

    b. raisins and praise ("Good boy")

c. Specify initial and intermed-

    c. movement toward the ball

iate responses directed toward achieving terminal response.

d. Differentially reinforce initial response until it occurs consistently.

e. Shift criteria for reinforcement to next intermediate response.

f. Continue this procedure of differential reinforcement and shifting criteria for reinforcement until the terminal behavior is achieved.

with any part of the body; touching the ball with the hands; holding the ball in the hands; moving the ball around in the air.

d. Any movement toward the ball with any part of the body was reinforced until it occurred consistently.

e. Reinforcement was given only when the child was touching the ball with his hands.

f. When the child was consistently touching the ball with his hands, the criterion for reinforcement was shifted and given only when the child was holding the ball in his hands. Reinforcement was then given only for moving the ball around in the air.

(2) 3. Describe how a DRO schedule can be used to decrease the frequency of a client's bragging about his sexual prowess.

Answer: Reinforcement would be given only when the client was doing something *other* than bragging about his sexual prowess. The therapist turns away from him and withholds verbal replies when the client talks about his sexual prowess. In contrast, the therapist looks directly at the client and responds verbally as soon as he talks about other topics. Thus, bragging about sexual exploits is subjected to extinction while other appropriate topics are positively reinforced.

(3) 4. Give an example of response differentiation, specifying an operant, the differentiated response, and the reinforcer.

Criteria for correct answer: Your answer must include (1) a class of responses whose members can be reinforced; (2) a specific response in that class that has been selectively reinforced over the others and occurs with greater strength; (3) the specific reinforcer involved.

Sample answer: When Joe speaks to his father about his problems, Joe's father rarely answers him. When Joe starts talking about running away from home, however, his father pays attention; that is, he questions Joe and warns him not to run away.

Operant: Verbal responses Joe can make to get a verbal response from his father.

Differentiated response: Joe talks more frequently about running away from home.

Reinforcer: Father's verbal responses (attention).

(2) 5. Using the information from Vignette 4, describe how the psychologist could use a DRO schedule to determine if the M & M's and points served as reinforcers for Mr. C.'s increased vocalizations, rather than the reinforcers being primarily the attention he received in the experimental situation.

Answer: The psychologist could employ a DRO schedule in which Mr. C. is given M & M's and points for any behavior *other than* vocalizing. If Mr. C.'s vocalizations decreased when these reinforcers were presented non-contingently, then the M & M's and points had acted as effective reinforcers for Mr. C.'s vocalizations. (The psychologist could further demonstrate the effectiveness of the M & M's and points by reconditioning Mr. C.'s vocalizations using these reinforcers.)

Criterion score: 14

CHAPTER 7

(3) 1 Using the information from Vignette 5, (1) describe the discrimination training procedure that was employed. (2) How were reinforcement and extinction involved in this discrimination training? (3) Describe the effects of this procedure.

Answers: (1) In Vignette 5, the counselor employed a discrimination training procedure with Mrs. M. whereby List A topics functioned as S^Ds and List B topics were S^Δs. (2) List A topics were reinforced by praise from the counselor. Talking about topics on List B was ignored and placed on an extinction schedule. (3) The response rate of List A topics increased and the response rate of List B topics decreased.

(3) 2. Jim, a retarded teenager, does not discriminate the Men's restroom sign from the Ladies' sign; that is, he sometimes walks into the Ladies' restroom, sometimes into the Men's. Give an example of an errorless discrimination training procedure you could use to teach Jim the appropriate discrimination.

Criteria for correct answer: Your answer must include (1) identification of the two stimuli, Men's restroom sign (S^D) and Ladies' restroom sign (S^Δ); (2) specification of the stimulus dimension to be varied gradually or faded; (3) reinforcement for correct responding.

Sample answer: Jim has been taught to discriminate large letters from small letters; that is, when shown two words, one written in small letters and one written in large letters, he chooses the word written in large letters. The therapist shows Jim two signs, the Men's restroom sign written in very large letters (S^D) and the Ladies' restroom sign written in small letters (S^Δ). When Jim chooses the Men's sign, the therapist praises him and gives him a nickel. The size of the letters of the Men's restroom sign is gradually decreased until they are the same size as the letters on the Ladies' sign. Jim continues to choose the Men's sign, however.

(5) 3. Describe a procedure for establishing a discrimination (nonerrorless). In your example, include one S^D, one S^Δ, and one response. How would you know when stimulus control had been achieved?

Criteria for correct answer: Your answer must specify one response, one S^D, and one S^Δ. The procedure consists of reinforcing the response in the presence of the S^D and allowing the response to occur initially in the presence of the S^Δ while withholding reinforcement. Stimulus control is achieved when the proper response is emitted only in the presence of the S^D and not in the presence of the S^Δ and when the latency between the S^D and the response is short.

Sample answer: Teaching a small child to call his father "Daddy" and not to call his uncle "Daddy." The father is the S^D for the child's saying "Daddy," a response that leads to reinforcement such as Father saying "Good" or hugging the child. The uncle is an S^Δ for the child saying "Daddy." Reinforcement is withheld when the child says "Daddy" upon seeing the uncle. When the child called his father (S^D) "Daddy" immediately upon seeing him, and did not call his uncle (S^Δ) "Daddy," stimulus control had been achieved.

(3) 4. Give an example of a stimulus generalization gradient that can be observed in an individual's behavior. What identifies this as a generalization gradient?

Criteria for correct answer: Your example must include a training S^D, a reinforcer, and at least two other stimuli. The individual's response rate is highest in the presence of the training S^D and occurs with decreasing frequency as the S^Ds become less similar to the training stimulus; this identifies it as a generalization *gradient*.

Sample answer: A teenage girl uses swear words when with one particular girlfriend who laughs in approval. The girlfriend is the S^D (training stimulus) for swearing. Her laughter is the reinforcement. The girl uses swear words most frequently with this girlfriend, slightly less frequently with other girlfriends, less frequently with boys her age, and with decreasing frequency with older boys and girls, parents and teachers.

Criterion score: 13.

CHAPTER 8

(4) 1. Give two examples of individuals with behavioral deficits and two examples of individuals with behavioral excesses.

Criteria for correct answers: Behavioral deficits refer to the absence or low frequency of appropriate behaviors. Behavioral excesses refer to high-frequency inappropriate behaviors.

Sample answers:

Behavioral deficits:

1. When someone compliments Joy, she puts her head down and remains silent.
2. A ten-year old retarded child only speaks three words.

Behavioral excesses:

1. Bill throws rocks at other children.
2. Carol runs away when she is introduced to strangers.

(4) 2. If a client tells you that her boyfriend is always late for their dates,

    a. Which of the two following questions would you ask her in order to obtain baseline measures of her complaint? (Circle the correct answers.)

       1. Why do you think he's always late?

       ②. How many minutes late is he?

       ③. How many times has he been late this month?

       4. What do you think his lateness means?

    b. Give two hypothetical answers to the questions you chose above that would provide assessment data indicating a baseline measure of the undesired behavior.

Criterion for correct answers: Your answers must provide specific data as to the frequency and/or duration of the problematic behavior.

Sample answers: He is 15 minutes late.

He has been late ten times this month.

(3) 3. From the information given in the following paragraph, identify Shirley's problematic response, its antecedent, and its negative consequences.

Shirley's boss frequently asks her to work late. Last week, he made four such requests. When her boss makes these requests, Shirley holds her head down and says, "O.K." She had unpleasant arguments with her husband twice over her working late, and on another night they arrived late to a play.

Answers: Shirley's problematic response(s): She holds her head down, says, "O.K."

Antecedent: Shirley's boss asks her to work late.

Negative consequences: Shirley had unpleasant arguments with her husband; they were late in arriving to a play.

(3) 4. From the information given in the paragraph below, identify the problematic response, its antecedent, and the probable positive reinforcers.

Children are playing ball in a group; Howard is sitting by himself. When Howard tells jokes about himself, the other children gather around and laugh at him. The social worker observes that the other children rarely speak to Howard unless he is making fun of himself.

Answers:

Problematic response: Howard tells jokes about himself.

Antecedent: Howard is sitting by himself while other children are playing ball.

Probable reinforcers: Children gather around and laugh at him.

Criterion score: 13.

CHAPTER 9

(4) 1. Using the information from Vignette 8, state four of Mr. L.'s problematic behaviors.

Answers: Mr. L. (1) mumbled, (2) looked down at the floor, (3) held his hand in front of his mouth, (4) spoke in a monotone, (5) drifted from one topic to another without waiting for a response, (6) talked only about his job on dates.

(1) 2. Specify one antecedent related to Mr. L.'s conversation with his employer.

Answer:

1. Mr. L. is seated across the desk from his boss.

2. Boss asks Mr. L. what he wants.

(2) 3. State two negative consequences of Mr. L.'s non-assertive behavior.

Answers: The negative consequences of Mr. L.'s non-assertive behaviors are:

1. Mr. L. does not have satisfying relationships with women; that is,

second dates are refused, a girl fell asleep while he was talking to her.
2. Mr. L. does not get his raise and promotion, remains in same position at same salary.

(1) 4. Using the information from Vignette 7, state a probable reinforcer maintaining Harold's drug taking.
Answer: Probable reinforcers maintaining Harold's drug taking include:
1. Harold listens to records with his friends.
2. He spends time with his girlfriend.
3. He avoids doing his homework.
4. He delays the nagging of his parents.

(3) 5. State an intermediate treatment goal for Mr. L. specifying (1) a desired response, (2) a relevant antecedent, and (3) a potential positive reinforcer.
Criteria for correct answers: Your answers must indicate that Mr. L. makes an alternative response in the presence of an antecedent that previously served as an S^D for non-assertive behaviors. A potential reinforcer must be delivered after performance of the desired response.
Sample answers:
Desired response: Mr. L. speaks in a pleasant tone of voice about a mutually interesting topic, such as a recent movie both he and the woman saw.
Relevant antecedent: having coffee at a restaurant with a woman.
Potential reinforcer: The woman responds favorably to Mr. L.; smiles at him.

Desired response: Mr. L. looks directly at his boss, speaks in a pleasant tone of voice, and clearly states his request or business.
Relevant antecedent: sitting across the desk from his boss.
Potential reinforcer: Boss agrees to Mr. L.'s stated request or business.

Criterion score: 10.

CHAPTER 10

(2) 1. An institutionalized mental patient, Mr. C., was given money during a verbal conditioning study. He dropped one coin on the floor and left the rest of the coins he had earned on the table. The psychologist concluded that money did not function as a generalized conditioned reinforcer for Mr. C. in the way that it does for most adults in our society. What could the psychologist do to establish the reinforcing value of money for Mr. C.?

Criteria for correct answer: Your answer must describe a procedure in which the psychologist pairs money with the delivery of known reinforcers so that the money serves as the discriminative stimulus (S^D) for the response of Mr. C.'s selecting an object to exchange for the coin. *Sample answer:* The psychologist shows Mr. C. a variety of items including cigarettes, candy, and cookies that are placed on a table. He gives Mr. C. a coin and tells him that he can exchange the money for any item that he points to. After Mr. C. selects the item he wishes, the psychologist asks Mr. C. to hand him the coin. The psychologist gives Mr. C. the item as soon as Mr. C. gives him the coin. The psychologist repeats this procedure several times and continues it during subsequent sessions.

(4) 2. You are a social worker involved in a community setting, and adolescents who have had one or two contacts with the police and juvenile authorities are referred to you. You station yourself in the low socio-economic neighborhood where these youths live because you plan to engage a group of them in activities that will help them stay out of trouble with the law, improve their academic performances, interview for and successfully hold jobs, and solve various interpersonal and family difficulties. Give two examples that indicate what you could do to establish yourself as a generalized conditioned reinforcer for these clients.

Criteria for correct answer: Your answer should include two examples that show the worker's arrangement of treatment conditions so that he is associated (as an S^D) with the delivery of a variety of unconditioned and conditioned positive reinforcers given on a non-contingent basis.

Sample answer: The worker could invite the youths to a meeting and provide a variety of refreshments such as soft drinks, cookies, and candy. These items are given non-contingently; that is, no specific behaviors are required of the clients to consume them. The worker could also take them for rides in the agency vehicle and to activities such as bowling. As these items and events appear reinforcing to the clients, they also become paired or associated with the worker who is the S^D for availability of the reinforcers. The worker thus begins to acquire reinforcing value for the clients.

(1) 3. In Vignette 4, the red light served as an S^D for Mr. C.'s vocalizations. It was paired with candy and praise from the psychologist. How could the psychologist determine whether the red light had become a conditioned reinforcer?

Answer: If presentation of the red light after a different response of Mr. C.'s increased the strength of that response, it would be a conditioned reinforcer. Or, the psychologist could withhold the other reinforcers, that is, candy, points, and praise, until the response strength of Mr. C.'s vocalizations decreased. Then the psychologist would present the red light immediately after a vocalization. If the response strength of the vocalizations increased, the red light would be a conditioned reinforcer.

(2) 4. State two advantages of using conditioned reinforcement over using primary reinforcement in maintaining behavioral change in a client's natural environment.

Answers:

1. An individual is less likely to satiate on a conditioned reinforcer.
2. Conditioned reinforcers are more abundantly available than primary reinforcers for desirable behavior in the natural environment. Generalization of desired behavior is, therefore, more likely to occur the more similar the reinforcers in the treatment environment are to reinforcers in the client's natural environment.

(4) 5. Give an example of a problem that can be analyzed as a stimulus-response chain. Include at least two stimulus-response units and label the appropriate components.

Criteria for correct answer: Your answer must include a series of behaviors linked by conditioned reinforcers that also serve as S^Ds for the following responses, and a terminal reinforcer that maintains the chain.

Sample answer: At parties, Joe is always either drinking or getting himself a drink. Some behaviors in this chain are shown in the following diagram:

S^D
party; sight of
people with drinks

R ⟶ S^{r+} · S^D

Joe goes to bar   sight of
liquor

R ⟶ S^{r+} · S^D

Joe pours   drink in
drink   hand

R ⟶ S^{R+}; S^{r+} · S^D

Joe   alcohol in   empty
drinks   mouth   glass

R ─────────▶

Joe goes to
bar . . .
the sequence
repeats

S^D = discriminative stimulus

$S^{r+} \cdot S^D$ = conditioned positive reinforcer that also serves as the discriminative stimulus for the following response

R = response

S^{R+} = primary positive reinforcer

Criterion score: 12.

CHAPTER 11

(3) 1. Give an example that describes how a modeling plus reinforcement procedure is used to develop and strengthen imitative behavior.

Criteria for correct answer: Your answer must include the following points: (1) a model who demonstrates appropriate behavior for the client (modeled stimulus), (2) a client who imitates the modeled stimulus, and (3) a reinforcer delivered after the client's appropriate imitation.

Sample answer: In Vignette 1, Mr. P. observed group members role-playing him and modeling appropriate behaviors in criticism situations. These models provided appropriate responses that served as S^ms (modeled stimuli) for Mr. P. to imitate. When Mr. P. imitated these appropriate behaviors in role-plays, he received positive reinforcement in the form of praise from the group members and therapist.

(3) 2. Give an example of the use of modeling in developing assertive behaviors in a group.

Criteria for correct answer: Your answer must include. (1) specification of problematic behaviors, (2) the use of a group member as a model who demonstrates appropriate responses, (3) imitation of the modeled stimulus by the client, and (4) a reinforcer delivered by group members after appropriate imitation.

Sample answer: Neil has difficulty asking girls to go out with him. He typically makes statements such as, "You wouldn't like to go to the movies Saturday night, would you?"; "I have two tickets to a play, if you wouldn't mind going." Neil speaks in a pleading, whining voice. These inappropriate responses were observed by group members during behavioral re-enactment of problematic situations. The therapist asked Jim, a group member, to model appropriate responses for Neil. Neil imitated the modeled responses and performed appropriate behaviors in role-plays. Group members reinforced Neil with praise for appropriate imitation.

(4) 3. Describe the use of a modeling procedure with prompts, reinforcement, and fading, given the following information: A therapist is trying to teach a retarded child to answer questions about his family. When the therapist asks the child, "How many brothers do you have?" the child does not answer. The child can talk and has in his repertoire all the words necessary to answer the question.

Criteria for correct answer: Your answer must include the following points: (1) the therapist models the correct response; (2) if the child still does not respond, the therapist models the correct response and prompts the child; (3) a specific reinforcer is given when the child correctly imitates the model; and (4) fading of the prompt and modeled stimulus when the child answers on his own.

Sample answer: The therapist asks the child, "How many brothers do you have?" When the child does not answer, the therapist models the correct answer, "I have four brothers." If the child still does not respond, the therapist models the correct answer again and prompts the child, "Now you say it, Tommy." When the child imitates the modeled stimulus, the therapist praises the child saying, "That's very good, Tommy." Gradually, the therapist fades out the prompt by saying it in a softer voice each time until the child says, "I have four brothers" in response to the question, "How many brothers do you have?"

Criterion score: 9.

CHAPTER 12

(3) 1. Give an example of each of the two types of punishment procedures and indicate how you would evaluate their effectiveness.

Criteria for correct answer: One example should specify the presentation of a punishing stimulus following a response; the second example should specify the withdrawal of a positive reinforcer following a response. In both cases, the effectiveness of the punishment is evaluated by observing a suppression or decrease in the strength of the punished response as compared with baseline measures.

Sample answers:

1. Mrs. Jones said to Mr. Jones, "You spend all your money on booze." Mr. Jones slapped Mrs. Jones across the face. Mrs. Jones stopped complaining to Mr. Jones about his spending money on liquor.

   The demonstrator made a face at the policeman and the policeman hit him with his club. The demonstrator stopped making faces at the policeman.

2. Sharon wore a short dress to school and her father withdrew her allowance for the week. Sharon did not wear a short dress to school again.

   Last week Tim came home a half hour late and his mother sent him to bed without his dinner. Since then Tim has come home on time.

(2) 2. Give an example that contrasts extinction with punishment by response-contingent removal of positive reinforcement.

   Criteria for correct answer: Your example must include the following two points: (1) Punishment is the removal of a reinforcer other than that which conditioned or maintains the target response; extinction is the withdrawal of the previously delivered positive reinforcer that conditioned the response. (2) Punishment results in an immediate suppression of the target response; extinction results in a gradual decrease in the strength of the target response.

   Sample answer: Mr. B. criticizes his wife for being overweight while they get ready for bed. Mrs. B. becomes angry and yells at him. This happens several times a week.

   Punishment: When Mr. B. criticizes Mrs. B., she refuses to have sexual intercourse with him. Mr. B. stops criticizing his wife about her weight.
   Extinction: When Mr. B. criticizes Mrs. B., she turns away from him and continues whatever she is doing. Mr. B. gradually criticizes her less frequently, as Mrs. B. continues to ignore him.

(5) 3. Give an example of how you could maximize the effectiveness of punishment with a client who gets off the subject during your interviews and rambles on another topic.

   Criteria for correct answer: Your answer should include the following points: (1) delivery of a punisher immediately after rambling responses; (2) punisher delivered each time rambling occurs; (3) punisher of sufficient intensity to suppress rambling; (4) specification of alternative, appropriate behaviors; (5) positive reinforcement of appropriate behaviors.

Sample answer: Each time the client begins to ramble, the therapist immediately says, "Stop! You are off the subject." The therapist should then specify what the client should talk about in order to provide S^Ds for client responses that the therapist can reinforce. The therapist could ask, "What were you doing when the problem occurred?" If answered appropriately, the therapist says, "That's getting at the problem. Please continue," reinforcing the client for staying on the topic. Client rambling decreases in frequency.

(3) 4. Using the information from Vignette 2, name the punishment procedure instituted as treatment by Mrs. D. with Stephen. Draw a paradigm of an incident that would lead her to use this procedure. Label the appropriate components.

Answers:

1. The procedure used was time-out.
2. A representative incident can be diagramed as follows:

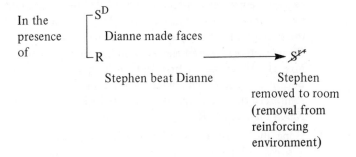

(1) 5. Give an example of punishment applied in a self-control contingency.

Criteria for correct answer:

Your example must include either self-administered response-contingent removal of a positive reinforcer or response-contingent presentation of a punishing stimulus.

Sample answers:

1. If I smoke more than one pack of cigarettes this week, I will send $25.00 to the American Cancer Society.
2. An individual carries an electronic cigarette case that is set to deliver a slight shock if opened at intervals of less than thirty minutes.

Criterion score: 13.

CHAPTER 13

(2) 1. Give an example contrasting the effects of punishment and negative reinforcement. Specify relevant responses and stimuli involved in each procedure.

Criteria for correct answers:
Your examples must demonstrate the effects of punishment in decreasing the strength of the punished response and negative reinforcement in increasing the strength of the escape or avoidance response.

Sample answers:
Punishment: A child eats with his fingers at the dinner table (R) and his mother slaps his fingers (S^{R-}); the child stops eating with his fingers. Negative reinforcement: A child eats with his fingers at the dinner table and his mother shouts at him (S^{r-}) until he eats with his spoon (R). Mother stops shouting (S^{r}), and the likelihood is increased that the child will eat with his spoon.

(3) 2. Give an example of escape behavior conditioned by negative reinforcement. Label relevant responses and stimuli.

Criteria for correct answer: Your example must indicate: (1) that a negative reinforcer is presented until (2) a specific response is made that reduces its effects or terminates it. (3) There must also be evidence that the strength of the escape response has increased.

Sample answer: Karen started whining for money to buy a soft drink. Mrs. Harris refused at first, but finally gave her the money and Karen bought a soda. Karen's whining for money (S^{r-}) served as a negative reinforcer that Mrs. Harris terminated (S^{r}) by her response of giving Karen the money (R).

(2) 3. Using the information from Vignette 3, describe the involvement of positive and negative reinforcement in the interaction between Carla and her mother prior to the social worker's intervention.

Answers:
Positive reinforcement for Carla: Mother put the toys away and promised to buy her new clothes.

Negative reinforcement for Mrs. H.: Carla screamed (S^{R-}) until her mother put her toys away and promised to buy her new clothes (R), the responses that terminated the screaming (S^{R-}).

(4) 4. Sylvia told her husband Harold, "Buy me a new car or I want a divorce." Harold bought her a new car and she stopped threatening to divorce him. Draw a paradigm that describes the avoidance behavior, labeling relevant components.

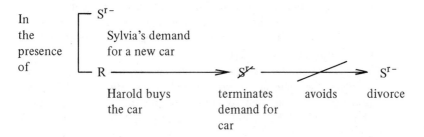

In the presence of

S^{r-}

Sylvia's demand for a new car

R → Harold buys the car

S^{r} terminates demand for car

avoids

S^{r-} divorce

Criterion score: 10.

CHAPTER 14

(3) 1. Using the information from Vignette 5, state one operant behavior and two possible respondent behaviors involved in Mrs. M.'s "being upset."
Answers: The operant behaviors involved in Mrs. M.'s "being upset" included: (1) running into her room and (2) locking the door.
Possible respondent behaviors include any autonomic responses such as increased heart rate, perspiration, face flushed, tears (any behaviors that were elicited by antecedent stimuli).

(7) 2. The following include examples of operant behaviors and respondent behaviors. Place an O in the space for those italicized behaviors that are operant, and an R for those that are respondent.

    a. 1. ___O___ One teenager in a treatment group *swears* at another boy. The second boy's face
       2. ___R___ *turns* red.
    b. 1. ___O___ You *ask* a client a question about his brother; you observe that his
       2. ___R___ breathing *quickens* and perspiration
       3. ___R___ *appears* on his forehead.
    c. 1. ___O___ You *give* Janet a piece of candy for completing her assignment. Carol
       2. ___O___ observes this and *starts whining*.

(2) 3. (1) Draw a paradigm showing respondent conditioning of the following phobia: A child is afraid of dentists. When he approaches a dentist's office, he begins to tremble, turns pale, breathes rapidly, then turns and runs away. This child has some dental problems that must be taken care of soon, or he may lose many of his teeth. (2) Describe an operant procedure for treating both operant and respondent features of this phobia.

Criteria for correct answers: 1. Your answer must include a paradigm showing the pairing of an unconditioned stimulus (UCS) with a previously neutral stimulus until the neutral stimulus acquires the ability to elicit the conditioned response (CR). (If the unconditioned stimulus was very intense, this might be accomplished on the basis of a single pairing.) 2. The operant procedure used to treat this phobia must involve the conditioning of operant behaviors that are incompatible with escape and avoidance in the phobic situation, as well as respondent behaviors incompatible with anxiety.

Sample answers: A paradigm showing respondent conditioning of the above phobia looks like this:

Before Conditioning

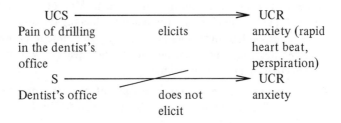

Respondent Conditioning

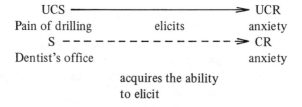

After Conditioning

Shaping via successive approximation can be used to condition operant behaviors incompatible with running away from the dentist's office. The therapist structures treatment so that the child makes successively closer approaches to the phobic stimulus (the dentist's office) and receives positive reinforcement as he successfully completes each step. The client should also be encouraged to talk about pleasant topics in order to establish physiological responses incompatible with trembling, rapid breathing, and turning pale in the feared situation.

(2) 4. Mr. F. is an alcoholic. He typically takes his first drink at 10:00 a.m. and drinks on and off during the day at work. When he comes home, he has three or four drinks before dinner, a few while watching television, and "a nightcap or two" before bed. Mr. F. is in danger of losing his job and his wife is threatening to leave him unless he stops drinking. Describe a respondent procedure that could be used to suppress Mr. F.'s excessive drinking.

Criteria for correct answer: Your answer must describe a procedure in which stimuli associated with alcohol are paired with unconditioned aversive stimuli until the conditioned stimuli elicit conditioned responses incompatible with alcohol drinking.

Sample answers: Covert sensitization is one procedure that can be used to suppress the excessive drinking. In covert sensitization, the client imagines himself in various drinking situations. These situations are then paired, also in the client's imagination, with highly aversive stimuli, such as insects crawling all over the alcohol and glass. These two scenes— the pleasant drinking situations and the highly aversive insects crawling— are paired until the alcohol drinking scenes elicit the unpleasant conditioned responses previously associated only with the insects.

Another aversive technique using shock as the UCS can also be used. For example, a picture of a bottle of alcohol, or the client's actually taking a drink, is paired repeatedly with shock until the picture or taking a drink elicits the unpleasant conditioned responses previously associated only with the shock.

Criterion score: 13.

CHAPTER 15

(3) 1. List three common obstacles to generalization of desired responses from the therapy situation to the client's environment.
Answers:
1. Dissimilarity between stimuli (S^Ds and/or CSs) in the therapy situation and the client's environment.

2. Reinforcement of undesirable responses in the natural environment.

3. Lack of reinforcement for desirable responses in the client's environment.

4. Desired responses insufficiently conditioned in the therapeutic environment.

(3) 2. In Vignette 4, Mr. C.'s verbal behavior was conditioned in a laboratory-like situation. (1) State one reason the conditioned behaviors might not generalize from the treatment situation to his on-the-ward behavior. (2) State two ways you could maximize successful generalization for Mr. C.

Answers:

1. Mr. C.'s verbal behavior might not generalize from the treatment setting to the ward for any of the following reasons:

   a. Ward staff may fail to reinforce Mr. C.'s speech when it occurs, so that his speaking is extinguished.

   b. S^Ds for speech on the ward might be dissimilar to treatment S^Ds for speech (e.g., there is no red light on the ward).

   c. Ward staff might reinforce quiet, inactive patient behaviors emitted by Mr. C.

   d. Mr. C.'s speaking might not have been sufficiently conditioned in treatment.

2. Successful generalization from therapy to the ward can be promoted by:

   a. Reinforcing ward staff for reinforcing Mr. C.'s verbal behavior on the ward.

   b. Altering reinforcement for Mr. C.'s speech from a continuous to an intermittent schedule of reinforcement that is more resistant to extinction and approximates the reinforcement schedule on the ward.

   c. The therapist could reinforce Mr. C.'s speech on the ward.

   d. Using more than one therapist to reinforce Mr. C.'s verbal behavior.

   e. After Mr. C. achieves criterion performance in speaking to the slides, conduct additional sessions to maintain Mr. C.'s verbal behavior at a high level—overtraining.

   f. Ward staff could reinforce Mr. C.'s verbal behavior in the treatment setting.

(4) 3. (1) State two behavioral assignments the marriage counselor gave Mrs. M. in Vignette 5. (2) State two reasons for a therapist's use of behavioral assignments in implementing an intervention program.

Answers:

1. The counselor gave Mrs. M. the following behavioral assignments:

    a. To make two lists of topics; one to discuss with her husband (List A), the other not to discuss with her husband (List B).

    b. To kiss Mr. M. when he came home from work and to ask him how his work had gone.

2. The following are reasons for using behavioral assignments in implementing an intervention program:

    a. Behavioral assignments give the client the opportunity to try out behaviors he discussed and practiced in the therapy session.

    b. Behavioral assignments structure a client's activities between therapy sessions so that progress towards the client's goals occurs not only during the therapy sessions, but also when the client is in his natural environment.

    c. Following the completion of an assignment, the client receives feedback from the therapist based on a specific task he has attempted.

    d. Behavioral assignments promote generalization of desired responses from therapy to the client's environment.

(2) 4. Using the information from Vignette 5, how could behavioral rehearsal be used to help Mrs. M. discuss a movie with Mr. M.? What is the rationale for using behavioral rehearsal?

Answers:

1. The counselor would instruct Mrs. M. in performing appropriate verbal and nonverbal responses involved in discussing a movie with Mr. M. The therapist would role-play Mr. M.; Mrs. M. would role-play herself in a simulated discussion of a movie. Mrs. M. would attempt to demonstrate appropriate behaviors in this discussion and to practice these behaviors. The counselor would praise her when she performed appropriately.

2. The rationale for using behavioral rehearsal is to provide an opportunity for the client to become more skillful in his or her ability to perform appropriate behaviors in the natural environment. Behavioral rehearsal promotes generalization of desired responses from therapy to the client's natural environment.

Criterion score: 11.

CHAPTER 16

(2) 1. State one possible resource and one barrier to goal attainment given the following treatment goal for Mr. L. in Vignette 8: Mr. L. appropriately asks his employer to consider his promised pay raise.

Answers:

Possible resources: Mr. L.'s stated cooperation and desire to improve his situation; support of co-workers; favorable employment record with the company.

Possible barriers: Co-workers discourage him; Mr. L. is reluctant to make an appointment to see his boss.

(2) 2. Identify an intervention strategy including two behavioral techniques and state the rationale for their use given the following treatment goals for Mr. L. in Vignette 8: establish and increase interpersonal skills such as (1) eye contact, (2) increased volume and frequent changes in pitch of voice, (3) staying on one topic at a time, and (4) appropriately responding to another person's comments.

Criteria for correct answers: The techniques you choose must be based on the goals of (1) establishing and increasing the frequency of the behaviors stated above; (2) modifying the intensity of speech.

Sample answers: An intervention strategy involving two behavioral techniques that could be used to achieve the above stated treatment goals for Mr. L. is as follows: modeling and behavioral rehearsal. Positive reinforcement could also be used to strengthen the new behaviors. (Shaping with verbal instructions can also be used, although it might take a longer time to achieve the treatment goals.)

Modeling was chosen as a means of demonstrating appropriate social skills to Mr. L. This technique is used to establish low-frequency behaviors and also to modify the intensity of Mr. L.'s speech. Behavioral rehearsal was used to give Mr. L. the opportunity to practice desired behaviors in a nonpunishing environment before he tried them in an actual situation and to promote generalization of the newly acquired behaviors.

(4) 3. Describe a behavioral contract that you could negotiate between the parents and two children of the Z. family based on the goals of decreased fighting between the children and increased rate of performance of specific chores.

Criteria for correct answer: The behavioral contract must specify the desired behaviors of both the parents and the children along with consequences of performance and nonperformance.

Sample contract: Joey and Frank will play cooperatively, and both will refrain from physical violence.

Parents will provide social reinforcement and points for cooperative play, and will attempt to provide equitable attention to the two boys. The points can be exchanged for allowance money and extra play time. Points will be removed from both boys for each occurrence of physical violence.

Joey will take out the garbage twice a week, and make his bed every day.

Frank will water the lawn once a week and make his bed every day.

Mr. and Mrs. Z. will take the children on an outing on Sunday afternoons, provided both children's chores are completed as scheduled during the week. If the chores have not been completed, there will be no outing.

(2) 4. Describe a method for evaluating the effectiveness of an assertive training procedure that could have been used with Mr. L.

Criteria for correct answer: Your evaluation method must include a measure of the strength of appropriately assertive behaviors before, during, and after treatment, both in the treatment situation and in the client's natural environment.

Sample answer: One way to obtain an objective measure of behavioral change would be to have Mr. L. role-play a social situation with the therapist or a female secretary. Mr. L. would be observed by the therapist in a similar conversation before, during, and after treatment, and the therapist could record appropriately assertive behaviors and their frequency in order to provide comparative measures evaluating the effectiveness of the intervention. A second source for obtaining this information would be data provided by Mr. L. before, during, and after treatment, concerning the frequency of his appropriately assertive behavior.

Criterion score: 9.

appendix 7
course post-test
answers

Answers for Vignette 1

(2) 1. State the inappropriate behaviors emitted by Mr. P. during criticism.
Answers:
Mr. P.
1. rapped his knuckles against each other and
2. made excuses. (Note: The other behaviors were elicited, not emitted.) (Chapters 2 and 14.)

(3) 2. How could a modeling plus reinforcement procedure have been used to help Mr. P. obtain a new job?
Answer: Group members modeled appropriate behaviors for Mr. P. in role-plays of job interviews. When Mr. P. imitated these appropriate behaviors in role-plays, he received positive reinforcement from the group members and therapist. (Chapter 11.)

(2) 3. What reinforcement was arranged for Mr. P. in the treatment situation, and what were the conditions for its delivery?
Answers: The therapist and group members praised Mr. P. as soon as he responded appropriately in role-plays. (Chapter 2.)

(4) 4. List Mr. P.'s respondent behaviors elicited by criticism.
Answers: The following respondent behaviors were elicited during criticism: (1) Mr. P.'s hands trembled, (2) his breathing became more rapid, (3) he perspired heavily, and (4) his face turned red. (Chapter 14.)

(2) 5. Describe the behavioral procedures that were used to promote generalization of desired behavior change from the group treatment setting to Mr. P.'s natural environment.
Answers:
1. Behavioral rehearsal was used in the group treatment setting to

provide Mr. P. with an opportunity to become more skillful in performing appropriate behaviors in his natural environment.

2. Behavioral assignments were given to Mr. P. so that he would practice appropriate behaviors learned in the group setting in his natural environment. (Chapter 15.)

Answers for Vignette 2

(5) 1. List five contingencies Mrs. D. carried out with Stephen and Dianne. *Answers:* (1) If Dianne teased and made faces at Stephen, the day's privileges such as ice cream and watching television would be removed. (2) If Stephen beat Dianne, he was told to go to his room. (3) If Stephen refused to go to his room, Mrs. D. would physically move Stephen to his room where he was to remain for fifteen minutes. (4) If Stephen kicked and cursed Mrs. D., the time in the room was extended by five minutes. (5) If he screamed or made loud noises while in the room, his time was extended by five minutes. (Chapters 4 and 12.)

(3) 2. Name the behavioral principle that was the basis for both time-out used with Stephen and the punishment used with Dianne. Name the reinforcers involved for Stephen and Dianne.
Answers: Both procedures involved response-contingent removal of positive reinforcers. The positive reinforcers for Stephen were Mrs. D.'s attention and Dianne's crying when Stephen beat her. The positive reinforcers for Dianne were privileges such as ice cream and television. (Chapter 12.)

(2) 3. The therapist told Mrs. D. to spend time with Stephen in the evenings and to read to him twice a week. His goal was to increase social behaviors emitted by mother and son that would be positively reinforced by each other. Describe two possible situations that would indicate that the therapist's goal was being achieved.
Criteria for correct answers: Your answers should include information that some behaviors related to time spent together by Mrs. D. and Stephen have increased over their previous rate. The behaviors should be positive or rewarding in contrast to the verbal reprimands and physical punishment by Mrs. D. and the cursing and kicking by Stephen that characterized their past interactions.
Samples answers: (1) Mrs. D. reports that Stephen is telling her many things about his school activities that he never talked about before. (2) Stephen asks for more nights of reading. (3) Mrs. D. reports speaking in a mild tone of voice to Stephen more often. (4) Mrs. D. reports that she puts her arm around Stephen more often. (Chapter 12.)

(6) 4. Describe a shaping procedure Mrs. D. could have used to establish cooperative play behaviors between Stephen and Dianne.

Criteria for correct answer: Your answer must include the following steps of a shaping procedure: (1) specification of the terminal behavior, (2) specification of reinforcers, (3) specification of initial and intermediate responses, (4) reinforcement of initial response until it occurs consistently, (5) shift criteria for reinforcement to next intermediate response, (6) continue to reinforce one response, then shift criteria to next intermediate response until terminal behavior is achieved.

Sample answers: The terminal behavior is that Stephen and Dianne appropriately play a game together for fifteen minutes without physical or verbal attacks. Reinforcers used are pennies and gumdrops. The initial response is they are both standing in the same room, engaged in separate activities. Intermediate responses include their sitting in the same room, playing different games; sitting next to each other, playing different games; asking and agreeing to play a game together. Initially, Mrs. D. would reinforce Stephen and Dianne when they were standing in the same room, playing different games. When those responses occurred consistently, Mrs. D. would shift the criterion for reinforcement to the next intermediate response, sitting in the same room, playing different games. When these responses occurred consistently, Mrs. D. would shift the criterion for reinforcement to the next intermediate response. This procedure of reinforcing one response until it occurs consistently, then shifting the criterion for reinforcement to the next intermediate response continues until the terminal behavior is achieved. (Mrs. D. could also model appropriate behaviors or use verbal instructions in conjunction with a shaping procedure.) (Chapter 6.)

Answers for Vignette 3

(2) 1. Specify the two measures used to determine movement toward the treatment goals.

Answers: The measures used to determine movement toward the treatment goals were (1) the decrease in frequency of Carla's screaming when told to put her toys away and (2) the increase in frequency of Carla's putting her toys away. (Chapter 16.)

(2) 2. State two factors that could operate during conditioning or extinction that would slow the rate of decrease of Carla's screaming.

Answers: (1) If Carla's mother were inconsistent in employing the extinction procedure, she would intermittently reinforce Carla's screaming, making it more resistant to extinction. (2) The rate of decrease of Carla's screaming would be influenced by the resistance to extinction determined by prior conditioning, that is, the schedule of reinforcement that maintained screaming prior to implementation of the extinction procedure. (3) If Carla were reinforced by her mother in other situations for screaming, the screaming might be more resistant to extinction. (4) If other individuals reinforced Carla's screaming, it would be more resistant to extinction. (Chapter 3 and 4.)

(4) 3. Describe the interaction between Carla and her mother in terms of positive and negative reinforcement. Draw a paradigm and label relevant components.

Answers: Carla's screaming was positively reinforced by her mother's putting the toys away and promising to buy her new clothes. Mrs. H.'s responses of putting the toys away and promising to buy Carla new clothes were negatively reinforced in that they terminated Carla's screaming. (Chapters 2 and 13.)

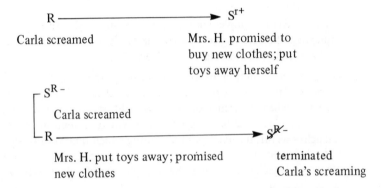

(2) 4. Name the operant procedure used to decrease Carla's screaming when she was aksed to put her toys away. Describe how it was implemented; that is, to which of Mrs. H.'s actions does the procedure refer?

Answers: Mrs. H. used an extinction procedure to decrease Carla's screaming. When Carla screamed about putting her toys away, Mrs. H. walked away from her. Mrs. H. also refrained from making promises to buy Carla new clothes and from putting Carla's toys away herself. (Chapter 3.)

(1) 5. What was the social worker's rationale for instructing Mrs. H. to praise Carla for putting her toys away?

Answers: In situations where undesirable behavior is decreased, it is important to establish and increase desirable behavior, incompatible with the undesirable behavior. The social worker, therefore, instructed Mrs. H. to praise and provide concrete rewards to Carla when she did put her toys away. (Chapter 3.)

Answers for Vignette 4

(2) 1. In the vignette, no goal is explicitly stated for treatment. State a possible treatment goal for Mr. C. and specify a measure that could be used to determine whether it was achieved.

Criterion for correct answer: The goal should indicate that Mr. C. vocalizes according to some observable, specific measure.

Sample answers: The goal for treatment could be stated as: (1) Mr. C. emits 125 verbal responses within a thirty-minute treatment session. (2) Mr. C. speaks five complete sentences during a thirty-minute treatment session. (3) Mr. C. responds to five out of six questions asked of him by the psychologist during a twenty-minute treatment session. (Chapter 9.)

(1) 2. What data should be collected before implementing the treatment described in the vignette?

Answer: Before implementing the treatment described, a baseline indicating the rate of Mr. C.'s vocalizations in the treatment setting as well as on the ward should be obtained. (Chapter 2.)

(3) 3. Describe the function of the red light. Name and briefly state the purpose of the operant procedure involving the red light.

Answers: When illuminated, the red light served as a discriminative stimulus (S^D) for verbal responses that would be reinforced. When the red light was off, it served as an $S^\triangle$ during which time vocalizations were not reinforced. The discrimination training procedure was used to teach Mr. C. to vocalize only when the red light was illuminated. (Chapter 7.)

(2) 4. Apply the concept of conditioned reinforcement to explain how Mr. C.'s vocalizations could have generalized to the ward from the treatment setting even though the unconditioned reinforcer, candy, was not given to him on the ward. What specifically did the psychologist do to promote the transfer of Mr. C.'s vocalizations to the ward?

Answers: The vocalizations were probably maintained by conditioned reinforcers on the ward, such as people responding to his speech, staff praising him for speaking, and other patients commenting favorably on his speech. The psychologist, by saying "Good," was using a conditioned reinforcer, praise, with the primary reinforcer, candy, to promote the shifting from unconditioned to conditioned reinforcers more readily available on the ward. (Chapter 10.)

(3) 5. Describe how the psychologist could use a DRO schedule to determine if the M & M's and points served as reinforcers for Mr. C.'s increased vocalizations, rather than the reinforcers being primarily the attention he received in the treatment situation.

Answer: The psychologist could have used a DRO schedule in which Mr. C. would be given M & M's and points for behaviors other than vocalizing. If Mr. C.'s vocalizations decreased when these objects were given non-contingently, the M & M's and points were positive reinforcers for Mr. C.'s vocalizations. (The psychologist could have further demonstrated the effectiveness of the M & M's and points as reinforcers by reconditioning Mr. C.'s vocalizations using these reinforcers.) (Chapter 6.)

Answers for Vignette 5

(4) 1. State four possible desired behaviors that could be included in treatment goals for Mrs. M. Indicate measures that could be used to evaluate movement toward those goals.

Answers: The following are possible desired behaviors that could be included in treatment goals with their measures for evaluating movement toward the goals: (1) Increase in frequency of Mrs. M.'s making breakfast for Mr. M. (2) Decrease in frequency of Mr. M.'s going out drinking with friends in the evenings. (3) Increase in frequency of Mr. and Mrs. M.'s going to movies or other entertainment together. (4) Increase in frequency of Mr. M.'s accompanying Mrs. M. on shopping trips. (5) Decrease in intensity and frequency of arguments between Mr. and Mrs. M. (6) Increase in frequency of pleasant conversation. (7) Increase in amount of time and frequency per week Mr. M. spends with Mrs. M. and the children watching television, going on trips, talking to each other. (Chapters 9 and 16.)

(2) 2. In behavioral terms, describe the rationale for the procedure involved in Mrs. M.'s drawing up two lists of topics.

Answer: Mrs. M. made a list of topics to discuss with Mr. M. (S^D), and a list of topics not to discuss with Mr. M. ($S^\triangle$). Items on the S^D list (List A) were discriminative stimuli for Mrs. M.'s responses that were reinforced by the counselor in role-play situations. Items on the $S^\triangle$ list (List B) were not reinforced by the counselor. The counselor used a discrimination training procedure to teach Mrs. M. to talk only about S^D topics to increase the frequency of pleasant conversation with Mr. M. and to decrease the frequency of their arguments involving List B topics. (Chapter 7.)

(2) 3. State two measures that could be used to evaluate the effectiveness of the discrimination training procedure employed by the counselor.

Answers:

1. Increase in frequency of speaking about List A topics.

2. Decrease in frequency of speaking about List B topics. (Chapters 7 and 16.)

(1) 4. How was Mr. M.'s leaving the house negatively reinforced?
Answer: By leaving the house, Mr. M. terminated Mrs. M.'s nagging and criticizing. Thus, his response of leaving the house was negatively reinforced. (Chapter 13.)

Answers for Vignette 6

(4) 1. Specify the target behaviors and their negative consequences for Mrs. G. and Mr. T.
Answers: The target behaviors were: (1) asking questions and making comments unrelated to topics being discussed; (2) talking continuously for five minutes or more without pausing for others to respond.
The negative consequences were: (1) ridicule and (2) exclusion from conversations held by other residents. (Chapter 8.)

(3) 2. State three measurable goals of the procedure carried out by the psychiatric nurse.
Answers: Goals of the treatment procedure were: (1) to decrease inappropriate questions and comments, (2) to increase Mrs. G.'s and Mr. T.'s appropriate speech during conversations, (3) to decrease the amount of time each spoke without a pause, and (4) to increase Mrs. G.'s and Mr. T.'s participation in appropriate conversations with other residents and staff. (Chapter 9.)

(2) 3. Describe two behavioral techniques the psychiatric nurse could use to help Mrs. G. and Mr. T. generalize appropriate verbal behavior outside the group.
The nurse could give Mrs. G. and Mr. T. behavioral assignments in which they would be required to practice the desired verbal behaviors outside the group setting; behavioral rehearsal could also be used in the group setting to allow Mrs. G. and Mr. T. to practice appropriate verbal behavior with reinforcement. (Chapter 15.)

(2) 4. Describe (a) a reinforcer that was given in the group to Mrs. G. and Mr. T. contingent on appropriate speech and (b) a possible reinforcer that would maintain their appropriate speech outside the group.
Answers: (a) The nurse and group members complimented and praised Mrs. G. and Mr. T. when they made appropriate statements during the conversation exercise. (b) Reinforcers outside the group could include other persons involving them in their conversations; staff or other residents reinforcing appropriate speech with praise, attention, interest. (Chapters 2 and 15.)

Answers for Vignette 7

(3) 1. Specify three antecedents to Harold's drug taking.
Answers: The antecedents to Harold's drug taking are: (1) Friends invite him over to listen to music and smoke marijuana. (2) Harold is with his girlfriend at her home. (3) Harold is home alone, looks in his notebook, and reads his class assignments. (Chapters 8 and 9.)

(2) 2. State two negative consequences possibly related to Harold's drug taking.
Answers: The negative consequences possibly related to Harold's drug taking are: (1) He fails to complete class assignments. (2) He is unprepared for class, having completed only part of none of his assignment. (3) He receives failing grades. (Chapter 8.)

(4) 3. State four negative consequences of Harold's failing grades.
Answers: The negative consequences of Harold's failing grades are: (1) He is grounded by his parents. (2) His parents nag him. (3) He is denied certain privileges such as watching television and going out with his friends. (4) His allowance is withheld. (Chapters 8 and 9.)

(2) 4. Specify two measures that could be used to evaluate movement toward treatment goals.
Answers:
1. Harold turns in an increased number of complete assignments.
2. Harold decreases the frequency and amount of his drug taking. (Chapter 9.)

(3) 5. State three possible reinforcers (positive or negative) maintaining Harold's drug taking.
Answers: Possible reinforcers maintaining Harold's drug taking include: (1) He spends time with his girlfriend. (2) He avoids doing his homework. (3) He escapes the nagging of his parents. (4) He listens to records and spends time with his friends. (Chapters 9 and 13.)

Answers for Vignette 8

(2) 1. State two desired behaviors that could be included in treatment goals appropriate to Mr. L.'s problem of non-assertion.
Answers: The following would be appropriate desired behaviors for Mr. L.: (1) Mr. L. asks his boss for a raise. (2) Mr. L. states his opinions to his boss. (3) Mr. L. speaks to his boss in a clear, firm voice, with his hands at his side. (4) Mr. L. speaks to a woman in a clear, firm voice with his hands at his side. (5) Mr. L. appropriately defends his rights in a conversation with his boss. (Chapter 9.)

(2) 2. Describe two role-playing techniques that could be used as part of Mr. L.'s treatment if he were participating in group therapy.

Answers: The following role-playing techniques could be used as part of Mr. L.'s treatment: (1) Modeling—a group member demonstrates appropriate behaviors in role-plays of problematic situations; Mr. L. appropriately imitates the modeled behaviors (and is positively reinforced). (2) Role-reversal—Mr. L. role-plays the part of his boss, for example, and another group member role-plays Mr. L. to demonstrate appropriate behaviors and to demonstrate how Mr. L.'s non-assertive behaviors serve as antecedents for his boss's responses. (3) Behavioral rehearsal—Mr. L. practices appropriate behaviors in role-plays of problematic situations and is reinforced by the therapist and group members for appropriate performance. (Chapter 11.)

(2) 3. Describe a procedure that Mr. L. could use to establish himself as a conditioned reinforcer for his dates.

Criteria for correct answer: Your answer should show Mr. L.'s arrangement of conditions so that he is associated (as an S^D) with a variety of unconditioned and conditioned positive reinforcers delivered on a non-contingent basis.

Sample answer: Mr. L. could invite a woman out for dinner, bring her flowers or candy, talk about her interests during the meal, and take her dancing afterwards. He does these things non-contingently, that is, no specific behaviors are required of the woman to obtain these rewards. As these items appear to be rewarding to the lady, Mr. L. becomes associated with their delivery; he is the S^D for her responses that lead to the availability of the probable reinforcers. Mr. L. thus begins to acquire reinforcing value for the woman. (Chapter 10.)

Total possible: 91.
Criterion score: 82.

appendix 8 summary of notational symbols and paradigms

SUMMARY OF SYMBOLS AND PARADIGMS

R = a response

S = a stimulus

S^+ = presentation of a positive reinforcer

S^{R+} = presentation of an unconditioned positive reinforcer

S^{r+} = presentation of a conditioned positive reinforcer

S^- = presentation of a punisher or a negative reinforcer

S^{R-} = presentation of an unconditioned punisher or an unconditioned negative reinforcer

S^{r-} = presentation of a conditioned punisher or a conditioned negative reinforcer

UCS = an unconditioned stimulus

UCR = an unconditioned response

S^D = a discriminative stimulus

S^m = a modeled stimulus

$\cancel{S}^+$ = removal of a positive reinforcer

$\cancel{S}^{R+}$ = removal of an unconditioned positive reinforcer

$\cancel{S}^{r+}$ = removal of a conditioned positive reinforcer

$\cancel{S}^-$ = termination, removal, or reduction of a negative reinforcer

$\cancel{S}^{R-}$ = termination, removal, or reduction of an unconditioned negative reinforcer

$\cancel{S}^{r-}$ = termination, removal, or reduction of a conditioned negative reinforcer

CS = a conditioned stimulus

CR = a conditioned response

⟶ = is followed by (operant)

⟶ = elicits (respondent)

⌐ = in the presence of

⟶̸ = is not followed by (operant)

⟶̸ = does not elicit (respondent)

Procedure: positive reinforcement
Effects: increase in
strength of R

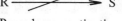

Procedure: extinction
Effects: decrease in
strength of R

In the
presence
of

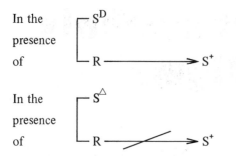

In the
presence
of

Effects: increase in strength of R in
the presence of S^D; decrease in
strength of R in the presence of $S^\triangle$

In the
presence
of

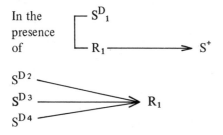

Procedure: stimulus generalization
Effects: R_1 occurs in the presence
of S^{D1} and is positively reinforced;
R_1 occurs in the presence of S^{D2},
S^{D3}, and S^{D4} without reinforcement

Procedure: punishment by presentation of a punisher
Effects: suppression of R

Procedure: punishment by removal
of a positive reinforcer
Effects: suppression of R

In the
presence
of

Procedure: negative reinforcement; escape conditioning
Effects: increase in strength of the
escape response, R

In the
presence
of

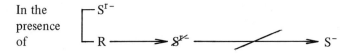

Procedure: negative reinforcement; avoidance conditioning
Effects: increase in strength of the
avoidance response, R

glossary

Accidental Contingency: An individual makes a response that is associated with a reinforcer on one occasion, but the response has no effect on the availability of that reinforcer on subsequent occasions. When an individual continues to emit this non-functional response, it is referred to as superstitious behavior.

Antecedent: An event that precedes and is closely associated with occurrence of a behavior.

Anxiety: An intense emotional response frequently characterized by physiological changes such as increased heart rate, perspiration, rapid breathing, and subjective statements of ill-ease or fear; it may generate escape or avoidance behaviors.

Assertive Training: A behavioral change technique used to correct social response deficits (e.g., mumbling, looking at the floor when speaking to someone, inappropriately agreeing with someone), and to increase appropriate assertive behaviors (e.g., speaking in a clear voice, looking at the person spoken to, and stating divergent views or opinions when appropriate).

Aversive Stimulus: An object or event that is identified as unpleasant, annoying, or painful; when given the opportunity, the individual will usually escape or avoid it.

Avoidance Behavior: Behavior that results in the termination, removal, or reduction of a negative reinforcer and that prevents the occurrence of a second negative reinforcer.

Backward Chaining: A behavioral change technique used to teach complex sequences of behavior. Stimulus-response units are successively conditioned, beginning with the last unit in the chain.

Baseline Data: Measures of response strength recorded prior to intervention, including rate, duration, intensity, latency and/or magnitude.

Baseline Rate; Baseline Level: The strength of a behavior prior to intervention or modification.

Behavior; Response: Any measurable movement or activity of an individual.

Behavioral Assessment: A strategy for obtaining specification of a client's situation and the formulation of behavioral change goals.

Behavioral Assignment: A specific task to be completed by the client between treatment sessions.

Behavioral Contingency: A statement that specifies the conditions under which certain consequences will follow a response.

Behavioral Contract: An agreement between two or more individuals in which the expected behaviors of each are specified along with the consequences for their performance or nonperformance.

Behavioral Deficit: Absence or low frequency of an appropriate behavior.

Behavioral Excess: A high-frequency inappropriate behavior.

Behavioral Re-enactment: A role-playing technique in which the client's problematic behavior and controlling conditions are assessed by observing him role-play an incident typical of his problem.

Behavioral Rehearsal: A role-playing technique in which the client practices desired behaviors that have been suggested and/or demonstrated by the therapist or group members.

Behavior Modification: The application of knowledge derived from the experimental analysis of behavior to human problems or situations.

Biofeedback: Auditory, visual and/or other sensory feedback regarding physiological states, such as heart rate, muscle tension, brain waves, skin temperature. It can be used in the operant control of autonomic functions. It can be applied in conjunction with behavioral techniques for relaxation training and the treatment of certain psychosomatic complaints.

Chains: (See stimulus-response chains.)

Classical Conditioning; Respondent Conditioning: Establishing or strengthening a response through pairing of a neutral stimulus with an unconditioned stimulus until the neutral stimulus acquires the ability to elicit a conditioned response.

Conditioned Aversive Stimulus: An unpleasant, annoying, or painful stimulus that has acquired these properties through pairing or association with an established aversive stimulus; when given the opportunity, the individual will usually escape or avoid it.

Conditioned Negative Reinforcer: A stimulus whose termination, removal, or reduction increases the strength of the response that terminated, removed, or reduced it; it has acquired these properties through pairing or association with an established negative reinforcer.

Conditioned Positive Reinforcer: A previously neutral or nonreinforcing stimulus whose presentation following a response will strengthen that response. It has become positively reinforcing through serving as an S^D for responses that were reinforced by established positive reinforcers.

Conditioned Punisher: A stimulus that has acquired the ability to suppress or decrease the strength of the response it follows through pairing with an established punisher; also, the removal of a conditioned positive reinforcer.

Conditioned Response (CR; R): In the respondent conditioning paradigm, a measurable activity, CR, elicited by a conditioned stimulus. The CR is similar to the unconditioned response. In the operant conditioning paradigm, the conditioned response, R, is a measurable activity that has been strengthened by reinforcement.

Conditioned Stimulus (CS): In the respondent conditioning paradigm, a previously neutral event that acquires the ability to elicit a conditioned response through pairing with an unconditioned stimulus.

Consequence: An event that follows a behavior and can influence the future likelihood of the behavior's recurrence; it can be reinforcing, punishing, or neutral.

Continuous Reinforcement Schedule (CRF): A reinforcement schedule in which a reinforcer is delivered each time the response occurs.

Contingency: (See behavioral contingency.)

Covert Sensitization: An avoidance conditioning method utilizing imaginal stimuli to decrease the strength of maladaptive approach behaviors; it involves respondent pairing of an aversive stimulus with the maladaptive situation.

Cumulative Recorder: An instrument that automatically records frequency of responses over time.

Deprivation: A condition in which an individual has not been exposed to a reinforcer for a specified period of time.

Differential Reinforcement: A procedure in which a certain response is followed by a reinforcer and reinforcement is withheld from other responses.

DRO Schedule: Differential reinforcement of behavior other than the target behavior. This schedule can be used as a control to determine the effectiveness of the reinforcer(s).

Discriminative Stimulus (S^D): An antecedent stimulus in whose presence a response is followed by a reinforcer.

Discrimination Training: A behavioral procedure in which a response is reinforced in the presence of S^D and extinguished in the presence of S^Δ.

Duration: A measure of response strength. The length of time a response occurs.

Errorless Discrimination Training: (See stimulus fading.)

Escape Behavior: Behavior that results in the termination, removal, or reduction of a negative reinforcer.

Ess-dee (S^D): (See discriminative stimulus.)

Ess-Delta (S$^\triangle$): (See S-delta.)

Extinction: Operant extinction—a previously delivered reinforcer for a response is withheld continuously (that is, each time the response occurs) until the response decreases in strength to its operant level or to a prespecified level. Respondent extinction—the conditioned stimulus is presented repeatedly, without presenting the unconditioned stimulus, until the conditioned stimulus no longer elicits the conditioned response.

Fading: (See stimulus fading.)

Fixed-Interval Schedule: An intermittent reinforcement schedule in which a reinforcer is delivered when a response is emitted after a designated period of time. For example, FI 2 min means that a reinforcer is delivered when a response is made after two minutes have passed.

Fixed-Ratio Schedule: An intermittent reinforcement schedule in which a prescribed number of responses must be emitted in order for a reinforcer to be delivered. For example, FR 10 indicates that a reinforcer is delivered after 10 responses have been emitted.

Frequency: The number of times a response occurs; frequency per time interval (response rate) is the most common datum used in recording response strength.

Generalized Conditioned Reinforcer: A previously neutral or nonreinforcing stimulus that has acquired the ability to increase response strength through association with established reinforcers. It usually refers to an object that can be exchanged for a variety of conditioned or unconditioned reinforcers.

Imitative Response: A response emitted in the presence of a modeled stimulus, topographically or physically similar to the modeled stimulus with regard to an observable dimension(s).

Intensity: A measure of response strength that is indicated in units such as grams, pounds, decibels.

Intermittent Reinforcement: Any schedule of reinforcement that is less than continuous. A response is reinforced on some occasions, and reinforcement for that response is withheld on other occasions.

Latency: A measure of response strength. The interval between presentation of a stimulus and occurrence of a response. In operant conditioning, the interval between presentation of the discriminative stimulus and emission of the response. In respondent conditioning, the interval between presentation of the unconditioned stimulus or conditioned stimulus and elicitation of the unconditioned response or conditioned response, respectively.

Magnitude: A measure of the strength of a respondent; usually obtained by measuring secretion of a gland or contraction of a muscle or blood vessel.

Model: An individual whose behavior serves as a cue for an imitative response made by another person that is similar to the behavior of the model.

Modeling Procedure; Model Presentation: An individual(s) is presented with a model who performs appropriate behaviors to be imitated.

Modeled Stimulus (S^m) The behavior of a model that sets the occasion for an imitative response.

Natural Environment: The people and physical surroundings in which an individual's adaptive and maladaptive behaviors are conditioned or maintained.

Negative Reinforcement: (1) Escape conditioning—a procedure in which a response that terminates, removes, or reduces the effect of a stimulus is strengthened. (2) Avoidance conditioning—a procedure in which a response that terminates, removes, or reduces the effects of a negative reinforcer and prevents the occurrence of a second negative reinforcer is strengthened.

Negative Reinforcement Contingency: A statement that dictates an "if . . . then" functional relationship involving the response that must be emitted in order to terminate, remove, or reduce the effects of a stimulus.

Negative Reinforcer: A stimulus whose termination, removal, or reduction increases the strength of the response that terminates, removes, or reduces its effect.

Neutral Stimulus: Respondent: A stimulus that does not elicit an unconditioned response or a conditioned response. Operant: A stimulus that does not increase or decrease the strength of a response it follows.

Operant: A response class, each member of which has the same or similar effect on the environment.

Operant Behavior: Behavior that is controlled by its consequences. The individual operates or acts on the environment to produce those consequences.

Operant Conditioning: Establishing or strengthening a response primarily by manipulation of its consequences, that is, positive or negative reinforcement.

Operant Level: The strength of a response prior to conditioning.

Paradigm: A set of notational symbols used to represent behavioral procedures and their effects.

Phobia: Maladaptive anxiety attached to a specific object; it involves a conditioned avoidance response.

Positive Reinforcement: A procedure in which a stimulus, presented after a response is emitted, increases the strength of that response.

Positive Reinforcement Contingency: A statement that dictates an "if . . . then" functional relationship involving the behavior that must be emitted in order for a positive reinforcer to be delivered.

Positive Reinforcer: A stimulus whose presentation following a response increases the strength of that response.

Premack Principle: Any behavior occurring more frequently than another behavior can serve as a reinforcer for the behavior that occurs less frequently.

Primary Aversive Stimulus: (See unconditioned aversive stimulus.)

Primary Negative Reinforcer: (See unconditioned negative reinforcer.)

Primary Positive Reinforcer: (See unconditioned positive reinforcer.)

Primary Punisher: (See unconditioned punisher.)

Punisher; Punishing Stimulus: A stimulus presented after a response that suppresses or decreases the strength of that response. Removal of a positive reinforcer is also referred to as a punisher or a punishing stimulus.

Punishment: Response-contingent presentation of a punisher or response-contingent removal of a positive reinforcer; it acts to suppress or decrease the strength of behaviors.

Punishment Contingency: A statement that dictates an "if . . . then" functional relationship involving the response that must be emitted in order for a punisher to be presented.

RAC-S: Acronym for *R*esponse, *A*ntecedents, *C*onsequences, *S*trength; the behavioral assessment schema used in this text.

Rate: A measure of response strength; response frequency per time unit.

Reinforcer: A stimulus whose presentation or removal following a response increases the strength of that response. (See positive reinforcer; negative reinforcer.)

Resistance to Extinction: A measure of response strength; usually measured by the number of responses emitted after reinforcement has been discontinued.

Respondent Behavior: Behavior that is controlled by its antecedents. An unconditioned stimulus or conditioned stimulus is presented to elicit an unconditioned response or conditioned response, respectively.

Respondent Conditioning; Classical Conditioning: Establishing or strengthening a response through pairing of a neutral stimulus with an unconditioned stimulus until the neutral stimulus acquires the ability to elicit a conditioned response.

Response; Behavior: Any measurable movement or activity of an individual.

Response Class: (See operant.)

Response Differentiation: The refinement of a response or the narrowing of a response class through differential reinforcement.

Response Strength: For operant behavior, measured by (1) frequency per time (rate), (2) latency, (3) intensity, and/or (4) duration. For respondent behavior, measured by (1) latency and/or (2) magnitude.

Response Topography: Description of a response according to its form, position, or movement.

Reward: An object or event that is identified as pleasant, satisfying, or desirable, and that the individual will seek out or approach.

Role Reversal: A role-play technique in which an individual role-plays the part of another person while the therapist or a group member role-plays his part.

Satiation: A condition in which an individual has been continuously presented with a reinforcer to the extent that it loses its reinforcing effect.

Schedule of Reinforcement: The frequency or pattern with which reinforcement is delivered for a given response. Types of reinforcement schedules include continuous, fixed-interval, fixed-ratio, variable-interval, variable-ratio, and DRO.

S-Dee (S^D): (See discriminative stimulus.)

S-Delta ($S^\triangle$): A stimulus in whose presence a response is not followed by a reinforcer.

Secondary Aversive Stimulus: (See conditioned aversive stimulus.)

Secondary Negative Reinforcer: (See conditioned negative reinforcer.)

Secondary Positive Reinforcer: (See conditioned positive reinforcer.)

Secondary Punisher: (See conditioned punisher.)

Self-Contingency Management: An individual arranges conditions so that his response is predictably followed by certain consequences, usually a positive reinforcer.

Self-Control: (See self-contingency management.)

Shaping via Successive Approximation: A behavioral procedure used to condition behaviors which never occur or occur with low frequency. Differential reinforcement is applied to strengthen behaviors progressively similar to the desired terminal behavior. Throughout the procedure, the criterion for reinforcement is shifted to include responses that more closely approximate the terminal behavior.

Simple Conditioned Reinforcer: A previously neutral or nonreinforcing stimulus that has acquired the ability to increase response strength through pairing or association with one particular established reinforcer; e.g., bus token.

Social Reinforcer: A reinforcing stimulus that becomes available through interaction with another individual(s). Attention, praise, and approval are examples of social reinforcers.

Spontaneous Recovery: The recurrence of a behavior that had previously undergone extinction. The behavior may recur at a future time under stimulus conditions similar to those under which conditioning occurred.

Stimulus (plural, Stimuli): Any object or event. It can include physical features of the environment as well as an individual's own behavior or the behavior of others. Stimuli can be discriminative, eliciting, reinforcing, punishing, or neutral.

Stimulus Control: A response reliably occurs only in the presence of S^D and not in the presence of $S^\triangle$; the interval between presentation of the S^D and the occurrence of the response (latency) is short.

Stimulus Fading: A behavioral technique in which the antecedent stimulus is gradually altered along one dimension until the response occurs in the presence of the desired stimulus. The same response continues to be emitted under gradually changing stimulus conditions with no errors or responses to $S^\triangle$.

Stimulus Generalization: A response conditioned in the presence of one stimulus (the original or training stimulus) will also occur in the presence of other similar, or functionally equivalent, stimuli without reinforcement.

Stimulus Generalization Gradient: The varying probability that a response will occur in the presence of a stimulus, depending on the similarity of the stimulus to the training stimulus. As the stimulus becomes increasingly different from the training stimulus, the likelihood of the response occurring in its presence decreases. As the stimulus becomes increasingly similar to the training stimulus, the likelihood of the response occurring in its presence increases.

Stimulus-Response Chains: Units of stimuli and responses that comprise complex sequences or patterns of behavior. Each unit consists of a discriminative stimulus, a response, and a conditioned reinforcer that also serves as the discriminative stimulus for the next response. The chain terminates with delivery of a reinforcer.

Straining the Ratio: A phenomenon occurring when a fixed-ratio schedule is increased too rapidly. A response extinguishes if the number of responses required for reinforcement is increased too rapidly.

Superstitious Behavior: Behavior that is strengthened by accidental association with a reinforcer. The behavior is not functionally related to delivery of the reinforcer and has no effect on the availability of that reinforcer on subsequent occasions. (See Accidental Contingency.)

Systematic Desensitization: A respondent method for treating phobias by counterposing deep muscle relaxation with a hierarchy of situations involving the phobic stimulus until it no longer elicits anxiety.

Target Response: The response that is observed or counted; the focus of modification.

Time-out: A behavioral technique of punishment by removal of a positive reinforcer(s). An individual is removed from the reinforcing situation immediately after the inappropriate behavior occurs and placed in an environment with minimal availability of reinforcement.

Token Economy: A planned reinforcement program in which individuals earn tokens or points for performing desired behaviors. These tokens or points can then be exchanged for a variety of objects or privileges.

Transfer of Change: The generalization of desired behaviors from the treatment setting to a client's natural environment.

Treatment Contract: A written or verbal statement of commitment between the therapist and client indicating that each will perform specific behaviors that can lead to resolution of the client's problem(s).

Treatment Planning: The therapist's pre-treatment and ongoing preparation in working with a client from intake to termination and follow-up.

Unconditioned Aversive Stimulus: A stimulus that is identified as unpleasant, annoying, or painful. It does not require pairing or association with another stimulus to acquire these properties. When given the opportunity, the individual will usually escape or avoid it.

Unconditioned Negative Reinforcer: A stimulus whose termination, removal, or reduction increases the strength of the response that terminated, removed, or reduced it without requiring prior pairing or association with another stimulus.

Unconditioned Positive Reinforcer: A stimulus whose presentation following a response will increase the strength of that response without requiring prior pairing or association with another stimulus.

Unconditioned Punisher: A stimulus whose presentation following a response suppresses or decreases the strength of that response without requiring prior pairing or association with another stimulus; also the removal of an unconditioned positive reinforcer.

Unconditioned Response (UCR): In the respondent conditioning paradigm, the response that is elicited by an unconditioned stimulus.

Unconditioned Stimulus (UCS): In the respondent conditioning paradigm, an object or event that elicits an unconditioned response without requiring prior pairing or association with another stimulus.

Variable-Interval Schedule: An intermittent reinforcement schedule in which a reinforcer is delivered when the response is made after an average amount of time has passed. For example, VI 5 min means that reinforcement is given when the response is emitted after an average of five minutes has passed, although the interval may range from 30 seconds to 10 minutes.

Variable-Ratio Schedule: An intermittent reinforcement schedule in which a reinforcer is delivered after an average number of responses is emitted. For example, VR 8 means that reinforcement is delivered after an average of eight responses has been emitted, although the ratio may range from 1 to 15.

index